How To  Buy

AN INSIDER'S GUIDE
TO MAKING MONEY
IN THE STOCK MARKET

JUSTIN MAMIS

FRASER PUBLISHING COMPANY
BURLINGTON, VERMONT

Copyright © 2001 by Justin Mamis

Published in 2001 by Fraser Publishing Company
A division of Fraser Management
P. O. Box 494
Burlington, VT 05402

ISBN: 0-87034-165-0

Originally published in 1982 by Farrar Straus Giroux, New York, NY (hardcover)

Library of Congress Cataloging-in-Publication Data

Mamis, Justin, 1929-
How to buy : an insider's guide to making money in the stock market / Justin Mamis.—
[2nd ed.]
p.cm.
ISBN 0-87034-165-0
1. Stocks—United States—Handbooks, manuals, etc. I. Title.

HG4921 .M325 2001
332.63'22—dc21

2001040242

Acknowledgment is made to the following publishers for their kind permission to reprint their charts: Commodity Research Bureau, Daily Graphs, Mansfield Chart Service, *The Professional Tape Reader*, Wertheim & Company. Acknowledgment is made to Dow Jones & Company for their kind permission to reprint two articles from *The Wall Street Journal*, © 1980 Dow Jones & Company, Inc.

Printed in the United States of America

Acknowledgments

What makes the stock market fascinating, apart from its potential for profit, is that it is a continuous learning experience. I want to thank some of the players who have shared their experiences and insights with me: Lewis Goodman, Edgar Kann, Lew Horowitz, George Lindsay, Ed Lowe, John Tortorella and Chris Castroviejo, Stan Weinstein, and my friends at Wertheim who have introduced me to the fascinating institutional sector of the marketplace.

FOREWORD

The other day, we listened to a professor being interviewed on TV about "the market." What fascinated us was that he wasn't talking about the market, as *we* know it. His comments centered on the Federal Reserve Board, on inflation or lack of same, on durable goods orders, and all manner of other economic factors (and from such matters he then presumed to know what stock prices were going to do). What people, in their infinite wisdom/madness, might do seemed to have nothing to do with it. That's the opposite of how we picture "our" market of buyers and sellers: like an old-fashioned farmer's market. Purveyors with goods to sell set up shop in the central town square (Wall Street) and put them on display (the ticker tape). Several farmers have similar-looking prosaic cabbages to sell; others have lots of different varieties of apples (big cap, small cap). At the same time, the populace wanders around to see if there is anything interesting to buy – highly desirable quality, or undiscovered bargain, or simply something they could use.

Some people will buy "at the market" right away, not wanting someone else to come along and snatch a desirable item away with a better bid; others will bide their time, hoping that by mid-afternoon the seller might reduce the price in the hopes of getting rid of his goods before the market closes for the day. That's the market we know: made up of a variety of different buyers and sellers, a variety of different goods and choice, a variety of motivations and information (or lack of same), an on-going stream of interest and activity. With so many people with so many different styles and opinions and tastes and pocketbooks and ways and means of deciding on what they want to do, it is a psychiatrist's dream of trying to understand it all at once … can't be done perfectly, but can be done relatively well.

We care about *that* market as it trades, with the fluctuating prices (and volume) telling us what's going on, and what the underlying psychology is. In a sense, we're trying to understand buyers and sellers, so as to be able to foretell what they might want to do next. In another sense, we're observing who's winning: the buyers or sellers, on the expectation that the discerned trend ought to continue. In still another sense, we are trying to establish which stocks are over-owned, and which are under-owned, and trying to observe, in various ways, when the trend from one to another may be changing, or has gone to such an extreme that it ought to be about to change. Nor do we need to know why – just when, and how, and what! We continue to believe, in fact, in one of the first things an NYSE floor trader ever taught us: "It's not the news that matters ... it's how the stock reacts to the news."

This book, and our other two volumes (*When to Sell*, and *The Nature of Risk*), describe our view of this marketplace. We've left untouched some of the original indicators described within, even though changing market styles have made some of them out-moded. (Odd-lot short-selling was supplanted by put and call buying, and options activity itself, in turn, has been shifted to second-tier indicator status with the advent of a vast number of new trading indexes such as QQQ for the Nasdaq 100.) You might read about those archaic indicators to get an idea of how sentiment has been measured in the past, so as to figure out how to deal with current ways sentiment is revealed ... keeping in mind that contrary opinion has been, is, and always will be the important stance.

When we opened up the original edition of *How to Buy* and saw at the outset the phrase, "the market fluctuates," we knew that the book did not need to be rewritten. Not only does the stock market still fluctuate, but *it does so in the same manner as it ever did* ... all of the talk about volatility and all of the manic technology swings of recent years being just remarkable extensions of such fluctuations. The manner in which the market does fluctuate, and how such fluctuations should be understood, seems more timeless than we would have believed in our youth – just as valid in coping with the manic rises and subsequent bubble burstings as when the market was relatively calmer. It still takes just as long to make a top, or a bottom (*which is the basis for this book*) as it ever did.

Keep in mind, as you read these pages, that a buyable bottom can only develop when everyone who wants to sell has sold – in other words, a buying opportunity represents contrary opinion to the prevailing selling. How do we get to that point where others want to sell? Simple – there has to be bad news at a bottom, for how else would prices get driven down? Not on 'good' news, surely, but on bad news, and not merely on bad news but on bad news that shareholders begin to feel can only get worse, or is never going to end. Ah, that's a buyable bottom: everyone else discouraged, scared; bad news haunting investors; and, of course, a share price that doesn't go down any more because everyone who wants to sell, or is finally scared into selling, has already done so.

In a book about *How to Buy* one needs contrary opinion to the prevailing scared sentiment in order even to start looking for a buying opportunity … a bottom which must be contrary – can't hear the media folk on CNBC and elsewhere talking about a bottom and expect to find it at one's elbow.

Don't think a stock is attractive just because it is down so far from its high, or that it is buyable just because it has become conspicuously strong for a day or two. Patience is required. Ask yourself, Who knows what? When did they know it, and Why is the stock acting that way? Remind yourself that you're not the only person in the country who is interested in a particular stock – if it's so great, why is it still going down? If it's so crummy, why has it begun to hold and even to turn upward? Being suspicious, being cynical, is a good way to practice being contrary. A bottom will not form, a buying opportunity will not appear, if everyone believes in it – "buying when you're crying" is a floor trader expression of what one has to do to make the best bottoming purchases.

There never has been, nor do we expect there ever will be, a bottom formed when buyers are enthusiastic … an intervening bounce perhaps, sharp and short-lived, but the psychology of bottoms, and especially longer-term buying opportunities, requires "scared." Indeed, good buying requires some nervousness that you might be wrong. What we are trying to convey in the pages of this book is various objective means – charts, indicators, sentiment analysis – to help you identify when, nervous as you may be, it is time to be the only one willing to buy at that moment. That's an exaggeration, of course, and it may happen to you only once in an entire investing career … but it is the "buy" attitude to strive for.

Justin Mamis   March 2001

CONTENTS

1

IT'S ONLY A GAME

I'm going to tell you things I know about the stock market that no one else knows, but what is most true about the market is something everyone knows: *it fluctuates.*

Every bit of the market's behavior, and all the information you need to deal with it, stems from that single simple fact. Yes, there are fortunes that have been made by those who got in on a stock early and stuck it out through innumerable declines and bear markets. This book is not about such rare instances. They are often offset by the stories you don't hear, of failure and mistakes in judgment. Besides, we are here not to discuss exceptions but to show you how to make money in the stock market without gimmicks, tricks, or systems, without enormous effort or time-consuming attention—solely by means of the information readily available to you.

"Can it be done?" is not the first question. Professionals do it all the time—or they wouldn't be professionals for long. Just like a rookie playing the game in the big leagues, a professional money manager or trader has got to produce or he is dropped from the team. No one fools around when capital is at stake. A pro either makes money in the market or finds a different profession.

Nor are we talking exclusively about those professionals who

3

have the advantage of paying much lower commission rates due to Exchange memberships. The proliferation of "discount" brokers has taken much of that sting away, and besides, some of the most successful professional traders we know gladly pay full commissions to brokers for intelligent opinions and good order executions. The trick in this business is not to make eighths and quarters but to go for the "big hits." Virtually the only extra advantage some of these professionals may have over a member of the public at large—and we're not sure this is truly an advantage—is access to "better" information (such as hot tips) a trifle faster. The batting average for hot tips proving true is dangerously low, however. More important, even when the information is accurate, it almost always can be discerned by non-professionals, too, as long as they know what clues to look for. If a stock is strong, it may signify that good news is about to be released, or merely that an institution has entered a big buy order on the Exchange floor—in which case the stock price will be vulnerable to fading as soon as that order is filled. We'll gladly show you the volume and price-action clues that can tell you, too, that "something may be going on," to help you decide whether the stock is worth buying. Remember, for someone to profit by what he knows—be it hot tip or intelligent analysis—he's got to go into the marketplace and act. This action will have an impact on the stock's price and its volume, thus creating an effect on the stock that we can perceive. This is the basis of all the information you will need to learn to make money in the stock market. If you find you are taking repeated losses instead, the problem is probably a personal (psychological) one, and you should place your money more safely elsewhere. So the question at the outset is not how you can make money but *should you be in the market at all?*

To Buy or Not to Buy

There is one reason why you shouldn't: you may not want to, or be able to, take the risk. Because the market fluctuates, your money is always being risked. Because you have to make a choice of what to buy, that risk is compounded by the added decision. This is true not only of stocks but, as so many banks, pension funds, and even professionals have found out to their sorrow, of the bond market as well. Bonds were once thought of, with almost a religious belief, as a safe place for investments, as "sleep at night" havens for funds, but a decade of declining prices, capped by the crash of 1980–81, has, we expect, destroyed that faith with a vengeance. Those with fiduciary responsibility for "widow and orphan" funds could only shrug that they had done the prudent, the proper, thing by investing in bonds, but the losses were just as real as if they'd been speculating in cats and dogs.

Even those who shunned supposedly risky investments by tucking their money away in fluctuation-free places like savings banks have been adversely affected by the curse of inflation. Without realizing it, they were actually gambling that their dollars would buy as much when returned to them, but they, too, lost, as an inflation pace of 10 percent and more exceeded the single-digit rate banks were willing to pay. Long-term bond rates include, theoretically, a premium for the pace of inflation, but bank interest rates can't do that. The best game plan, we suppose, if you fear risk, would be to buy short-term U.S. Treasury bills, rolling them over regularly and simply accepting whatever rate of interest is being paid at the time. As long as the country is still there, you'll at least be getting your capital back and earning something on it as an investment, letting economic forces make the interest-rate decision for you. So if you don't want to take any risk at all, but have excess capital you don't know what to do with, take yourself down to the nearest Federal Reserve Bank (or get the application forms by mail) and invest in three-month or six-month Treasury bills. If that's your course, you don't need to read any further in this book.

Those of us who want more, however, and are willing to take a risk to get more, must understand the nature of the risk. We're going to discuss later how to limit your risks by buying intelligently in terms of both timing and stock selection, but first you have to confront the nature of the marketplace. As long as there is fluctuation—whether you're dealing with bonds or stocks—there are choices to be made: what to do, and when to do it. It seems to us that what we are really talking about (with due apology to all those men in three-piece business suits with plush carpeted offices) is *playing* the market. That is, the market is a game.

Again, this is as true for bonds (or paintings, antiques, diamonds, real estate, for that matter), within their much more limited sphere, as it is for stocks. What we are describing is a form of gambling. *You are placing a bet on your judgment.* The odds may be good—and we'll try to make them better for you—but that doesn't take away the nature of what you are doing. There is a playing field—the market itself—and there are choices to be made, just as in roulette or at the race track. There are long shots, and safer (less volatile) alternatives that will yield less potential reward for your risk. There is the tension and anxiety that any gambler feels—and enjoys, once the bet is down and he can watch the ball spinning, or the horse sprinting down the home stretch, or the ticker tape running. Even someone who does no more than read the market results in the newspaper can't deny the rush of anticipation he feels as his eye runs down the column looking for Digital Equipment or Halliburton, or, when he sees a plus or minus sign, the elation or disappointment that follows. There is the cursing, or kissing, Lady Luck. There is the high of being a winner, the depression of being "down" via the stock's drop, and there is the frustration of having made no tactical mistake and still losing—for even professionals don't profit on every trade. The times when you'll buy because you think the market is going up, and then see the averages leap without your stock selections participating, can be the most aggravating of all. The market as a place to gamble can bring on even more anxiety than the track or the casino in the sense that, with a horse race or roulette wheel, a finite time—mere seconds or minutes—elapses and then you get a definitive answer as to whether you've won or lost, whereas the market goes on and on and on, constantly fluctuating and thus constantly changing your chances of winning or losing, and constantly creating the need to make yet another decision.

Make no mistake about it: every decision to buy, sell, hold; to pick stocks or bonds or real estate; to choose Digital or Halliburton or Verbatim, is a bet. You are gambling, whether you think of yourself as a long-term investor or a short-term speculator, or a broker convinces you that the stock market is a "nice" place for an American to invest in for retirement. Those concepts merely define the kind of gambler you are. Thus, if you are willing to assume some degree of risk, and understand that you are taking a gamble when you do, the next question becomes: Why the stock market?

Why Stocks?

This is America; there are a wide variety of investment choices and there is no need to bother with the stock market at all. You can go through life contentedly without buying a single share. So let's briefly consider some alternatives.

Bonds are a cousin of stocks. We've been picking on them as a supposedly safe investment in order to emphasize that everything contains a risk. As it happened, everyone who bought bonds for safety over the past decade and more had suffered a loss by mid-1981. It does no good to say it was just a paper loss; the loss was real, since, if the money had been invested otherwise (Treasury bills, for example), it could have been growing instead. And yet, even within this great bear market in bonds, there was a terrific trade to be made from the March 1980 lows well into June—with the proper timing.

Following is a chart of Treasury Bond futures, a relatively new commodity-like trading tool. While the financial futures market is a highly specialized and sophisticated game, you don't need to speculate in the futures but instead can use the chart to help gauge the potential direction for interest rates. At those times when there is intense concern about interest rates, the action in the financial futures market serves as an indicator for the stock market as well as the bond market. Note the huge price slide, so costly to supposedly conservative investors; the low in February (A); and the successful test of that low on March 28, 1980 (B).

This chart of the financial futures market showed a base similar to those you would see in stocks. This bullish action took place even as open-market interest rates were still rising, and at a time when conventional, professional, and published opinion insisted that rates were going higher instead. While deciding to act in the face of such widespread bearishness may have been difficult, the

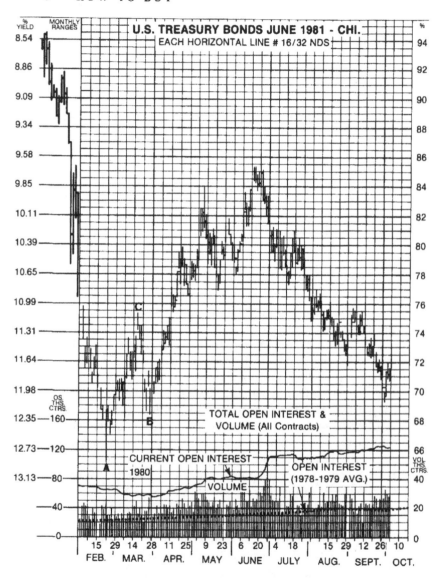

U.S. TREASURY BONDS JUNE 1981 - CHI.
EACH HORIZONTAL LINE # 16/32 NDS

TOTAL OPEN INTEREST &
VOLUME (All Contracts)

CURRENT OPEN INTEREST
1980

OPEN INTEREST
(1978-1979 AVG.)

VOLUME

choice itself was an easy "Should I, or shouldn't I?" That's the primary advantage of playing the bond market: you make your decision based on only one factor—which way interest rates will go. And the only thing you have to keep in mind is that because your decision is a bet on that direction, it is not without risk.

There used to be a belief on Wall Street that what was good for bonds was bad for stocks. That no longer seems to be true, although such a fashion, as with clothing, may come back into favor in the future. But increasing institutional sophistication, a devastating bear market in bonds, and a need for common stocks in a more balanced portfolio have changed the philosophy. Of late, easy money has led to rising bond prices as well as a favorable stock-market climate, while tight money has had negative effects on both sectors. There may be a time (as in late May 1981) when bonds are a good trade, but more often, given a choice of trading vehicles, it makes more sense to shoot for the potentially greater rewards stocks can offer. Note that if in March 1980 you had bought two-year Treasury notes yielding 15 percent, you would have snared a fine yield in a relatively riskless instrument, and could even have made a short-term capital gain within a month. But approximately three weeks later, from virtually the same type of chart formation (see page 134) in the Dow Industrial Average, you could have bought stocks at the right juncture for an ensuing 250-point rise.

On the other hand, during periods when interest rates are trending higher, you don't really want to own either bonds or stocks. These bearish times can be so destructive that all you ought to be concentrating on is preserving your capital so you can enter the game again at a later, less risky time. That means tucking your money into short-term, readily accessible top-quality havens such as Treasury bills. Even better, of course, for those willing to take the risk and play the game from every angle, would be to sell stocks short during such major bear trends. Your basic purpose is, first, to preserve capital and, second, to make it grow. That means betting when the risk is least, and not betting when the climate is dangerous, be it stocks or bonds, or both.

In sum, bonds and stocks often have become buyable at approximately the same time. Because the risks of holding bonds in an inflationary era have been proven to be as great as the risks of playing the stock market, we'd rather take our chances with stocks. If you can catch a significant price bottom, and *want* bonds for their yield, it pays to watch for such stand-out opportunities. (Some of the conditions we'll discuss later as associated with stock bottoms, such as panic, a market in disarray, and pronounced skepticism after a successful test of the low, can be applied to bonds with equal validity.) Certainly there are investors who have a need for such an assured income; you should see to it, though, that you are not lulled by the holding thereafter. Remember that you are playing a game; if you win one bet, don't lose the next. The smart thing to do in 1980, for example, would have been to buy equities a few weeks after the successful test of the low, in April, using bonds as just a short-term haven rather than as the conventional long-term "safe" investment.

As for other forms of investment, they have a laundry list of disadvantages. Such games as real estate, diamonds, antiques, paintings, etc., (1) are not liquid; (2) require special knowledge; (3) include steep dealer or middleman costs; (4) must be ferreted out before they become overly popular, thus increasing the speculative risk; and (5) are far less easy to establish a "right" price for. Consider, for example, that while an art dealer may put all his eggs into the art basket and never own a share of stock, his oft-repeated advice to the public is to buy only a painting you like—i.e., if you're wrong on the investment value, at least you'll have something pleasant to live with. But in the stock market you always know what someone is willing to pay for your shares, or what you will have to pay for something you want. You'll *always* have—and this is perhaps the most important advantage of stock trading—a readily liquid market. Stocks can be sold quickly, at a price close to the previous price, if you decide you don't want them any more.

Indeed, that is the best reason of all for gambling in stocks. Like those superhighway roadside restaurant signs, call it "Easy in, Easy out." You can get in the moment you decide you want to play, and out, if need be, as soon as you realize you were wrong or have enough of a profit. Or perhaps that's not the best reason after all. There is a lot to be said for—although few on Wall Street are willing to admit it—the excitement and fun of the gamble itself.

And while you are enjoying yourself, it's a sound bet for many reasons. The odds are relatively good, for example. Ten- or twenty-to-one payouts are rare, of course, but compare betting on a long shot at the track versus the favorite. The long shot would pay such high odds precisely because of the little likelihood of victory, whereas in the market the same analytical approach and judgment can be applied to Recognition Equipment as to IBM—and if REC looks like a good bet, it has just as much chance of being a winner as IBM. Nor does it have to be an all-out winner, as a long-shot horse has to be; as long as it racks up a decent profit, you'll be satisfied. What's more, because the stock market is a liquid arena, if you're wrong you can get out of your bet not only readily but with the bulk of your capital intact, unlike having only your losing long-shot ticket to show for your efforts after the race.

In addition, in the market it is possible to forecast tops and bottoms with reasonable accuracy. We've found—and we'll show you what to look for—that it is even easier to catch an important market bottom than a top, and that goes for timing individual stocks, too. The readily available information is much more consistently useful than the performance charts relied on for handicapping horses. Thus, the bet has a good deal of substance to it. It won't be flawless, and you'll have hot and cold streaks just like any other gambler, and you won't buy at the bottom eighth more than once in a lifetime, because that's pure luck. But as a place to bet your surplus money, stocks are relatively easy to understand, requiring some attention, but not all day every day. Anyone can learn to play the game reasonably well, and the monetary rewards are well worth it.

Playing the Market

Why have we argued in favor of playing the market when, if you've bought this book, you are undoubtedly already "in the market"? The answer is, we want you to feel comfortable with the game. Any of the conventional attitudes—such as the "own your own share of American business" basis for investing—will cause, and probably already has caused, losses. So too will guilt, suspicion, fear, anxiety, greed, and other emotions, while setting up the true playing field for you will make it easier to understand our point of view and to profit from it.

So let's define "playing the market" as using the stock market as the proper place to put your excess funds at the proper moment. That is, you begin with an absolutely free choice. You can enter the market whenever you feel the timing is right, and can withdraw or change your choices at any time. Even if you are truly a gambler at heart, and enjoy the fun of betting and the tensions of the game, you should always remember that *doing nothing is also a betting choice.* Too much money is lost unnecessarily by those gamblers who compulsively need to play something, anything, all the time.

The stock market is challenging, readily accessible, and easy to play—an ideal gambler's table at which you are pitted against a collective mind that often seems uncannily human. Playing the market is better than other gambles because it is far less subject to chance. The favorite wins only about a third of all races; the roulette ball falls we know not where; cards, too, are random. But the stock market, as we'll show you, has specific discernible features. That is, there are things to "know" about the market and about individual stocks that can shift the odds in your favor and help make them better bets. The main disadvantages are, as we've said, that it goes on and on and on, so that there is never a definitive moment when you know whether you are right or not, and there are times when you'll be a loser without making a tactical mistake. A good decision, it can be said, is not the same as a good outcome. You can act on what looks like a sensible bet at the time, only to see the evidence change on you. But at least you can change your bet, even if at a loss; try doing that when your horse stumbles out of the starting gate. There is, indeed, ample evidence out there to be seen and used; that's why we play the market.

As long as we're going to play, we need to define the game and its rules. Such guidelines are the basis for eliminating as many psychological impediments as possible, so as to reduce losses. Thus, the second important thing we have to say about the market is that, as long as it is going to fluctuate on us, *we need to distinguish between what is knowable and what is hope* or dream, or, at best, expectation.

Relying on the Facts

Time and time again, when we are asked for our advice on the market, people want to know "What's going to happen?"—where's the market going to go? how far? how long?—and while we could chat for hours about possibilities, probabilities, and even likelihoods, and yet not be sure, we can invariably answer a different question with ease: "What should I do today?" In other words, "How should I play the game right now?"—buy on a dip, sell into strength, stand pat, buy Du Pont, sell Motorola, etc. The actual betting decisions, in short, are much clearer than anything the crystal ball will show.

Amateurs believe in the market—that it is a "nice" place to make money grow—while professionals believe in the game. Foremost in this category are those who trade for their own, or their firm's account, either on the Exchange floor or from the firm's office (known as "upstairs" traders or, more formally, as Member Traders). These are pros who spend all day every day buying and selling; there may be as many different styles for such trading as there are traders, but in every instance the game they play is the same: buying a particular combination of letters (the ticker symbol) at a certain number (the price) in the expectation that they'll eventually be able to sell that same combination of letters at a higher number. Even the most virginal stock-market investor, strolling into a Merrill Lynch office for the first time, is doing exactly the same thing, even though he doesn't realize it, when he takes the broker's advice to buy American Telephone. True, he is buying a share in that company, and will have the voting rights to prove it as well as a dividend check as his share of its earnings, but he is actually placing a bet on the market action of T at the same time. The risk is that T's price may drop, creating a capital loss greater than the dividend received; the hope is that it will go higher. It may be a conservative bet, but a bet it is.

The professional may make his decision based on any number of factors, ranging from sheer tape-reading instinct to a hot tip from a friend; indeed, he may even buy something based on a conventional brokerage-house report extolling a particular stock. And while he may be unwilling to admit that he is gambling, he would probably recognize that his decisions are made within the context of a game, with profits and losses denoting whether he has won or lost. Nor does the time span matter. Whether it's the in-and-out activity of a floor trader or the longer-term orientation of a professional mutual-fund money manager, all either is trying to do is play the fluctuations for profit.

Obviously, since so many people lose so much money in the stock market, it isn't an easy game to play. You can't just stick a pin in the stock tables and be right often enough to stake real money on such a "system," nor should you play such an amateurish game as walking into a brokerage firm's office and buying whatever the salesman is peddling that day. There are dozens of different ways to play the game, but no matter what the style, it should be rooted in what is knowable, and not what can only be guessed at, or hoped for.

We hesitate to call what is knowable "facts" because the interpretation of those facts is always so quick to follow, but at least they start out by being specific and irrefutable—Halliburton closed on Friday at 100 1/2, up 2 3/8 from the previous day's closing price; the Odd-Lot Short-Sales Ratio for yesterday's trading was 1.40, and that was the highest in over five weeks; the daily bar chart of IBM shows that a budding, albeit small, head-and-shoulders bottom formation would be completed if the stock price crossed the "neckline" at 56; Digital Equipment pays no dividend; the latest quarterly earnings report for Inland Steel was $1.28 per share vs. $1.18 a year ago; the Federal Reserve Board's latest report showed Net Borrowed Reserves at $657 million; the Index of Leading Economic Indicators for May showed a record decline of 4.8 percent; and so on. All these are clear, factual items; the waters muddy only as interpretation of their significance begins.

Notice that there are, generally speaking, three categories of "facts." First, there are those that relate directly and exclusively to action within the stock market itself; these are known as technical data. Second, there are those that relate directly to the company and only indirectly to the stock market. Some investors use such corporate data to make buy-or-sell decisions; this is the fundamentalist approach. And third, there are those which pertain to the overall economy; while they are basically fundamental in nature, some, particularly the monetary data, have been adopted by technicians as useful indicators, too.

It is often said, by suspicious investors, that what is wrong with the technical view of the market—the notion that market behavior itself tells the story—is that all it has to go by is what's already happened. This, of course, is true. Technical analysis is based entirely on what is knowable: yesterday's price, not a hunch of tomorrow's. Any prediction is the analyst's opinion. The fundamentalists, however, disdaining the technical approach, feel more comfortable with earnings forecasts and economic predictions, because they believe that somehow in their analysis they are anticipating the future in a concrete way, apart from the vagaries of the market, by concentrating on the company instead. Saying that IBM should be bought if it crosses the neckline sounds more like hocus-pocus than saying IBM should be bought because, even though 1980 earnings will be up only 6 percent, the forecast is for a 23 percent gain in 1981. The problem with this apparently dignified approach is that it is both one step removed from the factual —based on future-earnings estimates rather than the already known earnings—and one step removed from the marketplace— based on the company rather than the stock.

Not only do such earnings estimates get "nickel and dimed" by the industry analysts—shaded this way and that as each quarter's actual report comes out—but fundamentalists also have to decide what buyers and sellers are going to do with the forecast once it becomes actualized. All sorts of should's and ought to's are used: IBM should earn $6.70 per share; IBM should sell this year at the same 11-times earnings it is currently selling at; IBM ought to sell at a higher price/earnings ratio next year because its earnings will then be rising rapidly again; and so on. Unfortunately, the market is not so obliging. Any number of things can go askew: the earnings forecast may be off by as little as a dime, surely accurate enough for a financial forecast, and yet the collective disappointment may produce a rush to sell; the earnings forecast may be on the money when reported, but no one may care, for those who did care have already bought on the forecast, or the market collectively believes that 10 times such earnings is ample enough, so the stock price goes nowhere; the earnings report may be a nickel better than expected, but just as the good news is released, the market has come under heavy selling pressure due to an international crisis, so IBM sells down regardless. In sum, the attempt to translate corporate matters into stock-market action is for the most part imprecise, because it fails to take into account other influencing factors. Many fundamentalists take refuge in the corporate world because the stock-market game continuously frustrates them. They can't deal with the market's fluctuations, so they end up buying shares in the company just because they like the company—and to hell with the market.

What we are seeing is that, at the root of it, the fundamentalists' shares are subject to technical factors regardless of their views. To be sure, they've played it safe by buying according to their theories; the investment committee can't criticize them for buying IBM even if it goes down, but they've risked their money by exposing it to technical factors without taking these factors into consideration when placing their bet. Consider, instead, the technical data: it's simple, even if our decisions about what to do with this data are not so easy. A look at the daily action chart as of Memorial Day 1980 shows that IBM has already broken a steep downtrend line and has been going sideways instead; if it can cross 56, it will complete a small head-and-shoulders bottom formation, and by reaching a price *higher* than the last previous rally high (at 55 3/4), it will inaugurate an uptrend instead. We don't know *why* sufficient buying has come in to improve the stock's technical picture—perhaps it is that earnings forecast; perhaps it's that the market itself has been quite strong for the two days prior, so that IBM begins to look like a "nice" stock still close enough to its low to seem "cheap"; or perhaps it's merely that traders think it is finally time for IBM to participate in the rally. But we don't know if we should try to anticipate that breakout (after all, the market, having already rallied sharply, is getting overbought), if we should actually wait until the breakout to buy, or if, instead, we should make the stock prove itself on the move, and then buy on a pullback. We do know that if IBM, as a market leader, looks increasingly positive —especially if similar improvement can be seen in several other blue-chip stocks—it is a healthy sign for the market's longer-term course, suggesting that any overbought condition will be tempo-

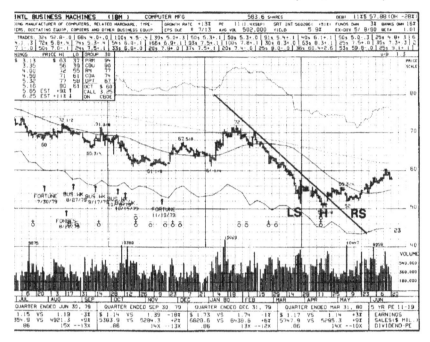

rary; but we still don't know whether to buy, or wait, or buy something else that may look even stronger. That is, the game isn't necessarily made easier by what we know. We still have risky decisions to make with our capital, but at least we are able to focus on what our choices are by sticking to what is readily knowable from the ticker tape and the newspaper.

Remember that all applicable information of any sort, whether it be the best earnings estimate or inside information on a takeover bid, must be translated into a money decision—whether to buy or hold or sell—in order for the possessor of that information to profit from it, and that action must take place in the market where we can see it. And since it seems reasonable that so-called big money is either smarter, or has access to better information, or both, the action to look for first is what big money decides to do. You may know nothing about the company itself, it may be just a ticker symbol to you, but market action—both volume and price change —can call your attention to the stock as a potential buy candidate.

At this point, if you want to, you can do all the fundamental analysis your conservative heart desires, but it is the technical analysis that has shifted the betting odds greatly in your favor.

Minimizing Your Risk

All we want to do, you see, is minimize the risk. As an astute floor trader once told us: "It's how much you don't lose, not how much you make" that determines stock-market success. Of course, the proper use of stop-loss orders (as discussed in detail in *When to Sell*) will get you out of a position that has turned out to be, to put it bluntly, wrong, but here we are primarily concerned about taking the least risk by making the best bet available to us at any given moment. In this instance all we know, based on the available evidence on that specific day, is that IBM is a potential place for betting money.

Obviously, someone is buying it. Here comes IBM across the tape in streams of activity: 55 1/4 1/4 1/4 1/4, now 55 3/8, back to 1/4, then 3/8 and—wow!—50,000 shares at 55 1/2. The temptation to jump on board is powerful; we sit on the edge of the chair. Imagine the pressure that would come across the phone line from a broker talking to a potential customer; reading the ticker tape while even innocently trying to entice the client into a commission-reaping purchase creates enormous tension to act before it is too late. (That, incidently, is how so many people manage to buy at the high for the day . . . and think they are personally jinxed.) IBM ticks back to 3/8, seems to be stuck there. Ah, we think, more hopefully than practically, it'll stop here and back off where we'll surely purchase it; we should have bought it last week, we berate ourself, when we spotted that head-and-shoulders bottom formation developing.

Of course, if we were dealing with, say, Recognition Equipment, we wouldn't mind missing it as much. There'll be other low-priced flyers. But IBM! We search the market for signs that the short-term rally is tired: TICK is faltering, but TRIN remains robust. Other leading issues are also stuck, but, damn, here come the oils, giving the action a new burst of life. IBM whacks away at 55 1/2, and now it begins to trade at 5/8. We sit back forlornly. The hell with it, we think, as if it has personally insulted us by going up before we bought it. If it won't cooperate by dipping, we'll wait for the upside breakout signal at 56. Hah, we don't even have to do that, we reason; since we are convinced that the overall market is getting overbought and will experience a correction, we'll damn well wait for the pullback after the breakout before buying. Except that— look at how impressive it is on the tape!—maybe we should buy a little now just to have it, and buy more on that by now ephemeral dip. Damn! then we should have done that back at 3/8, not now.

On and on our thoughts race, in rhythm to the clack of the ticker tape. We've become completely caught up in our emotions and our need to be perfect. Not only can we no longer make a simple decision about IBM, we've managed to miss the bullish action in REC, which we also wanted to buy, and, worse, we were so busy concentrating on buying—on being bullish—that we missed the chance to cash in our profit on Weyerhauser, which was on the top of our list to sell. Well, we "reason," if IBM stays strong, it'll carry the market with it, and we'll get a second chance to get out of WY. Thus, we've begun to compound our tactical errors; our emotional involvement has carried the day.

It can be even worse, as we've noted, if you are on the other end of the phone with a similarly emotional broker who not only wants to convey the flavor of the action to you but wants an order, too. And, perhaps worse yet, if you are out of touch and open the newspaper the next morning to see what has already become market history, the air will be full of curses of "should have" and "ought to have."

No, thanks.

It is to avoid these potentially destructive mind-churning effects that we've set out our three basic concepts. First, we've given you the playing field—a fluctuating marketplace—so that you can time your buying better and have the patience to wait, comfortable in the knowledge that the market game goes on and on. (IBM, for example, did indeed cross 56, but then it was again readily buyable under 55 as the market experienced its expected correction.) Second, we've introduced a playing style based on what is readily knowable—the "facts"—and while these "facts" may be in conflict (an increasingly overbought climate vs. the emergence of IBM as a buy candidate), you at least have the tools with which to make your decision. And third, by insisting that all market decisions have as their primary intent the reduction of risk, we can get rid of as many of our dangerous emotions as possible. After all, it's just a game. Let's enjoy it, not torture ourselves.

2

BUYING SENSIBLY
NOT EMOTIONALLY

Years ago, we watched a typical boardroom sitter in action. Retired, wrapped in an old cardigan sweater and puffing on his pipe, Harry stared at the tape all day in his neighborhood brokerage office. It was a place to go; it was social; and it provided race-track-type action, always intriguing because the market never stays the same. He'd watch quietly, sometimes for days, until a particular stock caught his eye. "Look at that Molly go," he'd say. Or: "Bessie's all over the tape like crazy." He was skilled at spotting a stock that had suddenly picked up a lot of activity and strength. "Wow, that Molly, up another quarter," he'd say, half to his broker nearby, half to himself. Or: "That Bessie's sure a strong stock." He'd start to edge forward in his chair as if he were at a burlesque show trying to get a closer look.

If the stock continued active and went up some more, its tape action would begin to drum into his head. "What do you think of Molly here?" he'd ask his broker, while never taking his eye off the tape. The broker might reply: "It's already up a lot." Or, less carefully: "Sure looks like something's going on." But Harry scarcely listened to the answer. He was already caught up in the action, rooting the stock on as if it were coming around the bend into the stretch. "There it goes," he'd say, his voice rising excitedly,

"5000 at 23, 23, 23, a quarter, it's in the clear!" By then, the stock might have been up a point or more already; by then, Harry was sitting on the edge of his chair. Finally he could bear the tension no longer. "Buy me a hundred," he'd cry out to his broker, "at the market."

Invariably, of course—it's the moral of this tale—Harry would pay the high price for the day, so frequently that he became an intra-office signal that the rally was over the moment he bought. He was a precise measure of dramatic tension during the race, and of the exhaustion at the end. By the time he was convinced he had a winner to bet on, the race was over for the day.

Unlike the sell side of the market, where the basic problem is getting the investor to act, to let go, the most serious buy-side problem is curbing such emotional spending attacks. If you've ever placed a bet at the race track and then decided, just before post time, "Oh, what the hell," and put an extra $2 down on one of your alternative choices—in effect, betting against yourself—you can see how easy it is to bet just because you can. The market window, so to speak, is always open while the tape is running. We all have an itchy wallet when we get caught up in the excitement of rising prices. Being carried away, so that you've just got to buy something, is not unlike behavior during an auction when the bidder goes far beyond his original intended price limit in the fever of the moment.

Indeed, we're talking about an auction market as the stock exchange defines it: a continuous auction market. There's a best bid and a lowest offer at all times. The price rises when another bidder comes in and takes the offer; prices fall when the seller is more aggressive. And after each transaction there is a new auction. The rules of priority and precedence come into effect and there is a fresh bid and a fresh offer, even if the actual prices remain the same. It is the specialist's responsibility to keep the auction continuous, as well as to ensure that the quoted market provides for fair and orderly trading. Excitement generated by the action on the tape, or more generalized excitement induced by reading about the market in the newspaper or being phoned by a broker, stimulates buying by those who fear they'll miss their chance. The market goes on and on, with new bets constantly being placed.

How a Floor Broker Buys

Suppose you are a floor broker who has just been given an order to buy 25,000 shares of IBM. You stride over to the post where IBM is traded, weighing, as you walk, what the overall market is doing (up, down, sideways), what you feel it might do, and ditto for IBM itself. You get a quotation and a size in the stock from the specialist: 57 1/2 bid for 5,000 shares; 2,000 offered at 57 3/4. Now, what do you do? If you wait, someone else might take those 2,000 shares ahead of you, so you buy them just to get started sensibly. But now you've caused the price to rise. The new auction market is quoted by the specialist as 57 1/2 bid for the same 5,000 shares; 500 shares offered at 57 7/8. Other potential buyers might rush in, or is a seller more likely? It isn't worth paying 57 7/8 because you'll be raising the price just for 500 more shares; you've got to calculate at what price level enough stock will come in for sale to enable you to fill the order, hoping you can avoid paying the high price for the day. Maybe, you think, you should just stand there and see if any sell orders come in, risking, however, that other buyers will take the shares at 57 7/8 and even at 58 ahead of you. So you, too, are itchy; should you, shouldn't you? Another 1,000 shares comes in for sale at 57 3/4 and you even buy 500 more at 57 5/8. But while you are standing there smugly, another floor broker marches in and buys the 500 shares offered at 57 7/8. "Three-quarters, eight," the specialist announces, giving the new auction market's best bid and lowest offer, followed by the size of each, "2000 by 10,000." And just as you are about to say "Take them," the other broker, instead of walking away with his 500 shares, takes the entire offer at 58 ahead of you. Playing the game is never easy.

A skillful floor broker has to be able to make spur-of-the-moment decisions all the time, knowing he'll be wrong sometimes, knowing that he, too, can get carried away by the excitement or frustration (hastily reaching up for shares above 58 because he's just missed the market), or lulled by an apparent success. Not all floor brokers are skillful, and some can butcher an order. But whatever the case, a broker's decisions in handling the orders he is entrusted with will affect the way the stock prints on the tape, and hence the way it moves and looks to all the rest of us simultaneously across the country on the ticker tape.

The Auction Market at Work

This action, and the infinite variations on it, from 100-share trades to big blocks, buying and selling, represents the auction market at work. The constant flow of orders helps to create what is known as the "book" in the stock. Literally, the specialist (the Exchange member who handles the market in that particular stock) maintains a ledger book—long and thin—in which are entered all the limited-price orders left with him that can't be executed "at the market," and to this book we'd add any orders being represented by brokers in the crowd. You decide to bid 58 on behalf of your order, and when a broker comes in with 20,000 to sell, you grab them, feeling relieved that you didn't really miss your chance after all. Except that he then asks the specialist at what price he can sell another 20,000 shares. "57 1/2," the specialist says, and suddenly you're embarrassed again, without really having done anything wrong. It's just the way the continuous auction market goes!

The facts of the book, and the action on the ticker tape, are available to you and Harry and huge institutions, and they are, at the moment of buying, all any of us has to go on. But because they *are* facts, they can help curb our tendency to become emotional, to fling our bet down wildly under pressure of the auction. We don't know why something is happening, but we do know what—and that's the only edge we can hope for. Sometimes, let's hope often, the available facts will help you to curb an itchy wallet and make a calmer, more objective decision.

By Exchange rule, the specialist must announce the size of the best bid and the lowest offer. This information can be obtained on the various interrogation machines brokers now have (such as Quotron, which is the one we are most familiar with, or Bunker Ramo). The same rule prohibits the specialist from disclosing the size of any bids below or offers above the current quoted market, although, of course, you can assume from experience that there'll be a lot more shares bid for or offered at the round number or at one half than at the odd fractions. Occasionally, a lazy or foolish or inept specialist may provide a quoted size of "one by one"—100 shares bid for; 100 shares offered—when you know from the trading activity that such a size simply can't be true. Sometimes such a size can represent sudden frenetic action that has scared the specialist; if the stock has by then already moved considerably, this quoted size is often a sign of exhaustion—the stock should retrace at least some of the move it has just had. At other times it can represent an attempt to protect a broker with a large order standing there, or may simply reflect a specialist who wants to play it safe. (Traders tend to shy away from such stocks because of the lack of full information readily available from the Exchange floor.) In any event, you can always ask your broker to get you the current size from the floor. As a bonus, you may sometimes be told a tidbit such as "Two competing buyers there," or "Bache has been a big buyer" or "Morgan Stanley's been selling all the way up." This may sound worthwhile, but it is actually little more than you can conclude from paying attention to the quotation and size yourself; it's just gossip. In other words, the way the stock actually trades in relation to the quotation is all you need to know.

We'll explain in detail how to use this "book" information in Chapter 7. Here we just want to depict for you the auction market itself, because it is at the core of the betting game. As the floor broker with the IBM buy order, no one is more itchy than you. You want to fill the order and get away from that post to do some more business, and you want to fill it without paying more than you should. This is where your ego is at stake, when you are more than just a messenger running around the floor buying and selling "at the market." So you have to take into your mind—instantly—all the information available. How far and how fast has the stock come up already; who else is buying; how much stock is offered, and at what price; how's the rest of the market; how urgent is your customer; and a host of other considerations. Then you have to decide what to do, as objectively as possible, with a curb on your natural impulse to just do and be done with it.

If that's what runs through a floor broker's mind, what about Harry? Virtually all this information is also available to him, and in exchange for what he lacks, he even has an advantage over the floor broker. Harry doesn't have to buy. He could sit back and say to himself: The stock is already straight up over a point without a downtick, so it's due for a fluctuation back down; there's only a few hundred shares offered, so no big buyer is apt to act right now; there's bound to be a lot of stock offered at the next round number either to act as a roadblock or to afford a chance to buy; etc. He could even pat himself on the back for having spotted a winner, shrug at having missed a chance at it, and vow to act more decisively the next time. For, instead of calling out what he was seeing, he could have bought the moment the action caught his eye on the tape, if he were going to be that kind of trader. At the race track it would be helpful if you could see the start before you bet—did your choice get away well, or did it stumble?—but you can't. Similarly, people who trade off the tape can't afford to wait. Harry, who thought he was waiting to be sure, more sure, and surest, actually was increasing his risk by letting the itchy feeling in him build up until he couldn't stand it any longer.

If you've ever stood on a New York City sidewalk and watched a three-card monte game, you may understand how this can happen. The dealer will have his patter and his slick hands; the crowd gathered around will even know there is a shill among them. But at a certain moment someone watching will become convinced that he can win the bet, that his eye has surely spotted which one of the three cards is "it." He gets so caught up in the excitement of the moment that he plunks down his $20 bill and picks, of course, the wrong card. It isn't even the greed to win the money, although that certainly is present. It is the need to be part of the excitement, the desire to be triumphantly right.

Nor does this attitude exist exclusively among the more active traders and tape watchers in the stock market. One of the amazing things about this country is the seemingly never-ending number of men and women who will just wander into a brokerage office with $5,000 or $10,000 or even $50,000 to invest as if that particular random day will miraculously turn out to be the perfect time to buy. What brings them in is not so much a sensible decision but a yearning. Greed for huge untoiled-for profits may be the bait, but it is the lure of participating in the excitement of gambling that gets the bet down. The potential rewards are greater than the savings bank can promise, and stocks certainly have more oomph.

Ask any addicted gambler how his sex life is, and you'll soon realize that the excitement of the bet is more than a substitute; it becomes the real thing. And the market has its own sexual terminology to add to the attraction. It does, after all, go up and down; people talk of getting married to a stock, of falling in love with technology or the oils; and what more potent symbol is there than the bull? Reading the financial pages begins to have the enticement that girlie magazines do, with the advantage that one doesn't have to be restricted to just looking; one can actually get involved. Be he sold-out bull or novice, the action is going on without him, so in he plunges. This is especially true during periods of speculative fever when not only the headlines are dramatic but everyone's neighbor, or the man in the locker room, the divorcee at the cocktail party, has a fabulous story of a conquest to tell. Who wouldn't want to take a fling, too? It is at such times that friends or casual acquaintances will often approach us, saying: "I've never been in the market—buying stocks scares me—but if you've got one stock you think is special . . ."

Harry, too, wants in. None of the other boardroom sitters are so alive as he has become at that moment, leaning forward in his chair. He wants to be on board for that stock's ride. "I own it, I own it," he can say as, in his daydream, the stock wins for him. All the "reason" that has kept him from buying sooner disappears. He can't endure watching any more. The temptation has been dangled in front of him, as in a three-card monte game. He is compelled to play.

Unfortunately, the urge to get in on the action most often strikes the typical investor very near the market's (or the stock's) top. Just as Harry leaned further and further forward in his chair until he couldn't stand it any longer, buyers leap in as a rising market increasingly catches their attention and demands their participation. One signal of a top, for example, is when a booming stock market leaps from the financial section to the front page of the newspapers. This rush to buy now that things look "sure" is as true of the so-called sophisticated institutions as it is of the public. A highly useful indicator has been developed that measures the way these "big boys" start tossing all their remaining cash reserves into the market as it gets closer and closer to the top, a top which is definable as the time when the buyers are all bought up.

Just take a look for a moment at this chart of the Mutual Fund Cash Ratio. It reflects a statistic published once a month (around the twentieth) that reveals the percentage of available buying power or, conversely, the degree to which mutual funds have so far spent their money for stocks. Notice that the lowest percentages of cash reserves—down to, and even under, the 5 percent-6 percent level—came at or just ahead of major market tops in 1965, in 1969, and most emphatically during 1972 and right at the peak of the market in January 1973, before the worst bear market since the '29 crash. More recently, a similar "bought-up" reading occurred in August–September 1976 when the Dow Jones Industrial Average peaked again over the 1,000 mark. Obviously, the higher the market goes, the more willing these institutions are to buy as much as possible. (Conversely, as we'll discuss in detail in Chapter 6, high readings—lots of available cash—occur at and thus help us identify

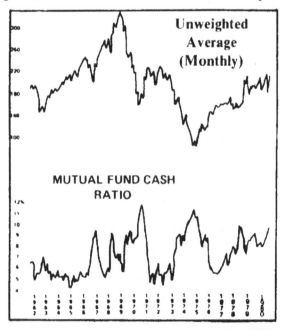

important buying opportunities, such as the over 10 percent readings in mid-1970, at the major low in late 1974, and at the Dow's double bottoms in 1978 and 1980.) Our point here is that rising prices create a gambling fever that affects even those who are supposed to know better.

All Those Itchy Wallets Near the Top

Our job is not only to show you when to buy, and how to buy more skillfully, but to keep you from buying emotionally. The ability to avoid buying at the wrong time is more important than trying to be right. In actual dollars, the losses from one overly emotional plunge can eat up the profits from two carefully selected winners. You can be right more often than not and still lose money. The floor broker with an order to execute is compelled to do more than just watch. He watches so as to be able to take more intelligent action. The typical investor or trader, however, becomes less objective the more he watches; the craving to be part of the excitement overpowers common sense.

The phenomenon of the itchy wallet is most virulently seen in a sold-out bull—the investor who is convinced the market is going higher, but finds himself on the sidelines without owning anything, having sold out his holdings during the previous downdraft or too soon in the rebound. Now he's got to own something, anything. The very ingredient—that the market is there and will always be there day after day, week after week—that should keep him calm and patient is the ingredient that causes him to want to buy something just to be a participant. After all, he's been paying attention, reading the paper every day, calling his broker. He wants something going for him, a bet that he can root for, get aggravated about, come alive with. No matter that the market is starting to look toppy; no matter that stocks are overbought; no matter that his last three bets have proven costly. He's still anxious to buy.

Of course, the market helps. It is typical of the late stages of a move—after a sustained advance, whether it's Harry's individual stock or the market in general—that stocks look their most exciting just as they've become dangerous. No one is immune when stock prices are leaping conspicuously, not the boardroom sitter, the nibbler on the other end of the broker's phone, the big institution, even the professional trader who is sure he can scalp one last point before he gets out. Everyone wants a piece of the action, to get his bet down. Everyone thinks if he doesn't buy right then and there, he'll miss out. So all the buying power gets used up, and there's no one left to buy, no one left to sell to. That's life at the top.

Although the urge to participate is strongest when the market is at its most exciting, many investors are willing to buy something regardless of the market climate. They don't give a second's thought to the fluctuations, or a moment's consideration to market timing, when a recommendation or a hot tip or extra cash comes their way. Indeed, certain institutions (pension or mutual funds, bank-trust departments, and the like) believe so religiously in the market that they follow a policy of being fully invested at all times. After all, it is their job to invest. As long as the game is played so incessantly, they feel obliged to be involved. So, too, the edgy onlooker. As soon as he has sold his position, he looks for something else to buy. Brokers, as salesmen, know from experience that the best way to get a customer to sell a holding is to lure him with a stock to switch to. Just as brokers always have something to recommend, even in a bear market, so, too, the outsider wants to keep betting. He'll play the game, without even considering the structure of the game. There's always a rationale behind this, like that of the gambler who, when asked why he bets in a game with loaded dice, replies: "It's the only game in town."

We will say this over and over again: as long as the market fluctuates as widely as it does, as perpetually as it does, there may never be a perfect time to buy a stock, but there will always be a better time and a worse time, when the odds are in your favor and when the odds are against you. It is this betting edge that we are constantly looking for. A sold-out bull, however, can't survive on that theory, because it requires patience, and perhaps long stretches of time without action; neither can brokers. For every broker who is willing to tell his customer, "I don't want you buying anything now; I just phoned to see how your golf game is," there are dozens who are afraid that if they advise their clients not to buy they might be wrong and see a stock go up without them. And besides, there's the commission they'd miss if they told you not to buy. But it's more than just the commission; many brokers don't want to take the chance of being wrong if the customer is willing to bet. Now that there is an active market in put and call options—the right to buy or sell at fixed prices for limited time spans—such brokers have an easy sales pitch: they pursuade their customers to bet via options because "you know how much you can lose." No, thanks.

It seems that brokers as well as their customers—call it human nature, if you want—are basically and perpetually bullish. Everything is tinged with that prejudice. The market, if not up today, will be up tomorrow. Sell recommendations, if any, are masked by the phrase "downgraded to a hold." But there is a never-ending quest for something to buy. "What d'ya like in the third race?" is translated to "Got a hot stock to buy today?" Once someone has joined the believers that the market is a place to play with money, he is always susceptible to buying. The lure, let us say, is how easy it seems to be to spot the winning card of the three being shuffled.

Of course, brokers have a good reason to keep the buy recommendations coming. A sold-out investor, bored and without a bet, might take his money and go to another firm. He might discover the virtues of real estate or Treasury bills. So the brokers rely on the faith of their clients: buy this, and if it doesn't work out well, let's hope you'll get bailed out on the next fluctuation up. The result is that, regardless of how long or how far the market has already been going up, or how vulnerable to a correction prices may be, brokerage houses continuously emit a steady stream of recommendations; the same is true for many advisory services. Even if they are editorially negative on the market climate in general, they'll try to dig up something, anything, to recommend. Actually, this is due only partially to a conviction that if they don't come up with something to recommend, the customer will go elsewhere; it also stems from a deep-rooted faith that the bullish side is the good side, the right side, the nice side. It is not just their job but their duty to keep recommending stocks to buy.

Both the sold-out bull and the novice, increasingly unable to bear being on the outside of the only game in town, have their anxieties fed by the broker's push to buy something. Nowadays a good salesman can get a wary potential client hooked by enticing him or her not with a hot tip but instead with those in-house high-yielding money funds. Out comes the money from the savings bank, and once the client is comfortable doing business with the firm, a simple recommendation of a stock or two—what's the harm in phoning, "just in case you have any interest"—comes forth. Let interest rates drop and stock prices leap, and even someone who didn't believe in buying stocks can get excited enough to place a bet.

Those Locked-Up Wallets Near Bottoms

We don't mean to pick on brokers in all this. The customer, of course, makes the decision to spend. The unfortunate phenomenon, however, is the companion fact that all those itchy wallets near tops get locked up near bottoms, so that the proverbial moth would fly out when they finally decide to loosen up. All those hitherto spendthrift bulls become tightwads just when buying is at its most sensible. Fear becomes the prevailing attitude precisely when the market is least risky. In contrast to casting caution to the winds, in his eagerness to buy as the market is running headlong (albeit excitingly) into a top, at bottoms the typical investor won't go near a stock. Oh, he'll nibble on the way down. If he's used to owning stocks, he'll buy his broker's seemingly sensible recommendations when the declining market seems to have paused. The big institutions will start to pick up stocks they think have fallen "far enough." And they'll all—odd-lotter and big money alike—try to guess the bottom because that betting game becomes, for a while, the path to continuing participation. But the primary sign of a real bottom is the pervasive fear that keeps prospective buyers on the sidelines. "Not yet," they cry out in protest. "Don't call me until it stops going down," they insist. "I'm not going to buy until I'm sure it is going back up again," is the final stubbornness. Brokerage offices are like morgues; no phones ring, and the brokers themselves are doing the crossword puzzle or reading the *Morning Telegraph* instead of *The Wall Street Journal.*

Of course, there's good reason for this fear. Not only is the news uniformly negative—lower earnings; poorer sales; unemployment up; forecasts of worse to come—but they've already lost plenty of money on the way down. Nor does it matter that they've heard the old expression: "Buy 'em when nobody else wants 'em." They may even accept it as a truism, but the typical customer will insist, "Let someone else be first."

Nor can you remind these investors, be they institutions or individuals, of an even more valid truism, that the market always discounts events—that is, it always looks ahead and, therefore, the decline has already anticipated the current negative news. It may have discounted *this*, the investors will insist, but the headlines (and forecasts) make a convincing case that there is even worse news to come. It's too soon to buy, right at the bottom. To be sure, market bottoms have historically been made at about the time a recession becomes generally acknowledged . . . not near its end. (The market's discounting ability has meant that people sold as they increasingly perceived impending economic trouble, and thus, by the time the actuality arrives, the bulk of such selling pressure is already past.) But suppose, those who are scared then argue, *this* one turns into a depression instead. All the market adages may be accurate in the abstract, but translating such words into action that contains a risk is extraordinarily difficult.

The reason is that at bottoms the place to be is out. On the way up, everyone wants to own stocks for the excitement, but on the way down, everyone wants to boast of having nothing to do with such a losing game. For some, too, there is, if not excitement, at least an emotional release, a sense of relief, that comes from finally dumping the stocks that have been causing so much discomfort. Having recently sold, who could turn around and buy? Any rally would look like a temporary technical deception, as other rallies did earlier in the decline, for now these investors want to be proven right for having sold.

The psychology of crowds has struck home again. The mob has been stampeding to the exits. When the game is betting on getting out, buying is inconceivable. It's easy to buy when everyone else is buying, but it is exceedingly difficult when you're the only one. An advisor, despite evidence in hand that he trusts, can feel as if he's gone way out on a lonely limb which just a little bit more selling activity could saw off. The market may have many of the same indications that past bottoms have had, but until prices actually start to rise again, buying can seem too dangerous to do anything more than think longingly about. After all, one of the sure indications of a true bottom is that just about everyone is scared. It is only hindsight that shows how little risk there really was.

Betting on the Upside Race

Once the uptrend becomes well established, placing bets is easier. A bull market makes buying stocks socially acceptable again. The stock market is now viewed as a proper place for excess capital: you can watch your money grow, collect dividends, take a flyer on a new issue and think of it as helping venture capitalism. And you are placing your bets not at the race track but in a place with carpets on the floor, where the brokers wear suits and ties. It may not seem like gambling at all, but beneath these apparent motivations lies the quest for excitement.

This participation in the grand market race upward can provide many different types of emotional satisfaction. Some enjoy the sheer thrill of the gamble, of betting on a stock to go up, and care primarily for having something to root for. Others are in psychic competition with neighbors or friends, or even with themselves, challenging their minds and egos to do well. Others, more secretive, enjoy the market as if it is another, livelier life that wives and office companions don't share. Still others feel the pleasure of being part of a club, are expansive about their dealings, even boastful. Just as people talk to strangers at race tracks ("The 8 horse, are you crazy? Look at the 6, a sure winner") they'd never say hello to anywhere else, the excitement of the club makes playing the market satisfying. "Buy me 100 shares" gets the bet down before the next tick appears on the tape.

But there are sensible times to buy stocks as well as emotional ones. As long as the market fluctuates, we want you to take advantage of its swings rather than let them take advantage of you. In succeeding chapters, we'll give you guidelines to help you buy near bottoms and to keep you from getting emotionally sucked in near tops. It isn't easy, but the path to successful market betting is to curb the hidden desire to participate in the excitement; to be as calm, cool, and objective as possible.

3

WHEN TO BUY

The market is the only gambling arena we know of where you have to bet while the action's in progress. At the race track, the pari-mutuel machines automatically lock at the cry of "They're off." At the roulette wheel, the croupier cries "Bets, please" before he spins the wheel. But once the opening gong sounds from above the floor of the New York Stock Exchange, prices continue to change all day; watching the tape becomes as addicting as eating peanuts at a cocktail party—you always want to see just one more tick and then another; it is increasingly hard to remain calm, cool, and objective. Indeed, the first buying opportunity we want to talk about plunges you right into the most hectic of all market situations.

Buying during a Selling Climax

Every once in a while, a buying opportunity comes along that's a bit like betting Man O'War to show. If you can read the signs right, a selling climax is just about as low-risk a chance to make a successful trade as you'll ever get. And yet it develops during the scariest of conditions.

What do we mean by a selling climax? The phrase has been

overused in recent years because, when prices are falling, many market commentators inevitably begin to anticipate one. But writing that "what this market needs to stop declining is a good selling climax," or "a selling climax appears imminent to clear the air," is, like a closely watched pot, why they so often refuse to materialize. A true selling climax is rare, but the so-called Hunt silver debacle, or Silver Thursday, is a recent example. The market had been declining severely for several weeks, from a top in early February 1980 all the way through March, taking the Dow Industrial Average down over 150 points. Previous support had been penetrated easily and the general climate had become one of fear. Then, on a Thursday afternoon (unusual, for most selling climaxes in the past have occurred on Tuesday mornings), the gloom became manifest. Rumors began to sweep the Exchange floor that something terrible was about to happen in the financial community. Trading in Bache shares was halted, and that magnified the rumors: the brokerage firm was about to go under because of the precarious position of all the silver contracts the Hunt brothers had bought on margin at Bache. It looked, even to a detached observer, as if a financial disaster was at hand, with a potential rippling effect that could spread to other brokerage firms and hence to the stock market itself.

By mid-afternoon, prices had fallen another 25 Dow points in waves of panic selling. The ticker tape was running extremely late. In large part, this reflected the sudden panic of small holders to get out at any price: the tape couldn't keep up with all the 100- and 200-share sell orders that needed to be printed. (To reduce the number of characters printing on the tape, Exchange policy is to announce "Volume Deleted," and if that doesn't help, the next step is "Repeat Sales Deleted"; any subsequent transactions at the same price are not printed on the tape.) When all such efforts fail to reduce tape lateness, but, instead, the panic causes even further delay, the practice has been to print "Flash Prices," in order to keep watchers posted as to the latest transaction prices. However, the widespread use of interrogation machines—which display current prices—has led to the elimination of the use of "Flash Prices" by the Exchange. Extreme tape lateness—let's say, twenty or more minutes late—as a measure of panic and dumping at any price, will have to be our signal of a climax. Such was the case that Thursday afternoon, with individual stocks down 5, even 10, points and the tape twenty-nine minutes late. Worse, it seemed increasingly likely that after the news was published that evening—with the potential that by then the news would be even worse than the rumors—the next day's trading would result in an even deeper price plunge. Virtually everyone was rushing to get out of the market exit at once.

Could you have bought stocks then? It would have been a matter of, as Kipling put it, "If you can keep your head when all about you are losing theirs." The selling proved to be climactic: panic everywhere, an almost total absence of buyers, the tape running drastically late, scare rumors abounding—those are the main ingredients. The sensible thing at that moment was not to join the stampeding mob but to consider doing the opposite. To be sure, the financial crisis could have snowballed, but a selling climax is not the time to be distracted by the news. The real question is, and always will be: If you didn't know anything about the rumors, what would the tape be saying?

Obviously, with prices having fallen so far so fast, you'd be looking not for confirmation that everything was awful but for clues, however faint, that the plunge at some point was being stemmed. We were lucky, having taken some losses earlier, for those sales produced freedom of mind as well as buying power. It's always harder to buy when one is already being racked with portfolio losses, because of the emotional entanglement. One invariably thinks one is participating merely by rooting for stocks already owned to rebound from such a crash. Better to have cash.

At a time like this, there isn't a moment to reflect on what might make a good long-term purchase. That's for another type of bottom. Instead of laughing gleefully at how far some of the stocks we'd recently sold had fallen, we began to monitor them more closely and, for added candidates, we asked the interrogation machine for its recap of those stocks showing the biggest percentage declines as of that moment. One stock was down 40 percent, another nearly 35 percent. Also on the list was Mesa Petroleum, not only down 10 points but, as a quick glance at its chart told us, back to a significant support level, where it had held during a previous major market decline. As soon as Mesa looked as if it might be holding at that same level again, we swallowed hard and bought some.

Immediately, the act of buying changed our perception from that of an incredulous observer to that of an active trader. And as our appetite for more was whetted as a result of acting, another interesting psychological push occurred. The floor broker's clerk who took that initial order said: "You're the only buyer on the floor." That wasn't quite true, of course, for by then we'd already begun to notice a few stocks refusing to go any lower, but those words did wonders for our ego, and hence for our courage. They challenged us to act on the adage: "Buy 'em when no one else wants 'em." So we quickly bought some more and, increasingly emboldened, more again. Within a few minutes, there was a mad scramble to buy all over the floor, causing the Dow Industrial Average to recoup its huge loss and close virtually unchanged for the day. It had proven to be a terrifically profitable selling climax for those able to see that the panic of others was a chance to buy.

Let's review the basic rules for such a buying opportunity, because, although rare, sooner or later you'll see such situations repeated in the future. Prices have to have been falling for an extended period beforehand; you can't get a selling climax near a market top. The instant panic generated by an advisory service's midnight sell signal on January 6, 1981, had elements of a climax in that the selling was on record-breaking volume, hysterical behavior, and an extremely late tape. Indeed, it would have been easy to make profitable trades by buying on the sharply lower prices of that day's opening, and then selling into the ensuing rebound. Nimble traders bought and sold quickly, but it was not a true buying opportunity. Because the January 6 selling occurred so close to the top, it was not truly climactic; stocks headed lower thereafter. In contrast, a true climax marks an important low; sellers are cleaned out. That's what makes it a low-risk buying opportunity.

Accordingly, a true climax must be preceded by a prolonged and steady decline, accompanied by deep-rooted gloom and a sense of doom. Finally, investors who have been tormented by the downtrend but have held on decide to disgorge their holdings because they've become convinced that prices can only get worse. Thus, in addition to such a prior extensive decline, stocks have to embark abruptly in a form of free fall. Often it is sparked by a specific financial crisis, such as rumors of a major bankruptcy or the silver fiasco, but then the dumping of stocks seems to pick up momentum on its own. It seems as if every tick on the tape is taking a stock lower, as if there are no bids around at all. It begins to look as if the only way to stem the decline would be to shut the Exchange down. Sometimes, as in May 1962, sharply lower opening prices, after a free fall the day before, mark the climactic low; in May 1970, the panic low was followed by a virtually unchanged opening the next trading day as evidence that the selling had been exhausted. In any event, not only is there a vacuum on the downside due to the absence of buyers, there is such a rush of sellers along the way that the tape runs extremely late. The panic grows. And when the ticker tape reaches the equivalent of "Flash Prices"—twenty minutes or more late—it is the clue that an extreme is being reached. Into such hysteria we want you to buy.

Of course it is not easy to remain calm in such circumstances. You have to put aside all the rumors, all the headlines real and imagined, and concentrate on the market action itself. Only the tape will tell you when the selling is ebbing and when buyers have begun to appear instead. Because the modern desk-top interrogation machine is a boon to traders at such times, serving as a surrogate to the tape, let's take a moment to discuss the information it can provide. (Brokers, of course, usually have such a machine in front of them, but even if you are just a customer on the other end of the phone, you should know what to ask your broker to ask the machine, and how to interpret the answers.) The quotation, size, and last sale arrive at the machine's display from different sources. First, there is the ticker tape itself, printing the actual transaction (the price at which it occurred, and the number of shares involved) in the correct sequence. Second, there is a separate quotation tape, revealing the bid and offer, and the size of that bid and offer. Third, there is the last sale information, which comes not from the tape itself but nowadays as it goes *into* the computer which drives the tape.

When a transaction occurs, a reporter employed by the Exchange records it on a "mark-sense" card designed so the computer can "read" it. There is room for three such transactions as well as an updated quotation supplied by or overheard from the specialist in the stock. The card is fed into the reader and hence into the computer; this then drives both the ticker and the quotation tape. It may take a while for the actual transaction to appear on the ticker tape, but as soon as the information is fed into the computer, it can be retrieved by the interrogation machine. All you have to do is ask.

The typical machine can provide a wealth of information. Most important, it tells us the latest available quotation in the stock, the number of shares bid for and offered, and the last sale price. On the customary busy opening, or during a selling climax, the tape is to one degree or another late. That's all there is to it. Once the quotation tape is caught up after the opening, it is almost always current thereafter because there are far fewer changes to record from moment to moment, although sometimes the reporter will fail to pick up a change in the quotation, causing it to lag a price change. What's more, if you ask the machine about a stock, it doesn't give you the last sale that printed on the tape but, rather, the last sale fed into the computer and the current quotation as well.

Many machines can be programed with a "market-minder" feature that enables the user to list certain stocks on the screen. The price changes for the stocks being monitored are up-to-the-minute. Each price represents the latest sale, since the information is procured as it is fed into the computer rather than after the transaction is printed on the ticker tape. Thus, the latest price change is revealed without our having to ask for it, as the "market minder" updates automatically. By watching the "market minder" as it blinks its changes, or by asking the machine for its data on a particular stock, we can track price changes closely despite an hysterical market. Mesa might be selling at 44 on a tape running twenty-nine minutes late, but if you had asked the machine for MSA during that silver-selling climax, it would have reported "− 39 7/8" as the last sale, for example, with a quotation of 39 5/8 bid, offered at 40. As soon as the ticker tape starts to run seriously late, it becomes useless. In the old days the only recourse a trader had at such a time was to watch the "Flash Prices" as they appeared on the tape to learn what was happening on the floor of the Exchange. But now the desk-top machine solves that problem.

Your eye catches MSA on the tape falling in the space of a few minutes: from 43, to 42 1/2, to 42; you know that it is collapsing along with all the other stocks. But the tape is so late that these prices have no relevance. The machine, however, reports that MSA's last trade was at −39 5/8, while the quotation has become 39 1/2 bid, offered at 39 3/4. That is, since last you checked, someone has sold to the previous bid at 5/8. At this moment you still have absolutely nothing to go on.

When it comes to deciding when to buy a stock, and which one to buy, there are a multitude of factors to consider. Compared to the one factor we're concerned with here, they may seem almost cosmic in nature, for now we must pay attention to only the most minute aspect of the marketplace: a single tick. Is it up or down from the previous different price? In our example, the machine shows a −39 5/8, so we know from the minus sign that the last sale was a downtick. Were it to read +39 5/8, we could reason that in the meantime the stock had sold even lower—at 39 1/2, say— but that someone had come in next to buy at 39 5/8. This may sound rather casual, but it is useful to think always of a minus, or down, tick, as being initiated by a seller, while a plus, or up, tick has been initiated by a buyer. In other words, a seller has to hit the bid—down—while a buyer has to take the offer—up. We want to know who is the initiator because this speaks to the dynamics of the situation.

At this moment, all we can watch for are these tiny clues: perhaps a couple of plus ticks, representing the willingness of someone, at last, to buy in the midst of the panic. Sometimes the clue is nothing more than a shift in the quotation. We're watching this intensely because we want to act at the first sign that the stock has ceased going down. We don't want to guess at the low—let someone else be that lucky—but with the market in a complete rout and Mesa already down more than 10 points, we'll take any clue as meaningful. Actually, there are now rapid price changes of +39 3/4, +39 7/8, −39 5/8, +39 3/4, and the quotation has improved to 39 5/8 bid, offered at 39 7/8. Those brief hints of stabilization are all you have to go on. A buy order is rushed down to the floor and shares are purchased on the offer at 39 7/8. It wasn't the absolute low, but considering that the stock leapt right back up within the next several minutes to close over 45 and reached 48 the next morning, you've been amply rewarded by paying close attention to detail.

Even though that is a true enough story, it isn't as easy as it may sound. During a selling climax you need to monitor not only one stock but several different issues—market leaders as well as those stocks you might want to buy—to see if the trend is truly, even if only on a small scale, shifting all over the Exchange floor. What we've just described for Mesa should be equally visible in General Motors, IBM, and Georgia Pacific. Once you sense that the trend is there, it's time to act. And there is nothing like being instantly right to help you feed more buy orders to the floor, despite the apparent risk.

There is always a risk in the stock market. Otherwise, there'd be no excitement to the bet. But a true selling climax, if you time your purchases precisely, offers that rare chance to buy with the least risk possible. The opportunity is, however, not only rare but short-lived in nature. Stocks bounce back up as wildly as they came down, because now there has been a vacuum left overhead. Just about all the potential sellers have already dumped in their panic to get out, and there is very little stock offered for the next several points on the path back up. After the silver-panic climax, the rebound lasted about four trading days and carried the Dow Industrial Average upward another 60 points. Thereafter, however, the market began to retreat again and over the next three weeks gave back almost all that it had gained. This inevitable fluctuation back down is known as a "test of the low"—and it is on this test that we get our next sensible chance to buy.

Buying on the Test of the Low

Indeed, the subsequent test has its own elements of reduced risk, and presents a calmer chance to buy for longer-term objectives. What makes buying on the test of the low desirable is that it is accompanied by an array of favorable indicator signals and individual stock-chart improvements, rather than the isolation of trying to keep your head during the hysteria and gloom of a selling climax. By this time you've had a chance to see which stocks are proving themselves to be stronger than the market—the newly emerging leaders—and you can more comfortably pick out the issues you ought to be able to hold during a whole new bull trend.

It's a bit embarrassing to admit, but the fact is that at this point there are suddenly a few strong stocks that should have been bought already. We don't mean they got missed because they are obscure; they could be Du Pont or Texaco. But, in the midst of a bear market, one's viewpoint is not geared to spotting incipient bullish stocks; the resistance to further decline which had begun even while the averages were still slipping becomes apparent only after a rally heightens the look of the chart and shows that base building for a new advance had already developed. The realization that there are at long last some worthwhile stocks to buy is one of the post-climactic clues that the market is actually changing trend from down to up. Other factors, too, come together to help identify a buying opportunity based on a test of the prior low. The consensus must still be one of anxiety and pervasive bearishness, and sentiment indicators, such as odd-lot shorting and put-option buying, will intensify. The recent rebound will be dismissed as purely technical in nature—that is, it occurred because the market got oversold and was "due" for a bounce. The economic news and expectations will continue to be a source of fear, perhaps increasingly so. As prices start to slide again, it will look as if the bear trend is about to be resumed in full force.

Here's what readers of *The Wall Street Journal* were told on Monday morning, April 21, 1980, under the headline "Strategists Advocate Defensive Moves to Meet Recession." The article began: "Wall Street strategists are manning the barricades and plotting defensive moves to grapple with the recession at hand . . . The most forceful among the strategists are those warning against committing new funds to stocks until the full impact of the recession is seen in corporate earnings and balance sheets . . . Others are advocating total avoidance of both bonds and stocks until evidence is obtained as to the severity of the downturn . . . The stock market is still in a 'dangerous phase, where the potential decline for individual securities is great.' " Later in the article, the director of research for a major mutual-fund organization was quoted: "The market will stay in a fairly narrow channel between 740 and 800 in the Dow Jones Industrial Average, but if events move rapidly in the recession, the market could break below 740." What brought this bearishness out in full force was that the market had declined 28 Dow points during the preceding week. Indeed, following the publication of these opinions, it fell another 12 points on that Monday.

But that very day's low marked the successful test of the prior selling-climax low. For the remaining four trading days of the week, the Dow Industrial Average leapt over 50 points across the 800 level. Nevertheless, that show of strength didn't change the consensus much, for the April 28 *Wall Street Journal* reported: "Caution Is Prevalent Among Advisors Despite the Rally." It was the same old anxiety, yet the market had already launched a powerful bull move which was to carry over 200 additional Dow points and last well into the autumn before any signs of trouble set in. Fear and worry about inflation, or recession, or whatever the bugaboo of the day happens to be, will invariably be found at important market bottoms.

Obviously, the behavior of stocks themselves will tell a more important story than the headlines, because the market consistently has forecast events much better than the economists have. Remember, one of the market's characteristics is that it discounts; the bad news has been anticipated by those who sold back at the prior top. But you can't assume that prices will turn upward simply because almost everyone has become pessimistic. Nor do we want just to guess when to step in and buy during a decline, even if we have a sense that it is shaping up as the necessary test of the prior climactic low (rather than a renewal of the decline). The practical message has to come from the market itself, via the indicators, which we will discuss in a later chapter. Under the surface appearance of a renewed decline in the averages, one or more indicators will begin to tell a different story of what is happening. We look to two different types of indicators to provide such evidence. Certain sentiment indicators (odd-lot or specialist short-selling, for example) can tell us if the consensus has become intensely bearish —so we can consider becoming bullish instead. And the internal

An Appraisal: Strategists Advocate Defensive Moves to Meet Recession

By GENE G. MARCIAL

Wall Street strategists are manning the "barricades" and plotting defensive moves to grapple with the recession at hand. But there isn't any unanimity in the battle plans.

The most forceful among the strategists, however, are those warning against committing new funds to stocks until the full impact of the recession is seen in corporate earnings and balance sheets.

Others are advocating total avoidance of both bonds and stocks until evidence is obtained as to the severity of the downturn.

"It's fairly clear that a recession began in March and that we are in a very steep deceleration pace at the moment," says Eric Miller, senior vice president and chairman of investment policy at Donaldson, Lufkin & Jenrette Securities Corp.

"The key question is how deep the recession will be," says Charles Miller, president of Advisory Funds Inc., a Houston-based investment counseling company. The stock market, he says, is still in a "dangerous phase, where the potential decline for individual securities is great." Individual companies face very poor earnings in the next year and a half, Mr. Miller believes, warning that liquidity squeezes will reduce significantly growth of dividends or will cause dividend cuts.

Abreast of the Market

In spite of the slippage of interest rates last week, with some commercial banks cutting their prime, or minimum, rate to 19½% from 20%, some analysts aren't fully convinced the worst is over. "We are advising clients to sit very tight in cash equivalents," says Anthony L. Adams, managing partner at QSR Advisory Corp., a New York investment concern. "Bonds are still tricky despite the big rally in bond prices last week," he says. He is convinced that both stocks and bonds remain volatile and that it wouldn't pay to make long-term commitments in either.

Analysts say there is a deep sense of unease among investors on the question of how long and how steep the recession will

be, and how long it will take to make an effective impact on inflation. "The fear is nobody knows which companies will break under the pressure of liquidity constriction and earnings slide," says Monte Gordon, director of research of Dreyfus Corp. On that basis, he doesn't expect the market to move forward in the next three months.

"The market will stay in a fairly narrow channel, between 740 and 800 in the Dow Jones industrial average, but if events move rapidly in the recession, the market could break below 740," warns Mr. Gordon.

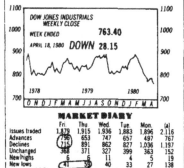

DOW JONES INDUSTRIALS WEEKLY CLOSE

WEEK ENDED APRIL 18, 1980 **763.40 DOWN 28.15**

MARKET DIARY

	Fri.	Thu.	Wed.	Tue.	Mon.	(a)
Issues traded	1,879	1,915	1,936	1,883	1,896	2,116
Advances	796	653	747	657	497	767
Declines	715	891	862	827	1,036	1,197
Unchanged	368	371	327	399	363	152
New highs	6	6	11	4	5	19
New lows	41	59	40	33	27	138

(a) Summary for the week ended April 18, 1980.

DOW JONES CLOSING AVERAGES

	1980	Friday Change	%	1979	Yr. Ago % Chg.	Since Dec. 31	%
Ind ...	763.40	−5.49	−0.71	856.98	−10.92	−75.34	−8.98
Trn ...	238.17	−2.68	−1.11	231.01	+ 3.10	−14.22	−5.63
Utl ...	106.60	−0.37	−0.35	102.74	+ 3.76		
Cmp ..	279.02	−2.14	−0.76	292.65	− 4.66	−19.30	−6.47

Ex-dividends of Columbia Gas System 65 cents lowered the utility average by 0.20.

The above ex-dividends lowered the composite average by 0.10.

OTHER MARKET INDICATORS

		1980	— Change —		1979
N.Y.S.E.	Composite	57.21	−0.24	−0.42%	57.09
	Industrial	64.38	−0.35	−0.54%	63.14
	Utility	35.73	+0.04	+0.11%	38.34
	Transportation	47.10	−0.46	−0.97%	45.63
	Financial	56.95	+0.04	+0.07%	59.47
Amer. Ex. Mkt. Val. Index		235.72	+0.53	+0.23%	180.82
Nasdaq OTC Composite		134.66	+0.11	+0.08%	133.67
	Industrial	156.78	−0.06	−0.04%	147.75
	Insurance	142.19	+0.10	+0.07%	142.80
	Banks	97.05	+0.66	+0.69%	107.29
Stand. & Poor's 500		100.55	−0.50	−0.49%	101.23
	400 Industrial	112.44	−0.62	−0.55%	112.90

TRADING ACTIVITY

Volume of advancing stocks on N.Y.S.E., 9,810,000 shares; volume of declining stocks, 12,920,000. On American S.E., volume of advancing stocks, 1,090,000; volume of declining stocks, 1,030,000. Nasdaq volume of advancing stocks, 3,279,200; volume of declining stocks, 3,289,500.

indicators (such as the advance/decline line or the high/low statistics) provide a reliable guide to timing, by giving specific signals when the market has become much better than the falling averages are making it look. The same indicators don't always work at similar bottoms, but all bottoms have in common the fact that at least some indicators will begin giving off bullish signals despite declining prices.

Remember, we don't need absolute proof. The previous low and bounce has already encouraged us to start searching for signs of a change in trend. But what makes this climate different from those minor rally phases during the prior path downward? First, there is the climactic action—heavy-volume dumping. Second, the fear and panic has created, at last, a bearish consensus. Instead of the attitude, early in the decline, that it was survivable, investors have not only thrown in the towel but many have switched to the short side (or have stepped up their buying of put options as a bet on a further decline). But, third, we've begun to see certain buyable stocks, the leading action of which serves to confirm that we're on the right track. All we're really looking for now is evidence that the market is getting better internally despite the decline. The best such evidence comes from divergences between the Dow Industrial Average and various indicators. The all-important rule to remember is that *it doesn't matter what the divergences are; any divergence is meaningful.* This is not magical; a divergence means that some facet of the market no longer is in unison with the previously pervasive downtrend; the bearish monolith is breaking apart at last.

For example, the test of the low created on the climactic action of that silver scare produced exactly the kind of divergences needed for an important buy signal. On Monday, April 21, the drop of 12 points in the Dow Industrial Average produced a new closing low below the close of that panic day three weeks earlier. How would you have known, especially if you'd read all those scare words in that morning's *Wall Street Journal,* that the decline wasn't going to continue, even accelerate, instead? Well, for one thing, as the tables attached to the articles reveal, on the previous Friday the blue-chip average was off 5.46 points, yet there were only 41 new lows compared to 59 the day before. For another, despite the drop in the Dow that Friday, more stocks advanced than declined. Thus,

An Appraisal: Caution Is Prevalent Among Advisers Despite the Rally

By VICTOR J. HILLERY

Although many investment officers have been heartened by the stock market's recent action, the recession's unknown dimensions are making them reluctant to rush back into equities.

There's also a renewed anxiety about Middle East developments in the wake of the abortive U.S. rescue effort in Iran.

"We want to participate in the longer-run growth potential of selected equities, but we don't feel that the time for maximum commitment is here yet," asserts Daniel S. Ahearn, senior vice president and investment policy committee chairman at Wellington Management Co., Boston.

He's concerned that the "coming recession may be deeper and last longer than most people appear to expect." He fears that, with a combination of deteriorating profit margins and a substantial slowdown in unit sales growth, profits could decline this year and in 1981.

"We don't think the stock market has discounted two years of weak corporate profits," he asserts.

In addition, he thinks that even with a severe recession it will be difficult to reduce inflation below a double-digit level. "And this raises the possibility of tighter wage and price controls," he says. "It also would limit any decline in long-term interest rates."

Abreast of the Market

Mr. Ahearn is troubled, too, by the "uncertainties connected with Iran and Afghanistan and the excessive cartel price for international oil."

In this atmosphere, Wellington Management, which supervises $4.9 billion in mutual funds and counsel accounts and advises on another $3.9 billion, expects the market "to continue extraordinarily volatile." Wellington's aggressive equity accounts are about 80% invested and its stock-bond balanced accounts are about 60% in equities.

Continuing market volatility also is expected by H.O. (Harry) Johnston, senior investment officer of St. Louis Union Trust Co. He attributes this to lack of investor confidence that's fostered by the unknowns surrounding the recession and inflation.

Investors will be disturbed, he suggests, by dividend reductions and omissions and possibly a few bankruptcies. Another threatening cloud, he adds, is the possible "politicizing" of the Federal Reserve in this election year, diverting it from its targets.

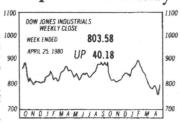

DOW JONES INDUSTRIALS
WEEKLY CLOSE

WEEK ENDED **803.58**
APRIL 25, 1980 UP **40.18**

MARKET DIARY

	Fri.	Thu.	Wed.	Tue.	Mon.	(a)
Issues traded	1,828	1,852	1,921	1,918	1,905	2,124
Advances	662	1,021	1,087	1,402	470	1,533
Declines	779	498	488	261	1,036	428
Unchanged	387	333	346	255	399	163
New highs	9	10	12	5	2	24
New lows	19	20	18	38	85	141

(a) Summary for the week ended April 25, 1980

DOW JONES CLOSING AVERAGES

	---------- Friday ----------			Yr. Ago	---- Since ----	
	1980	Change	%	1979	% Chg. Dec. 31	%
Ind ...	803.58	+6.48	+0.81	856.64	-6.19 -35.16	-4.19
Trn ...	241.19	+0.20	+0.08	230.86	+4.48 -11.20	-4.44
Utl ...	108.56	-0.51	-0.47	101.18	+7.29 + 1.96	+1.84
Cmp ..	288.73	+1.07	+0.37	291.78	-1.05 - 9.59	-3.22

Ex-dividends of Inco Ltd. 18 cents and F.W. Woolworth Co. 45 cents lowered the industrial average by 0.51.
Ex-dividend of Chessie System 64 cents lowered the transportation average by 0.29.
The above ex-dividends lowered the composite average by 0.20.

OTHER MARKET INDICATORS

	1980	- Change -		1979
N.Y.S.E. Composite	59.73	+0.35	+0.59%	57.40
Industrial	67.73	+0.57	+0.85%	63.75
Utility	36.35	-0.07	-0.19%	37.87
Transportation	48.13	+0.07	+0.15%	45.87
Financial	58.30	-0.26	-0.44%	59.45
Amer. Ex. Mkt. Val. Index	249.31	+1.40	+0.57%	183.65
Nasdaq OTC Composite	137.92	-0.77	-0.56%	134.37
Industrial	161.42	-0.93	-0.57%	149.60
Insurance	144.34	-1.27	-0.87%	142.65
Banks	98.37	-0.52	-0.53%	107.10
Stand. & Poor's 500	105.16	+0.76	+0.73%	101.80
400 Industrial	118.13	+1.07	+0.91%	113.82

TRADING ACTIVITY

Volume of advancing stocks on N.Y.S.E., 14,300,000 shares; volume of declining stocks, 10,140,000. On American S.E., volume of advancing stocks, 1,970,000; volume of declining stocks, 1,140,000. Nasdaq volume of advancing stocks, 2,443,400; volume of declining stocks, 4,611,900.

lready present for an impending reversal. And
21, when the Dow dropped another 12 points to
89 new lows, compared to 698 on the day, three
e climactic low. In short, the market action of
/as far better than the Dow Industrial Average
made it look. It was time to buy.

Tests of the low come in two varieties. The first type is when the
Dow makes a new closing low but, as in 1980, the indicators divert
in blatant fashion. Another example of this occurred in 1962 on the
heels of a classic selling climax at the end of May. Following the
initial rebound, the DJIA actually slid to a new low about three
weeks later. But there were many favorable indicators around;
odd-lot short sales, for example, indicating the extreme bearishness
of small traders, had reached over 6 percent for a very bullish
reading, and the High/Low Differential refused to confirm the
May lows, thus creating a bullish divergence.

In 1970 we saw an example of the second type, a successful test
of the Dow's May low. During the next decline, which culminated
in early July, the blue-chip average held well, but the Advance/De-
cline Line went to a new low, producing a favorable divergence.
This bottom, in addition, was accompanied by positive sentiment
readings—high odd-lot (amateur) short-selling and the lowest specialist (professional) short-selling ratios since 1962. What is interesting about such a divergence is that when the Advance/Decline
Line makes a new low, it encourages the bears to believe they are
right, since they see those falling prices in many stocks. But what
they miss is that there has been a divergence, and, consistently
through market history, *any divergence signals a change in trend.*

A buy-signal divergence also happened in 1974, as the biggest
bear market since '29 neared its end. The DJIA hit its initial low
in October (also anticipated by high odd-lot and low specialist
short-selling). But following a modest rally, it looked to many
pessimistic investors as if the decline were resuming in full force.
They were convinced they were right when the Dow made a double
bottom (closing at virtually the same level as had been reached in
October), while the Advance/Decline continued to go lower. This
bullish divergence was confirmed by the High/Low Differential,
which showed far better readings on the December low than had

been registered on the first low, indicating that many stocks had already begun to resist any further decline.

The net result of such signals is that you can be comfortable buying even though the prevailing climate is so gloomy. New lows, whether in the Dow average or the Advance/Decline Line, keep almost everyone else too scared to compete with you. You actually can "buy 'em when nobody else wants 'em."

What misleads most people is that they tend to believe that when the initial rally fizzles it marks a true failure. They are still in tune with the prior bear trend, and this is reinforced by the prevalent bad news and gloomy comments such as those quoted above from the *Journal*'s "Abreast of the Market" column, and reinforced even after the rise has begun by continued fear and disbelief (see the *Journal*'s April 28 column as well). Thus a renewed decline confirms their fears, especially since they've just seen what started out to be an exciting rebound actually fail. But stocks never—and even in the perverse market this particular "never" is safe to use —turn around and go straight back up well. A V-shaped pattern will always fail. In fact, one of the useful measures of a rally that will prove to be only a modest bear-market rebound is that it comes from such a reversal. It is only when there is a subsequent test of the low that it becomes safe to buy for more than a quick trade.

This is the way a major bottom forms, after a cleanout of fearful selling and a test which provides evidence that individual stocks have begun to hold despite the bad news. In addition to the various divergence and sentiment indicators, there is another tool to help you identify an important bottom and keep you out of all false rallies until the time is ripe to buy. The moving average of the Dow Industrial Average (or the moving average of an individual stock) is so much like a shadow that we too often merely glance at it when we should be scrutinizing it. In effect, a moving average represents both past price change and the rate of change, and it is applied to a chart which depicts current price action. It has been described belittlingly as no more than the wake of a ship, and that's all it is —until it becomes useful.

One fancy computer-based service we know of thinks its computer is so smart that it can establish an exact number of days for a moving average appropriate to each individual stock or market average—23, or 9, or 32 days—with little regard for the fact that the marketplace is never so simple, consistent, or accommodating. The standard methods of calculation not only work consistently enough for our purposes, but they have the advantage of being relatively easy to compute or are readily available in published chart services. For our money, these longer-term moving-average lines work far more often than random expectation could have it. However, we have never found any similar consistency in the shorter-term moving averages which can also be found in chart services: the 30-day or 50-day calculations. We ignore them in our own trading and will ignore them here.

But the longer-term moving-average line is a consistently useful tool both for stocks and for averages. What it does best is tell you where you are in the trend. Such a moving average is calculated in various ways by different chart services. Mansfield, supplying weekly bar charts, uses a weighted 30-week method; that's the approximate equivalent of 150 trading days, with the latest week given 30 times the weight of the price that dates back 30 weeks. The weighting tends to make it turn direction faster—and to be crossed on the up or down side earlier—so Mansfield's moving average is a leading line, a factor we find helpful since we prefer early clues, even though that means occasional false starts. Trendline, printing daily bar charts, provides a moving average based on an unweighted 150-day trading span. Daily Graphs, while similarly printing daily bar charts, uses 200 trading days, also unweighted. As a result, its line is the last of the three to bottom and to start turning upward; those additional days require a longer time span to start swinging around, as older higher numbers are dropped and new ones replace them.

Despite these differences in calculation, all three charts are useful, and not so far apart from each other as to be conflicting or contradictory. A clearly defined moving-average line—that is, one that has remained uncrossed for a considerable length of time—is valid in any of these services. While Mansfield charts can provide untrammeled breakouts— a decisive move up across the line—and thus can be rewardingly early, often the actual individual stock breakout on heavy volume comes thereafter on a crossing of the daily chart's moving-average line. The fresh perspective obtained by checking out a reading on another chart is often a useful analytical approach.

Here's a Mansfield chart of the Dow Industrial Average during the bear market of 1977. A top was reached in September 1976 (A), and the moving-average line—the dark line on the chart—at that point began to arc over and dip down. Although there was a brief upside interlude at year end (B), thereafter the trend of the market was clearly down. As the bear market gathered momentum, the long-term moving-average line was evidence of direction and contained the decline all the way down. Mid-year rally attempts (C) were halted at the line—which serves as resistance—and then the decline accelerated. Near year end (D), an attempt to stabilize looked momentarily promising, but again the rally attempts failed, twice, at the line, and in January 1978 (E) the decline resumed.

As such a serious decline unfolds, the moving-average line starts trailing the price action because there are still many high-level inputs included in the calculation. So long as this picture exists, the primary trend is down, and this is all the warning you should need

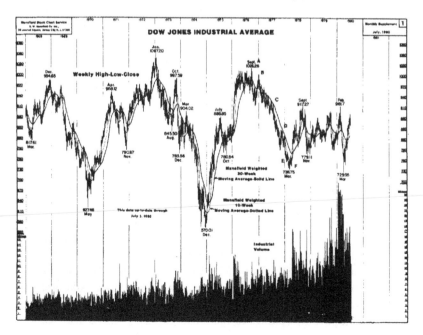

to avoid the temptation to buy. The moving-average line, in its function as a form of resistance, acts like a jailer, keeping its prisoner within bounds. (The reason is that the individual components of the average, too, have rallied only up to their resistance levels, where heavy supply for sale stops any further advance.) Intervening rallies may redress a particularly wide spread between the two, but because the moving-average line is a form of resistance, it may sometimes be nudged, but will almost always remain uncrossed by price action or, if crossed slightly, will nevertheless continue to identify the direction of the trend by still heading downward. *So long as the moving-average line is pointing downward, it is too soon to buy.*

Finally, the decline has been so severe and the market average (or individual stock price) has come down far enough to have left its long-term moving average behind and, of course, well above the current price level. This was the case in November 1977 (D), when a rally made it back only to the line before failing, and then again in March 1978. This time, however, the action was accompanied by considerable improvement in various indicators and in individual stock action. It seemed as if only the Dow components were weak, but even then there was a brief and successful test (F) of the 736 low. When the rally finally came, it burst out across the moving-average line, which then immediately reversed direction. As it headed upward, it signaled that the bear trend was over and a new uptrend had begun.

Such reversals take effect very rapidly in terms of the market averages. The shift from heading downward to turning up is, therefore, almost always a coincident, rather than a leading, clue. What it does define for us is the direction of the trend, and the rule is: Stay out as long as it is pointing downward; start buying when it reverses. If the moving average is far away, you are assured that nothing more than a bear-market rally is brewing.

But with an individual stock, the action usually takes longer. The stock begins to move sideways: rallying, declining, rallying, declining. These gyrations enable the longer-term moving-average line to catch up with the current price action as higher old prices are dropped and replaced with the latest, much lower prices. Thus, the straight-down plunge of the moving-average line is also being arrested. At first it loses its rate of decline and then starts to arc sideways, although, of course, it remains above the current price level. The more the price action gyrates, the more time the moving-average line has to cease heading down and to move sideways itself. Therefore, the bigger the base being formed by the stock the better, as buyers step in to help it increasingly resist further decline, for it gives the moving-average line ample time to catch up. Now it is quite possible, even at this juncture, that all we have is a consolidation of the prior decline, and that the stock will rally only up to the moving-average line before falling again. You are well warned not to believe in this action so long as the moving-average line is still heading downward. Don't try to guess a bottom yet, because there's a lot more worrisome action ahead, and there's no need to tie your money up yet. But once the picture begins to change, the situation becomes viable. This doesn't happen overnight in an individual stock, which is why the longer-term moving-average line is better for our purposes. Often, the first rally or two will fail under or just at the moving-average line. But if a base has begun to form, it will bring with it a loss of downside momentum in the trailing moving average, and create a potential change in trend.

The following chart of General Electric during the same period is a simple example. You can see that a potential inverse head-and-shoulders bottom (a chart formation that resembles an upside-down human head and shoulders, with the head as the lowest point, relatively balanced with sell-offs, or "shoulders," on either side) began to materialize in early 1978. The moving-average line (A) was still heading sharply down, warning that it was no time to buy. The first rally from what eventually turned out to be the left-shoulder low at about 45 failed at 48, and another leg of the decline set in, carrying to just under 44, and ultimately proving to be the head of the bottom formation. The second rally also halted near 48, but by this time the moving-average line had reached that price level, serving as additional resistance for the moment. Note that during this extended sideways action the moving-average line had time to lose downward momentum and to start turning sideways. Another dip came, but this time only to 46, for both a successful test of the low and the creation of a right shoulder. To complete the inverse head-and-shoulders formation, or base, in the

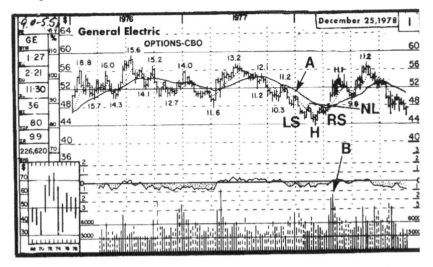

stock, we could now also draw a neckline connecting the two rally peaks, noting that the moving-average line was at approximately the same price level—just under 48. Thus, when General Electric moved decisively across that level, on increased volume (see point B, which depicts the significant increase in trading activity), it was staging an important upside breakout across both the hitherto downtrending moving-average line and the neckline, which had halted the two prior rallies.

The Breakout Buy

Such breakouts to the upside mark the third opportunity in a cycle for intelligent and objective buying. Our focus now shifts from general market timing to that of individual issues. We are constantly on the lookout for breakout potentials because they occur frequently and provide an excellent opportunity to time our purchases to the precise moment the trend is turning from down to up. You can see on the chart of the Dow Industrial Average that the upside breakout works well as a general market buy signal, too, but we still need to decide which stocks to buy. The presence of individual stock charts with such potential, especially, as was the case at the 1978 bottom, when early leaders are already breaking out on the upside even as the DJIA is still sliding, can help you anticipate the upside breakout in the average itself. But, more important, such charts give you desirable buy candidates. You may fret that you've missed the time to buy if the secondary test of the low has come and gone, but the breakout itself still provides the definitive opportunity, because it is proof positive as to direction. It signals a worthwhile move ahead.

But before we come to the moment of the breakout, let's discuss the base-building action. A base begins as sideways action as buyers step forward to absorb shares late sellers are still anxious to unload. You may wonder why buying during this period isn't good enough. After all, you'd be buying close to the low and hence could get a better price. Well, for one thing, as long as the long-term moving average is still pointing downward, the base could turn out instead to be just a consolidation along the path of a soon-to-be-resumed decline. Furthermore, we always want to be as sure as possible when we place our bet, and that means waiting for the breakout to prove both an actual trend reversal and strength. Having waited this long, we're willing to pay a couple of points for the insurance. At a major bottom, these few points are trivial. In addition, waiting for the breakout means that our money can be held safely on the sidelines until the last possible moment—buying just as the dynamic phase begins. Obviously, if you see a chart such as the General Electric, with a reasonably clear head-and-shoulders bottom pattern and a moving-average line that has begun to arc sideways, it is possible to anticipate. But buying still wasn't safe while the head was being formed, for the new low has continued the downtrend; anticipation can only be done when a right shoulder serves as a successful test of the low, and when there is a lot of supporting evidence.

Sometimes base building takes no set pattern. More often, though, it is identifiable. The General Electric picture is a near perfect head-and-shoulders bottom. But you can also see that it is an ascending triangle, formed by an uptrend line connecting the low of the head and the secondary test low of the right shoulder. Often, a third dip before the breakout will help confirm that pattern of an ascending triangle. The upper line of such a triangle is, of course, the neckline connecting the rally peaks. Occasionally, you'll spot a symmetrical triangle instead, wherein the rally peaks are successively lower and the sell-off lows are successively higher, depicting in chart form the battle between buyers increasingly raising their bids and sellers willing to take lower and lower prices for their shares. What we have—it is the nature of a base—is this tug-of-war between these two forces; since it comes after an extensive decline, we are looking for evidence that the buyers are beginning to win; successively higher lows indicate that the tide of this war is increasingly shifting to their side. However, sometimes, just when you think all is clear, and that a low has been established, there'll be one last whack down to a new low that looks as if the decline has resumed instead, but it will prove to be a shakeout, a false breakdown, with the next move up being quite powerful (probably because that final burst of selling has left an even bigger vacuum of supply overhead).

In any event, the characteristics of a base are, regardless of any discernible pattern, an extended sideways movement replete with fluctuations up and down (the more dynamic the better), a longer-term moving-average line that has ceased going down and has now arced to within striking distance overhead, and a couple of aborted rally peaks that have hitherto held back any further advance. Base action can be jagged; failures to make a new low certainly help define a base, and it is an increasingly bullish sign when any attempt to renew the decline holds at a successively higher level. But bearish failures are not so much the key ingredient of bottoms as bullish failures define a top. We'd say, rather, that the key ingredient of a bottom is the successful upside breakout.

Because, in our philosophy, the breakout buy is the best opportunity for taking objective action in individual stocks, let's look at it in more detail. *Our first rule* is that we want the market, and not our own action, to prove that we're on the right track. If our own anticipatory buying causes the breakout itself, we are guessing that it is okay rather than betting with the confidence we would have if we saw substantial buying from elsewhere. In order to prove the validity of our choice and the timing, *the second rule* is that volume is required as proof. Too little attention is paid to volume, yet it is an essential ingredient. As the old adage has it: "It takes buying to put a stock up, while stocks can fall of their own weight." That means you need to see a considerable increase in volume to verify the breakout. Almost every instance of an upside breakout from a potential bottom formation that has petered out and eventually failed to produce a profitable rise has as its warning clue inadequate volume on the upside. Take a look at the substantial increase in volume the week the Dow Industrial Average staged its market breakout in April 1978, and the similar sharply increased pace of trading that accompanied General Electric's breakout. Volume proves strength.

Our third rule is that a true breakout does not start from the bottom. Sorry about that, because it means you won't be buying so ego-gratifyingly close to the low. But if a stock starts rising from its low, the chances are great that it will already be tired (overbought) by the time it reaches the breakout point. It won't have enough strength left to produce a vigorous, valid move. It'll probably fizzle. That's all to the good. We really don't want it to go shooting up through the breakout point (such as the neckline) so late in the rise; yet another failure near that breakout point will help reinforce that particular level as an even more significant breakout point. Hesitation just under the breakout point, as the stock regroups its forces, is highly desirable.

The odds have shifted so much by now in favor of such an upside breakout that you may be tempted to act regardless. Let's suppose the stock has come up to the breakout point again and has again backed off. This time, though, it doesn't dip as far; buyers have become more aggressive. (This may take the form of the right shoulder of a head-and-shoulders bottom, or a dip that holds near the rising trend line of a triangle formation. These are successful tests of the low; the more the better, and best if each succeeding dip halts at a higher price than the previous one.) You may see increased volume appear in the trading activity, as buyers step up their dealings more intensely; a noticeable increase in trading for a few days just under the breakout point can be a useful clue that the stock is poised to go. Overhead supply is being eaten up. Sometimes, however, the opposite develops. Volume may dwindle to its lowest point during the base-building phase. In the former instance, the increased volume comes as buyers pay eighths and quarters more and then withdraw temporarily. In the latter instance, the stock, instead, will drift down that eighth or quarter, but because by then there is very little selling pressure left, there will be no further follow-through on the downside. In either case, *price action alerts, but volume is the confirmation.*

The accompanying daily chart of GCA Corporation for 1980 is an interesting variation worth studying. Despite the severe market decline that February and March, GCA managed to stay above its long-term moving-average line, which was still rising. So, to begin with, we had a favorable climate; such relative strength is highly bullish. The low was made at 21 on the silver-selling climax, and a new base began to form; when the next low was slightly higher, at 21 5/8, we could draw a slightly rising trend line connecting these two lows, and when the ensuing rally failed at a lower level than the prior rally's 26 3/8, we could draw a slightly descending upper line, thus creating a small triangle formation. A third dip to a low at point A confirmed the validity of the lower trend line, and shortly thereafter the stock charged across the upper line for a decisive upside breakout, confirmed, as you can see, by sharply higher volume (B). Incidentally, note that a rough measurement of

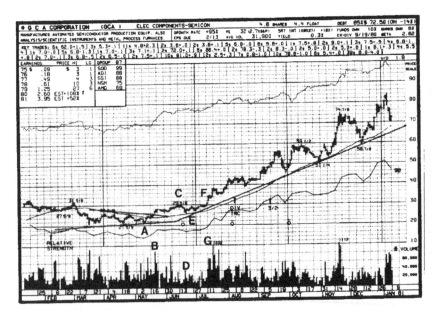

the width of this triangle—21 to 26 3/8, or approximately 5 points
—when added to the breakout level near 24 1/2, came remarkably
close to anticipating that rally's first target. The rally stopped at
29 5/8 (C) and the stock began trading sideways, just under resistance left over from the February top. What happened next often
develops within a market climate that is becoming increasingly
bullish—instead of the small base, the entire area begins to look
like another, bigger base, with a new breakout point. Note that in
June the stock dipped down to support (E) at the previous breakout
point, still holding comfortably above the long-term moving-average line, which had begun to rise again. What's more, during this
period, volume (D) dipped to a significantly low level, indicating
a sold-out situation. All this in itself would be favorable enough,
but you can also see that the action around point E has its counter-
part in the sideways action, with a low of 27 5/8, during February.
Call the winter action the left shoulder, and the June action the
right shoulder, with the head identified as the triangle formation
that sparked the trend reversal. Last, a trend line can be drawn
connecting the two prior highs at 31 5/8 and 29 5/8. You can see
that this neckline of the head-and-shoulders bottom formation, and
the resistance at the round number of 30, kept the stock going
sideways into July until GCA at last staged another breakout (F)
across those twin, but temporary, problems. This breakout proved
explosive, with volume (G) zooming massively to provide positive
confirmation that a big move was being launched. Thus, an early
buyer could have paid around 26 by jumping in on the upside
breakout from the triangle formation; a more careful, patient buyer
could have bought after the pullback (E), and especially as volume
diminished so favorably, at around 28. But notice how late you
could have bought the stock—seemingly late, that is—for even if
you had paid as much as 34 after breakout confirmation, you were
still on board for a run to 84.

Here we have an example of how rising volume just before the
initial breakout can indicate impending upward force, and how
during the second, more extensive base formation, low volume is
bullish just before that upside breakout. No matter which clue you
look for, keep an eye on volume as you begin to spot potential
breakouts. These breakouts are your third good-buying opportu-

nity of the cycle. Indeed, the more such potential and actual break-outs you spot, the more buyable the entire market is; they serve as a market indicator in themselves, with the advantage that they don't all occur at once. Miss one and look for another. You are still in the early stages of the bull move, and the risk is minimal.

The Pullback Buy

But there is more. Let's now discuss the fourth good-buying opportunity: the pullback. There are several degrees of pullback—one of which is the way GCA pulled back to support after the initial breakout—so let's study the sequence. The initial breakout occurs as buyers eagerly grab all the stock in sight, at a price level where sellers have finally been exhausted. In the vacuum, the price temporarily runs away. Eventually, however, buyers will cease to take the stock up any higher; it has gotten too rich too soon for them. The stock dries up on the tape; there is a downtick or two; a few sellers show up and hit the bid. The result is that there is customarily a quick pullback toward the breakout price level, often within fifteen minutes or half an hour after the breakout occurred. It is fast; it is mild; and it is temporary. Waiting for such a quick pullback is a sensible method of buying. The advantage is that you'll actually have seen the stock prove itself by breaking out with vigor on a confirming substantial increase in activity; if you've wanted to buy the stock and have so far missed the moment, or if the activity itself alerted you, this is a quick chance to buy.

Brief in nature, such a pullback should be followed by renewed upside action. Interestingly, there is often a subsequent pullback a few days, or even two or three weeks, later. Often, this is because there are layers of resistance overhead. In 1980, the Dow Industrial Average, for example, broke out across 800, ran into resistance near 830 (about where its moving-average line was, too), and pulled back to just under 800 about three weeks later, before setting sail again. In GCA, as we've seen, the pullback came about two weeks after the initial upside breakout from the triangle formation, hit the top of the breakout level, and helped form an even bigger base.

The pullback is usual, not unusual, action. The important thing to remember is that the breakout level has now become serious support. A good stock will never give you a chance to buy at a bargain level, so you'll have to raise your bid a bit, but you aren't in this game for eighths and quarters. Because no stock goes up in a straight line, both the brief intra-day pullback and the subsequent test of the new support level provide the fourth low-risk buying opportunity of the cycle.

In a true bull market, there will be many potential choices, and it will be hard to go completely wrong. But we aren't in this as a guessing game. We want as many facts as possible, not hopes or hunches, and proven strength is the most desirable fact of all. Of course, there will never be enough proof; the next tick on the tape may be down. But when we see the stock charge across a previous resistance mark, on increased trading activity, the market is announcing as best it can that here is a stock that wants to go up. What is the point in trying to guess the bottom for a weak stock? Why look for something that ought to move, might move, should move, but isn't moving? To bet on a laggard is to assume added risk, even though it might seem safer because it is still so close to its low. In the stock market, laggards are the risky bets because there's apt to be a good reason they haven't moved yet—big money doesn't want them, for whatever reason—just as there is a reason a horse goes off at long-shot odds at the track; it hasn't proved itself in the company of the other bets. And you have an advantage over the race-track bettor: the stock favorite will pay off point for point with any other pick, whereas the favorite at the track has appropriately low odds. So why worry about why the laggard isn't moving? Let it prove itself first by forming a base, by establishing its own worthwhile breakout point. The entire game is to bet on what is knowable. We don't know it all, perhaps we don't even know very much, but surely we can identify a stock that is becoming strong.

That doesn't mean you should reach up for a stock after it has already doubled. Sure that's strength, but it has become dangerously late. There is a law of diminishing return (and increasing risk) the higher a stock goes, a risk that is compounded in any stock that has gone for a while without a meaningful correction within its uptrend.

Relatively early in the unfolding bull trend, there will be a succession of individual stocks breaking out. Even groups that emerge a bit afterwards can go a long way. Apply several guidelines: Does the stock have a legitimate base, large enough to support a full-fledged move before running into overhead resistance? Is there a sensible entry point (the breakout) to provide evidence that it is turning strong? Is there group confirmation? Eventually, you'll be searching harder and harder for new ideas. That in itself becomes a primary warning signal. The less there is to buy, the less reason to act. You are down to the last few apples in the barrel and it is time to back off and let others play the game without you.

Buying on the Correction

After the breakout phase, and its accompanying temporary pullback, of the cycle, there is only one last buying opportunity: on the correction. Corrections are the inevitable fluctuations that come in a stock which has risen a certain amount and now needs a rest; buyers are tired, while sellers come to the fore to cash in their profits. Such a correction should prove as temporary as the earlier pullback, but since we are now buying along the way up, the risk has increased. By this time, then, you must apply one simple rule: *Buy with the longer-term trend, but against the short-term trend.*

This rule should help you resist the temptation of chasing a stock, reaching up for it emotionally, and perhaps paying an at least temporarily high price. When the trend, for both the market and an individual stock, is up, the buy side is the side to be on. No one should sell short against that primary trend. But you only want to buy on a correction—the fluctuation back down. That is, you buy against the short-term downtrend, stepping in to bid as the price of the stock approaches support. This support can be a rising trend line, or the by now rising moving-average line, or the area where the stock consolidated previously before launching a new rise; often it is a combination of these factors. In addition to the ability to hold support, during this type of short-term downtrend, volume should try up noticeably. A stop-loss order—an order to sell if the stock declines further instead of resuming its rise—must also be placed just under such support, or at the point where the trend line or moving-average line would be broken decisively, for protection.

A glance back at the previous illustrations will show that both the Dow Industrial Average and an individual stock like General Electric came back to the moving-average lines during corrections and, given a chance to prove that they were holding properly, were indicating that it was okay to buy. Similarly, we've drawn in an uptrend line for GCA that connects correction lows. Note at the 51 1/4 correction low how much volume dried up, indicating an absence of selling pressure. This was also true during the correction which culminated at a low of 58 7/8 in December—a low made just about at the top of the prior sideways consolidation which served as good support. That's enough successful corrections for our money. Personally, we find such buying difficult and believe the only sensible way to take on the added risk of buying so far into the uptrend is to concentrate almost exclusively on proven strong stocks. Buy the best, rather than guess, and, of course, make sure you protect your capital with a stop-loss order.

Remember that you are always going to be influenced by the stock's recent price. If the stock is up from 20 to 25, you are going to feel it is too late to buy—yet the major move might be just beginning. GCA is an example of how "late" you could have bought and still enjoyed a huge rise. The criterion for buying stock should not be where the stock has been so much as is the stock strong. In full-fledged bull moves, stocks have a habit of going much further up than seems reasonably possible. You want to buy stocks that are hard to buy; they refuse to come all the way back down to support, or to your bid; you have to reach up to fill your order. Indeed, the market is not reasonable. It can be as perverse to your benefit as it can, so it seems, be out to get you. As long as you do your buying at the low-risk times in the cycle, don't hesitate. Buy as soon as the message is clear. Only boardroom sitters wait for one more tick as proof, until buying becomes dangerous.

4

WHEN NOT TO BUY

To play any game well, you've got to be unencumbered by fear of losing. The difference between a top tennis star and the rest of the entrants in a tournament is not the strokes themselves, Billie Jean King once said, but that the great player plays to win while all the others try hard not to lose. It's okay to lose in the stock market; sometimes it can't be helped, and even the shrewdest take their lumps, as even Borg loses matches. So don't take a loss as such a blow to your ego that it distorts your next decision. That losing involves dollars, and not chips or Monopoly paper, means you shouldn't be betting the grocery money, but it doesn't change how you should play the game.

Investors may think they are placing their bets to win, but often that's not the case. Sometimes they buy stocks merely because they seem safe. You've heard, and perhaps even made, the remark: "After all, how much lower can it go?" as an attempt to defend a seemingly low-risk purchase. At the other extreme, an investor sometimes buys a stock because it has already risen so much, so well, that he reasons it's surely got to be a winner. Many investors come pouring into the market late because they keep waiting to be sure they aren't going to lose. They take rising prices as an indication that buying is finally a safe bet. There's less fear of being wrong after a prolonged rise, since buying seems so successful. But the same investors who will rush in and buy near tops will hesitate near bottoms, when buying is for a fact low-risk, because what's not yet absolutely proven seems unsafe to them. They see the recent past of falling prices as a threat; the downtrend seems bound to continue, just as a recent past of rising prices makes it seem as if the market will go up forever. Indeed, many who ask for advice, or subscribe to a service for its opinions, will then watch the recommended stock rise day after day, and only after it has gone up substantially will they decide that the recommendation was "right" and finally buy it.

None of this is necessary if we learn some objectivity. In the preceding chapter, we pointed out several sensible times to buy. Now let's examine the times during a market cycle when restraint is the better part of valor.

Don't Buy Late in the Rally

It may be late in an uptrend, but no one really knows that except natural-born pessimists and cynics. A sold-out bull doesn't know it, because he's sitting there sorry he sold so soon; stocks are still going up, and a few stocks are leaping. Someone who's held on to his stocks doesn't know it, because he's thrilled with the rise. It may be too soon for talk that the market is going to the moon, but the Street exudes an air of confidence and prosperity. There's just been a "normal" correction, but now the market is indeed going higher, and chances are, if you buy a stock, it'll go even higher along with the averages. Chances are, though, that you'll eventually lose money with such purchases even though they are right!

Oh, there's a possibility that you'll pick a stock that will have such a big rise you'll be able to get out with a gain, but the odds are increasingly against you. Indeed, because fewer and fewer stocks participate well in the late stages of a bull market, the chance has mathematically increased that you'll pick a stock that is a dud. But here's how you can be right and still lose money.

Let's start with the Dow Industrial Average. Suppose it has been rallying over the course of three or four months to reach 960, sold off to 910 in that normal correction, and now looks as if it is ready for another move to a new recovery high. The rally comes as expected and carries all the way to Dow 1,000. That, as you can see, is a 10 percent rise. Surely you should be able to make money on such a move.

Now let's match that 10 percent rise to an individual stock. You've been shrewd. You didn't fall for the temptation to buy a laggard that hasn't yet responded; you didn't get sucked into a previous big winner that has already become tired. Suppose, instead, that you buy a stock that does even better than the Dow and rises 15 percent; that means you were right. The stock rises from 20 to 23—that's 15 percent—but after commissions on a 100-share transaction, you haven't made much more than $200—*if* you buy at the low and sell at the high. But of course nobody does that. Let's say you came close to the low, paying 20 1/4, but when the stock gets to 23 you don't sell. After all, at that time the market was still strong, the stock was still strong, and you didn't take that risk with your own money just so the broker would make almost as much in commissions, with no risk, as you would on the trade. It looks as if you've got a stock that can go still higher, even though a normal dip is in the works. So you hold.

And here's what the stock does next: dips to 21 1/2 (a normal one-half retracement of the advance), rallies to 22 3/4 (looks like it is going through to a new high, but it dies), dips to 22 (okay, it's still holding well), inches back up to 22 1/2 (fizzles again), but by the time you decide to sell, it has eased back to 22 (so you'll sell on the next rally), but then it keeps on drifting down to 21 (oh, oh, there goes the profit), bounces to 21 3/4 (damn it, you'll wait for 22 1/2), fades to 19 1/2 as the Dow, too, slips back down to its own support. Now you've got a loss instead, even though you bought the stock and were right because it went up 15 percent so quickly.

Of course, if you'd bought 100 shares of a $100 stock instead, and caught that 15 percent gain, you could still have come away from the trade with a few hundred bucks' profit—if you'd been nimble, and if you think that such a profit is worth risking that much capital. And you might even have bought a stock that leapt 20 percent or 30 percent during that rally. We don't want to take that away from you. But remember that when such rallies occur after the market has already had a substantial rise—such as the September–December 1980 or March–April 1981 periods—it can be accompanied by a lagging Advance/Decline Line. That is, late in a rise, fewer and fewer stocks join in. And, typically, you'll begin to see fewer stocks make new highs than had been able to during the previous rally. These, of course, are the signs of deterioration that indicate a top is forming. We don't want to call a top until the indicators give actual statistical signals—why try to anticipate indicators that are already by nature anticipatory?—but we do want to show why it is increasingly hard to make even a trading profit so late in the uptrend. The mathematical odds are against you: fewer stocks rising, fewer new highs, and the chance that, even if you are right, you can't get out in time with a profit worth taking the risk for.

Here's an example that we picked out as a possible illustration of the breakout buy in the previous chapter. As you can see, Digital Equipment had an obvious breakout point at 66 1/8 (A)—two rally peaks and its long-term moving-average line were focused there. It hesitated just under that level, broke out to 70, had a buyable

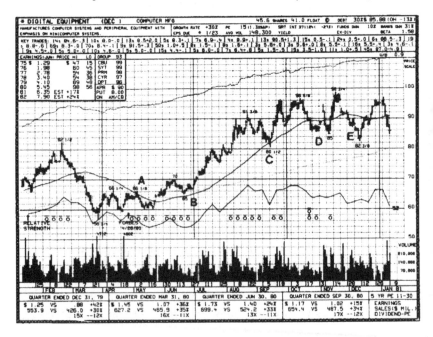

pullback (B) to the new support level, and then took off strongly. Traders could still have bought on the correction when it came back to 80 1/2 (C) because that action held favorably just above the small sideways consolidation action in July and August. Note, too, that at this time the rising long-term moving-average line was still far away. On this move, therefore, a trader could have succeeded in taking about a 15 percent gain.

But on the subsequent dip to point D, the situation is not so clear. It was that much later in the market's uptrend, for one thing, and for another, that quick trip up a few points and back down to 85 raises the question of how stable the uptrend might still be. Nevertheless, had you bought around the 86 level, you would have been rewarded with a new high. But although that was a 15 percent rally again, if you hadn't sold promptly—and why would you have, when the stock had just made a new high?—the gap on the downside thereafter would have taken away half your profit before you could have gotten out, and if you didn't, the stock then dipped to a low (E) below your purchase price. As you can see, although there were profitable trades for the nimble, the risk of buying increased substantially as the bull trend matured.

It's difficult to tell when late becomes too late. Obviously, when the Dow Industrial Average is up 230 points in the course of just a few months, it has already had a substantial move. The danger, after such an extensive rise, is that when a downtrend occurs, the market can look as if it is experiencing just another correction, with the bull trend still intact. That's when you'll begin to read in *The Wall Street Journal* and elsewhere the opposite of what you read near the bottom (as quoted in the previous chapter): that the big institutions, banks, and related sages have finally decided that the bull market is for real, and that they're using the dip to buy a lot of stock. The consensus will make you feel comfortable, too, but don't let it influence you! Oh, there are professional traders who'll try to scalp a few points any time the market is going to bounce, but it is an exercise performed because they are sitting in front of the tape and are supposed to do, do, do, all the time. In reality, the market is living on borrowed time.

Better to be bored, better to be sitting on the sidelines, however impatiently, watching. But one problem that develops at this time in the cycle is having too much money. If you've been shrewdly taking profits now that the market has run up so far for so long, you are sitting with a lot of buying power plus the smugness that goes along with having taken worthwhile gains. This can create a profligate feeling of "Oh, what the hell, I can afford a little loss. After all, I'm playing with their money." But it isn't their money; it's yours. Such late phases of a bull cycle are as tempting as they are dangerous. Beware of the lure of the excitement; don't join the complacent crowd; put your money away. If you keep gambling at this point in the cycle, you'll be distracted from what should be your fresh concentration on the sell side. It's hard to be buying and still think of selling other stocks or even of selling certain issues short, as well. Just because you have an itchy wallet doesn't mean you have to follow the crowd or get caught up in the market excitement so near the top. It's the three-card monte game all over again.

Watch Out for the Downtrend

But now we've passed the top, and prices have already begun to slide. Remember that as the top was being formed, the market was subject to brief selling squalls. Each time it bounced back, perhaps even reaching new highs in the averages, and with a few stocks conspicuously strong. Thus, when the next correction unfolds, it can look temptingly like another dip, perhaps a seemingly better cleanout, leading, it seems, to a chance to jump on board with a recently swinging stock at a better price. The stock was overextended before, but now it has corrected, so it seems safe again. What you've missed in this situation is that the market trend is changing. Fewer stocks are going to make new highs; more are going to turn into downtrends. To be sure, there'll be another upward fluctuation, but it is likely to be a failing rally now. Part of that rally has to be conceded because you won't buy at the low of the correction. So there won't be as much room to garner a profit, and if the upside failure comes upon you sooner than expected, it can easily result in a loss instead. Look at the chart of Digital Equipment again. The chart shows that there was a trading profit to be made in December from the low at 82 3/8 to the rally peak in the 94–96 area. But warning signs were already there: yet another lower low made on that correction, plus the increasingly close moving-average line. Hindsight says it was okay for the nimble, but we say it was far too risky a bet for our money. The odds are no longer in your favor.

The average investor can't be blamed too much for this buying error. Enthusiasm for stocks is not only widespread but growing, and even a more experienced player—and, typically, brokerage-house advice—is geared to buying the apparent bargains on such a dip. It may not even be clear that the market or individual stock has already topped out until you see the failing rally. One way to protect yourself against a forthcoming plunge is through the proper use of stop-loss orders. The first rule applies before you buy —that is, you don't buy at all unless a stop-loss order to sell can be sensibly placed—just below a previous low, or just under a trend line or moving-average line—within approximately 10 percent of the purchase price. If the stock is selling at a higher level, it is warning of an already overextended situation. In the example of Digital, that would mean a stop placed at 79 7/8, just under the prior low at 80 1/2 and under the important round number. That is so far away that it would have kept you from jumping into the stock when it was trading in the 90s, where garnering a profit would have been exceedingly difficult. We believe it is important to enter the stop order to sell if the stock breaks below the particular danger point on a "good till cancelled" basis—that is, leave the order entered as protection. Our experience is that if it is only a mental stop point, it is all too easy to rationalize holding, as you convince yourself that you'll surely sell the stock on the next rally instead. Learn to get out fast if you are wrong. Cutting your losses is vital at this point in the cycle, because in innocence or eagerness you may have bought very early in a whole new bear market, believing erroneously that the first dip was just another correction.

One of the problems at this point in the cycle is that the economic news is generally optimistic: booming earnings, a blooming economy, etc. Many investors, having bought, rely on such news to justify their purchases even as the price dips into the loss column. But the market knows. Remember: it discounts events. It's begun to go down because it foresees trouble ahead. The boom is peaking, and what lies ahead is a recession instead. In reading all this good news, keep in mind that what's important is not the news itself but how the market responds to it. Once good news ceases to have a favorable effect, or to produce further stock-price gains, you can be sure the upside has lost its potential.

In the next stage, prices begin to tumble more vigorously. You've still got an itchy wallet, anxious to snap up what will look like terrific bargains compared to the prior peaks, and you'll begin to believe that surely this has been enough of a correction. There'll be minor rally attempts, and each new decline may look as if it's the last. But be careful. You have certain guidelines to keep you safe. As soon as, and as long as, there are a succession of lower highs and lower lows, the market is in an established downtrend. It will not turn overnight; it will not shoot straight back up. The long-term moving average, by now pointing down, should serve as a reminder of the overall trend. Once you've had a sell signal, don't buy just because lower prices look appealing.

Don't Try to Guess the Bottom

The next point in the cycle when itchy buyers begin to make costly mistakes is when they try to guess the bottom. Why anyone feels the urge to make such a stab in the dark is hard to fathom. There's no hurry; the market itself will tell us when it has become safer. But no, buyer after buyer has to take a flyer. "I'll buy some now, and more if [read: when] it goes lower" is a favorite expression of overeager bulls.

True, someone has to start buying. If you were managing a billion-dollar portfolio for a pension fund, you couldn't wait to buy everything at the most desirable time. Once an individual stock begins to make buying sense, you'd have to be the one to step in first. It is that beginning buying that the rest of us would see. "Du Pont," we'd murmur, "is sure holding well here, while everything else is plunging." Maybe once that buy order is filled, the stock will resume its slide, but perhaps the stock has some appeal that will attract other interests. The more such buying, the more the stock would start to hold against the market—that is, show relative strength—alerting us. Obviously, the few stocks that begin to do this are most likely to have particularly cogent underlying reasons for such purchases against the trend; that's why they usually prove to be the leaders in the next upturn. Such rare issues stand out as they begin to form bases. But it is the base we want to see first. To throw a dart at the stock tables and hope that the day you bought will be the bottom is sheer folly—guessing without evidence.

Many itchy wallets get emptied during this guessing game. Premature buyers get stuck with losses as the correction continues. The decline, of course, picks up momentum late in the game, so the losses get even worse. The premature buyer gets scared. That makes it doubly hard to buy stocks at the true bottom. First, of course, the hitherto available buying power has been dissipated. Second, even if there's some cash left, those who own stocks already and have suffered with them are reluctant to buy any more, just when they should. They'll be participating in any rally by rooting for the stocks they bought prematurely to bounce back up to the price they paid . . . and are likely to sell out when they are even again; the combination of buying too soon and paying the price for such a mistake typically creates a disbelief in the real bottom. "Once burned, twice shy" prevents too many investors from acting precisely when they should loosen their purse strings at last.

Avoid That Bad Bet

In sum, there are three main times to avoid doing any new buying. First, late in the uptrend, when the odds have begun to shift against you. An intermediate rally—a fluctuation of some time and distance—nevertheless has a limited life. Eventually it is no longer wise to search for a different place for your money. It's a bit like searching through the bottom of the barrel to see if there's one apple left that might still be juicy. It is much more logical to assume that the laggards have been left behind for good reason than to hope you can find the one overlooked potential winner. Second, on the way down, when prices can seem tempting in comparison with their recent peaks. Do not get lured by what will then be a prevailing complacency that it's just another correction. Third, don't take a stab at catching the bottom. Wait for actual proof—a base always has to form before a true reversal.

We're talking about avoiding a bad bet. To be sure, you'll stand around with your hands in your pockets, fingering that wallet and thinking you've got the cash to take a chance on something. Having too much available buying power can cost you. Learn to turn your back on temptation and walk away. The cycle is more powerful than your attempt to defy it. We're not arguing differently than you would if your buddy made a big hit at the track and still wanted to bet the eighth and ninth races. Wouldn't you tell him to take his winnings and go home? Too many investors remain too eager near the top, and stay eager far too long in the ensuing drop. Sold-out bulls are virtually a textbook definition of impatience. But the tape over and over again will show the wisdom of waiting. The market will go to an extreme on the downside, too. Don't try to jump on every little rally just to play the game. Let others spend their money first to tell you what you need to know. Let stocks themselves, and not emotion, speak at the bottom.

5

MARKET TIMING VS. STOCK SELECTION

Does all this sound a bit too easy? Giving advice on paper can always make it seem as if all you have to do is follow instructions. But attacking the stock market correctly is like trying to put together a Christmas toy from the printed instructions: it isn't as simple to do as it reads. And yet it isn't hard, either. As long as you don't curse yourself for not being perfect, you'll find that it is possible to come to grips with the market even in all its perversities, to analyze its future possibilities, and to make sensible bets. But that still doesn't mean you'll make money at it.

In the stock market, it is possible to be right and still lose money. The previous chapter discussed an all-too-typical example: predicting accurately that the market is going to rally, buying a stock that promptly goes up with the market, and still winding up with a loss. In that case, the basic flaw was buying so late in the cycle. At other times you can be even more right about the market but still lose: it shoots up powerfully, but the stock you've chosen languishes (while others you might have bought instead do quite well). Or the market doesn't look too healthy, so you sensibly wait, only to watch the one stock you really had your eye on go up in defiance of the averages.

The possibilities for risk are endless. Even when you know what you are doing, trying to coordinate so many different factors makes playing the market a constant challenge. Still, in our opinion, it is possible to be right about the overall course of the market about 90 percent of the time. Lest that sound like bragging, we hasten to add that one of the main reasons you can be right about the market so often is that you are free to change your mind. Whenever you see that the market isn't doing what you predicted, you can make a fresh decision, thus always staying in approximate gear with what is actually happening. The only rule for accurate analysis is that you can't afford to be stubborn. The ego battle that arises when the market isn't doing what it ought to be doing is one you'll always lose if you insist the market has to conform. It won't. It can always be more willful than you can afford to be stubborn. Indeed, we have an aphorism regarding this kind of ego crisis that you might want to tack up on your bulletin board: *When the market does the unexpected, it is doubly significant.*

But no matter what the market does, all you have to go on is the observable evidence. Try to sort out what is factual from what is subjective. Is the chart of the Dow Industrial Average forming a potential base? Where is resistance? Where is support? What's the direction of the long-term moving-average line? Are the odd-lotters shorting heavily or not? In answering these and a host of similar questions, you've got to keep your own hopes out of the judgment: are you already long, or short; have you already trumpeted your opinion only to see a different possibility now looming? Are you too willing to seize on the opinions of others because they agree with yours, or can you be independently objective? Look at the available evidence, decide on what action seems most likely, and then ask yourself what it would take for the market to prove you wrong.

That's the hardest question to ask yourself. After all, you've already made up your mind; now we're asking you to question your decision *after* you've supposedly evaluated all the evidence. What we want is for you to find the stop-loss point in your reasoning, so you won't stubbornly cling to an opinion too long. The market, after all, isn't in business to prove you right; in fact, it sometimes seems the opposite is true.

It is, of course, easier to change your mind about the short-term course than the longer-term. If you expect the market to open lower tomorrow morning and instead it opens higher, it's clear that you were wrong. Now you have to decide what that means. Every input, virtually every tick on the tape, can affect what you think is likely to happen next, and it is entirely legitimate to change your opinion when there are new inputs. Indeed, you are irresponsibly stubborn if you don't.

Sooner or later, though, you're going to have to act on your market opinions, and that's a different story. Then the question of being right translates, not into the abstract problem of what is the market going to do, but into the specific one of what *you* are going to do to participate. Here again, at the outset, it isn't too hard to be right in theory. We've found, over the years, that when we make a list of buy candidates, we'll be right at least 70 percent of the time: two robust winners, say; five that are approximately in gear with the rally; two flat, and one dud. It's easy, until we have to pick from among them the one or two stocks we can afford to buy. Having the opinion is far easier than actually placing the bet.

Selling stocks is different. Since you already own a specific issue, your choice is extremely limited: you either sell, or you continue to hold. If you don't like the market climate, or the stock you own has begun to top out and looks vulnerable, the answer is simple: you've got to sell. The biggest problem is an emotional one: being able to let go.

But you never *have* to buy. Perhaps you are uncomfortable with the overall market; perhaps you believe it is okay, but aren't thrilled by the stocks on your buy list; perhaps you really want to buy but you think the market has gotten temporarily overbought, suggesting that you might be better off waiting for a dip. As a prospective buyer you have choices beyond whether or not to buy: namely, which stocks to buy among the different candidates. While it can be emotionally harder to bring yourself to sell, buying is objectively more difficult, because of the multiplicity and complexity of decisions involved.

The question on the buy side is not how to be right. If you follow our guidelines, you'll find that it is relatively easy to be right often enough. The strain lies in trying to incorporate all the available inputs into your practical decision of when, which, and how. That's why one frequently hears arguments over whether it is better to follow market timing—gearing whatever buying you do to coincide with favorable general market indicators—or to follow stock selection, ignoring the general market and concentrating on the individual stock itself. That philosophical debate is really an attempt to narrow the difficulties of the decision-making process. Adherents of one school or the other are blocking out, or avoiding, the difficulties inherent in the required additional inputs. They think it will make their job easier—or they've failed so often on one score that they opt for the other philosophy as being safer.

Market Timing

There are those who believe exclusively in market timing. In the dangerous world of the stock market, it may seem the safest path is to identify significant market swings and ignore all other problems. When the indicators speak—enough. These believers try to time the market itself as if it were a single entity—usually as measured by the Dow Industrial Average—when it supposedly is turning from up to down or down to up. It seems easiest to make such calls because the evidence is at its most convincing, and can be especially gratifying because the call is usually being made against the consensus opinion. The market timer can afford to wait until sufficient evidence is in without having to fret at all about the possibly differing action of a particular individual stock. Give us, for example, a conspicuous divergence between the Dow Industrial Average and such key indicators as the Advance/Decline Line and the High/Low Differential, toss a couple of suddenly favorable sentiment indicators into the equation, and we'll call a bottom confidently. That's what a market timer does, and then expects any and all stocks to obey that prediction.

The problem is, stocks are not so obedient; they don't all move up and down in lockstep with the averages. In the early stages of a bear market, some stocks will continue to rise; they won't get their come-uppance until late in the decline. And market bottoms are even less accommodating. Individual issues make their bases and stage their rallies in their own good time . . . or fail to participate at all. A pure market timer can say sell everything and be secure in the knowledge that he is protecting his clients from the ravages of a bear market, but he can't ever say buy everything and be useful. Market timing can be easy, and can make the forecaster look like a hero, but it isn't the practical answer.

But, you may remind us, didn't we ourselves join the ranks of market timers when we advocated buying stocks not only on a selling climax but at the next turning point, too: the test of the low? True, indeed. Such calls are market timing at its best. But they only open the door by telling us *when* to buy; figuring out *what* to buy is at least as important. It's all right for the hero to send a telegram to clients: "Bottom reached Go 100 percent Long." But at the other end of that message to become fully invested we've still got to pick which stocks to buy, unless we just place a bet on the Dow Industrial Average with the London bookie who handles such wagers.

While market timing can be heroic at the right moment, such major turning points are relatively rare. At other times, there is less to say. Suppose the forecast is lukewarm—then what do you do? It's the best the market will allow for, at that juncture, but is it enough to act on? Or suppose it is a short-term buy signal, within a still dangerous bear trend. Should you buy, or stay out? The problem with relying exclusively on market timing is that there are too many moments in the cycle when trying to pin a bull or bear label on such a vast composite may be entirely misleading. Suppose the market has entered a trading period when it is neither animal? Suppose you make a correct bearish call for the blue-chip average, but secondary stocks prove to be winners, as was the case in January 1978? The market might be making a top for months on end, as from September 1980 to April 1981, when timing rallies could be exceedingly dangerous, however accurate. Similarly, one could go broke successfully timing rebounds within a major downtrend; fortunes were lost by those who bought for the August–October 1973 bear-market rally. Or you might call the market bearish because it looks as if the selling is about to resume (for example, November 1974), only to find out that it has turned into a successful test of the prior low. To persist in trying to make a judgment, to be stubborn about timing above all else, may blind you to what is actually happening to the stocks themselves.

Stock Selection

In frustration, many investors turn to the alternative approach. A large contingent of those who believe exclusively in stock selection will insist that the market can't be timed at all. That means, of course, that they've been so completely wrong at several important turning points that they've thrown up their hands and decided that the only path to righteousness is via stock selection instead. If they can only pick the perfect stock, they reason, they can ignore the fact that the market fluctuates. Value will out, they insist. True, a certain few have a nose for ferreting out bargains and have the patience, and the extra money to spend while waiting, to be successful at this approach over the years (even though bear markets are just as painful in the interim). And it is possible for a hedge-fund manager, able to play both sides of the market, to pick strong stocks to buy and to sell short weak ones, and thus to ride all the trends without worrying about market timing at all. But, more often, stock selectors are virtuously willing to sit with supposedly undervalued stocks year after year while apparently overvalued stocks go shooting up and up and up.

One of the biggest flaws of this approach is that its practicioners tend to search for what their arbitrary criteria say is undervalued, insisting they'll be right "someday." That is, they buy what isn't moving rather than what is. As a result, they frequently get left behind during a rally, while, of course, a serious decline will hand them losses as their selections get even cheaper. What they have done is substitute their own criteria as to what makes a stock a bargain for the market's more objective judgment as to what to buy.

Other stock selectors are more fashion-oriented. They ignore the market trend and concentrate on picking apparently desirable stocks, but they opt for what has become fashionable, the currently "in" groups that have stories attached to them. The problem here, of course, is that they have joined the crowd late, only buying when the selections have become conspicuously okay, socially acceptable, so to speak. Often, such buying is done on the first decline off the top, when the hitherto hot stocks seem cheap compared to their recent highs. They've ignored what is happening in the market and —even if they pick well—will wind up with losses.

But, you'll remind us, if we don't believe in the theory of stock selection, why have we espoused the virtue of picking individual stocks on breakouts and pullbacks? Surely that is stock selection? And it is. But it is of a different kind, letting the market tell us what to select, and when.

A Blend of the Two Techniques

Rather than opting exclusively for one or the other of these two philosophies, or insisting that sometimes one and sometimes the other approach applies, what we should aim for is a blending of the two techniques. The market is always an intellectual battle of trying to coordinate what we perceive about the long- and short-term trends, and what we perceive about how individual stocks are going to perform within these trends. The market is infinitely complicated, and regardless of how easy it may be to be right about this single factor or that, it is incredibly hard to unify all the factors into a tactical whole.

Let's start with the stocks themselves. After all, they are the trees of the market forest. The performance of individual stocks is what pays off for us. Tracking individual stocks is a means toward sensible stock selection—how else would we know what to buy when market timing signals said to act?—but the information gained from such work can be a valuable indicator in itself. In February and March 1978, for example, many individual stocks were turning upward out of exciting base formations, while the Dow Industrial Average was continuing to slide. What was actually happening was that only a handful of widely held stocks, mainly Dow components, were still in downtrends. Week after week, more and more secondary stocks were becoming bullish. Anyone keeping close track of individual stocks would have found a few irresistible buys, regardless of market timing, and thus would have been prepared both intellectually and practically to believe in the massive upside breakout that finally occurred in April 1978 (see chart in Chapter 3, p. 51), when the DJIA leaped across its long-term moving-average line. That's the best example in recent years of how stock selection is also a component of market timing.

With that experience in mind, we recommend that anyone more than peripherally involved in the stock market should keep a few individual stock charts. In the first place, it will help you develop your interpretive skills, and will allow you far more effectively to "read" the charts in such services as Daily Graphs, Trendline, or Mansfield. In the second place, you'll get a feel for what stocks actually are doing, rather than what they seem to be doing, and that will become its own indicator. In March 1978, you would have seen the market's potential for an upside explosion, simply because you'd have noticed that the charts right under your own fingertips were screaming: "Buy me, buy me." Any divergence between what many stocks are doing compared to what the Dow Industrial Average is doing is an excellent indicator.

We keep a number of our own daily charts. Our own preference is the do-it-yourself daily bar chart as described in the bible of charting books: Edwards and Magee's *Technical Analysis of Stock Trends* (often available in second-hand bookstores), plotted on the semi-logarithmic paper available from the John Magee, Inc., service. We rely on the Mansfield service for weekly charts instead of keeping our own, and refer to Daily Graphs or Trendline to get a daily view, when we want one, of those stocks we don't chart ourselves. We keep back newspaper pages so that if a stock looks exciting we can quickly make up our own chart on it—and will always do so before we buy that stock. This is vital analytical work (more important than reading annual reports) if the stock market is your vocation, and if it is an avocation, it is a matter of how seriously you take the investing of your money. The only rule we suggest is that you never chart more stocks than you can comfortably keep up with; a dozen or two may be sufficient to increase materially your feel for what is happening in the market. If you start getting behind by keeping too many, you'll eventually give up in frustration. Try to plot the stocks you are particularly interested in, along with several market leaders, such as IBM and General Motors. Your own charts, (or the charts you scan in the available services) can be highly useful in pinpointing market timing, as well as in creating a basis for your own stock selection. If you have a list of buyable stocks that is plentiful and exciting, you'll know you're on to something special. If, on the other hand, it looks as if the market should rally but there are only a handful of stocks on your buy list, or if the list is composed of obscure names, or if General Motors and similar major companies are on the negative side, something is wrong; the rally may come, but it is apt to be feeble, extremely narrow, or very late in the game.

Of course, at the same time you are watching individual stocks, you are also keeping track of the important market indicators. Many of the indicators worth tracking are based on the overall action of individual stocks. How many of them are advancing, compared to the number declining? How many are able to make new highs? How many odd-lot shares are being sold short? The Advance/Decline Line, the High/Low Differential, and similar indicators are actually summaries of what individual stocks are doing. By revealing what stocks as a multitude are doing, these indicators provide historical, empirical evidence for what kind of readings consistently accompany important buy points; in other words, for market timing.

Thus, although we've started with stock selection, we are back to market timing. The two techniques taken together best indicate the kind of climate in which you can place low-risk bets. In the good old days (1953–66), when the long-term trend was bullish, people thought that sooner or later the rising market would bail them out of any mistake. Even now, there is a belief that it is okay to own a stock even if it isn't performing well, because eventually it will go up. But if the market is heading into a top, the worst thing you can do is to hold on to an already weak stock; it is guaranteed to be a leader on the downside. The best way to avoid such a predicament is to make sure you pay attention to market timing as well as stock selection. There will be different criteria for which stocks to buy at each of our different buying opportunities—the most deeply oversold at selling climaxes; those showing relative strength at the test of the low; and then, on an individual basis, those breaking out and pulling back properly, thereafter—but, as a rule, true stock selection cannot be done apart from sensible market timing. Let's discuss how this can work.

Here's a chart of the Dow Industrial Average during the winter

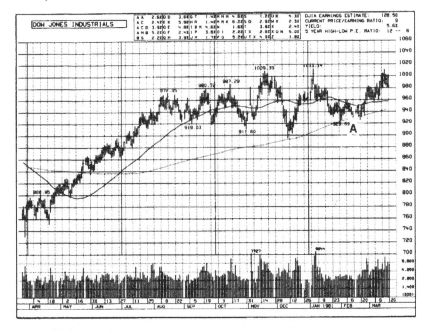

of 1981. In January and February it had a potentially dangerous look, needing only to crack down below its moving-average line (A). Many analysts expected the market to break below that broad trading range, so many, in fact, that the percentage of bearish advisory services rose spectacularly. Other sentiment indicators— heavy odd-lot short-selling and extremely high put-option buying, representing bets by the trading public on the market's going down —also pointed to the extreme pessimism around. Such readings argued that these bears were unlikely to be gratified, but they weren't timing anything on the upside.

Within this context, many individual stocks began to act well. Here's an example. USI's earnings were falling badly; the third quarter had been reported as 14¢ vs. 46¢ per share, accelerating a decline that had begun several quarters before. Yet the stock was already holding around $8 per share even as the general market (see the preceding chart of the Dow) was whacked by two severe declines—in December 1980 and January 1981. If you didn't know anything more than what was on this chart—which is, after all,

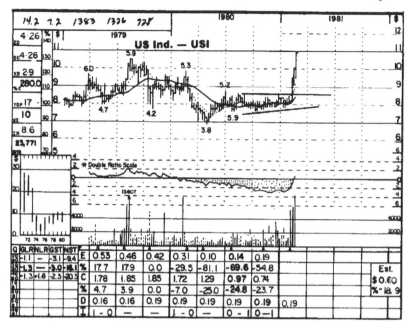

nothing more than the tape action condensed and depicted in graphic form—of something identified only by its ticker symbol USI, you'd jot it down on your list of buy candidates. But if you knew the company, you'd have quickly shied away, for not only were earnings already down, but in the midst of that gloomy market climate, fourth-quarter results were reported at 19¢ vs. 42¢ per share. Surely that would have scared any fundamentalist away. Yet, within days after those bad earning figures were released, the stock moved—up! We still don't know why, but obviously someone with a lot of buying power was right in buying plenty of shares around 8 for months prior to the upside breakout.

There was only one reason to buy this stock—its strength. When it comes to stock selection, we need to start with some concrete criteria, not opinions, not stories, but proof in the marketplace. Not only were there fundamental reasons not to bother, the company was highly speculative. Yet there was a clue to alert you to USI's potential as a buy candidate in that refusal to sell lower despite the bad earnings report. As soon as it started to break out above those two prior peaks at 8 5/8 on heavy volume, not only was the question answered as to whether to buy, so was the question of when. The stock, in a sense, selected itself.

We only want a stock that someone else cares about. Once we take a stock out of the vacuum of fundamental analysis and put it in the marketplace, it competes with all other stocks for our buying attention. How is it doing compared with all other stocks? If the story behind the recommendation or research (or hot tip) is so good —and it has finally filtered down to us—then why isn't the stock proving that potential? Or will it do so in the not so distant future? What was so special about USI that it kept finding buyers even though the market—in terms of the averages—had fallen sharply twice in six weeks? Not only don't we know, but we don't need to know. The stock announced itself first as worth keeping an eye on, and then as buyable. Strength begets strength.

But a move like USI's may be an isolated case. We'd never buy it even on such a clear-cut breakout if the market climate were truly bearish. At that point, however, other stocks—indeed, many

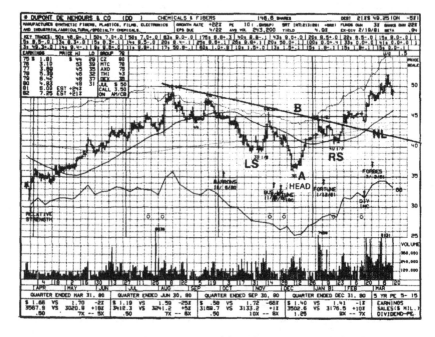

other stocks—were starting to look good, too. Opposite is a chart of Du Pont. There was no particular story (earnings for the latest quarter were flat); it seemed to be just a staid old stock, but . . . The first thing to notice is that it held (A), in December, at support —that is, above the small base which formed at the culmination of the prior major decline. But this may have escaped your attention until, several weeks later, DD held at a much higher level, so that the chart suddenly could be seen as a head-and-shoulders bottom. Moreover, the neckline (B) also represented a very important downtrend line (two points can make a trend line, but third and fourth points confirm the line (B) and give it far greater validity). Wasn't it intriguing that at a time when the consensus was bearish —meaning that the sentiment indicators had reached bullish readings—stocks like Du Pont suddenly looked buyable? You can see that if you spotted several such market leaders with similarly favorable patterns, this would become an indicator in itself, helping to confirm what the sentiment indicators were also saying—that the market was going to confound all those who were betting that it was about to go down. Your list has furnished you not only with sensible stock selection but with aids to market timing, too, because the upside breakouts helped signal a rising market.

Those who worship fundamentals miss this. They are busy off in the abstract world of the company rather than seeing the dynamics of the race being run. Consider, for example, the price/earnings approach, as depicted by the ratio between these two factors. Do you pick a stock that is selling at a supposedly "too high" 30 times earnings because its earnings are soaring 50 percent a year? Will the stock continue at such a ratio, or are you paying too high a price? Who is to decide in any intrinsic way? Or do you buy a stock selling at a ratio of 3 because it seems like such a bargain? And how vulnerable are you, in either case, if something goes wrong? Or consider another approach, full of filters to screen out likely buy candidates: the company must have a net worth of so much, an assets-to-liabilities ratio of no more than such and such, a price so much less than book value, an earnings growth rate of so much per year over the past five years, and so on. And once you've compiled a list based on these criteria, how do you know when to buy, or which one?

These, and similar, approaches are a never-ending struggle to find some way to relate what is knowable about the company to the action of the stock. Yet that action is already plain to see. The ticker tape provides full disclosure; the newspaper stock tables provide the full day's summary; the published chart services provide a graphic representation. In order to figure out whether a stock is under- or overvalued, the reference becomes the fluctuating stock price. But when the decision must be made to buy or not, the real action is put aside again in favor of the company's statistics instead. Will you sleep better owning a weak, undervalued stock or owning a stock zooming upward into overvalued territory? Oh, maybe you won't sleep so well with a skyrocketing stock because then you'll have to worry about when to sell, but that problem is dealt with in another book. Right here, what we want to establish is that, given a choice—and the market always provides that—we want to buy *strength* because it is the only objective proof we have.

You can have your own style. To us the strength is proven, in the Du Pont example, when, in succession, it validates support, holds higher than that low on the next dip, forms a bullish chart pattern, and then breaks out. Others might wait to see the strength of the breakout and then buy on the pullback. Still others might buy earlier, as the right shoulder was being formed, because the market indicators had turned favorable and Du Pont was a stock they really wanted to own. It doesn't really matter in the long run, so long as you make sure the market action verifies what you'd like to do before you do it. In contrast to mere opinions about a company, a stock's strength or weakness are observable facts, just as are support and resistance levels, trend and moving-average lines, etc. If you buy a weak stock, you are guessing that it won't go any lower, when lower it has been going; you are fighting the tape. Aren't you interested in buying a stock that will go up? Then why not make it a rule only to buy a stock that is already proving it can do just that?

You'll argue that the strong stock is already up. True. You don't get the same payoff from a horse that is leading the race as you do when it is still in the starting gate. Actually, studies have shown that stocks which have doubled are more likely to double again than any other ascertainable group. Many stocks, although seemingly already up a lot, are still early in their moves. Prices, you'll remember, always go to an excess. But there is more to it than that. We aren't asking you to buy a stock near the end of its move, but as it proves itself. We haven't bought at the bottom, and have indeed given away a precious few points from the low, but we have gained the assurance that the stock is alive, with empirical evidence that others, with plenty of buying power, are willing to bet on that particular stock.

It's possible to be wrong; the market permits no perfection. After we buy, the stock may falter, fade, fail. That's why, despite the value of stock selection, we want the added confirmation of market timing. If the overall market climate isn't in gear, you'd be safer skipping even so intriguing an individual selection as USI or Du Pont was at that time. At the moment you buy—rather than with the aid of hindsight—all you know is that those issues are relatively strong. A bearish or even a lukewarm market climate should cause you to hold back. But a conjunction of favorable market indicators at the time the stock starts breaking out might be all the signal you need.

Using the Technical Data

How, then, do we find the best stocks to buy? Not the way those who insist on stock selection alone customarily proceed. They believe that there is some way to ascertain value—indeed, they use the phrase "intrinsic value" as if there is some mathematically definable absolute worth for a stock that not only will keep the stock safe from harm but ought to lead it to go up in price sooner or later. Thus, they believe, rather contradictorily, that eventually the market itself will determine a proper price, but they don't want to accept that at the present moment the market is already determining such a price.

True, the company whose stock you're eyeing in all likelihood isn't going into bankruptcy, will continue paying its dividend, will keep increasing its business, or will snap back from a temporary problem. And, equally true, you may have spotted something in the balance sheet of the company that makes it relatively more of a bargain than other companies. A company selling at $30, with $20 per share's worth of liquid assets apart from its going business, may be said to have a certain kind of value. And, of course, there are companies whose appeal lies in their potential for earnings growth, such as a drug company with a new drug coming onstream, or a mundane machine-tool company turning into a leader in robotics. These stocks may be *potentially* buyable, but in no instance is there any way mathematically to calculate an intrinsic value—worth is only what the marketplace determines. It is only when something happens to the stock in the marketplace that any such value becomes profitable rather than potential.

Fundamental research goes on all the time. It is far more important in extent, and in its effect on buying decisions, than the technical approach. Indeed, it creates the decisions that in the end influence the charts we see. This is becoming increasingly so as institutions dominate market activity. Analysts at many different brokerage firms will follow a company, while at the other end the investing institution will have its own analyst not only reviewing those brokerage reports but often doing his own analyses besides. All this may then result in the company's name being put on the institution's buy list. It is then up to the portfolio manager to make a decision. As you can surmise, therefore, with all the different steps involved, the impact of even the greatest story will rarely hit the market all at once. The result is that, without having the vaguest idea of what the story is—although often we can do our own analysis or make a supposition—we can begin to see the effect on the stock's price action. What technical analysis of an individual stock does, in a sense, is let fundamentalists do the work, while we watch to see if the story has potential—that is, do others believe —and when it might be reasonably safe to act.

This recalls the professional trader's adage that what's important isn't the news itself but how the market reacts to the news. For example, the market has anticipated something negative about a company, so the price sells down; when the news is finally announced, all the selling may have already happened; if the stock remains unaffected (as USI was), it has reacted favorably to the bad news. However, if the news is a surprise, and the stock sells down, then it has reacted negatively. Thus, the manner of the response is more important for our purposes than the news itself. In this case the news is the analyst's work, the firm's report, the buy recommendation. Time after time, when we mention to an institutional-portfolio manager that we like the looks of a particular stock's chart, he'll reply that "there's a good story around on it." Well, we could have surmised that, because it is axiomatic that for a stock to have a bullish chart pattern there has to have been good buying going on. No one has access to all the Street's analyses and opinions, or gets them ahead of everyone else, or even absorbs the available information promptly, but that doesn't matter, because we can see the stock's action instantaneously, completely, and continually, by looking at the collective judgment. The tape, and by extension the chart, tells us if there are more buyers than sellers. And that's all we need to know.

Without the technical information in front of us, we'd have no means of checking empirically on what is essentially both the analyst's opinion and the degree of belief in it as a viable reason to buy the stock. Expectations change, or can be disappointed, or wrong; the forecast can be right enough, but perhaps no one cares; perhaps most of the buying has been done already; perhaps the seller believes a different thesis, or simply decides to take advantage of the new buyers to unload a big position for some unrelated reason. Obviously, there will be better, or more exciting, stories than others. A stock that is said to be reasonably priced isn't worth buying; there has to be an expectation of, and a reason for, a move to a higher price. But whereas the fundamental recommendation exists in an abstract world, technical analysis exists in the marketplace. It, too, looks at expectations: is the base big enough, is there a potential breakout ahead, is there room for the stock to move before meeting resistance? It identifies those stocks for which good buying has already established that the fundamental analysis (or hot tip, for that matter) has been accepted as viable, but also adds the necessary ingredient that the stock can actually go up.

What's more, most of this analytical work is affected by the market. When a stock is selling down, it is perceived to be in trouble; when it is rising, expectations soar, too. As a stock is forming a top, there are no fundamental warnings. All is good news, and the first decline is seen as nothing more than a normal correction. Typically, it isn't until several months later that the reasons the stock has been declining become apparent. Thus, the fundamental analyst is at first blind to the dangers the market is warning of and later forgets that at some point the stock is going to begin to anticipate a turnaround instead. Tell him that the stock is building a base and he'll scoff, saying the company still isn't doing well.

Such was the case with Northern Telecom. The stock had a high of 48 in January 1980, and by May, analysts were estimating $3.80 per share for that year and $4.50 for 1981. But, as you can see on the chart, NT renewed its already serious downtrend when it broke down below 33 in October 1980; the reason it suffered its eventual 20-point drop was a huge write-off for the fourth quarter that turned 1980's anticipated profit into a whopping $5.44 per-share loss instead. The chart had spoken first, just as it did thereafter, when NT then began to etch out an almost textbook-perfect head-and-shoulders bottom. But even while the right shoulder was being formed, those same analysts were insisting that the stock should be avoided because, to quote one, "the company still has too many

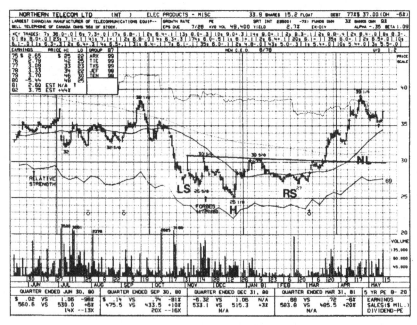

problems." Indeed, that was true; first-quarter results for '81 showed lower earnings of 68¢ vs. 72¢ per share. But by the time that news was announced, the stock had already broken out across the neckline (and its long-term moving-average line), and the news caused only a 2-point temporary dip. This story wouldn't be complete without adding that the fundamental analysts who had shrugged off the bullish technical picture in February were busily recommending the stock at 38 in April.

This is a classic case of knowing too much about the company (its current problems) and understanding too little about the marketplace (that it anticipates change). But fundamental analysis is affected by the market in another way, too. If the stock existed in a vacuum, an opinion that earnings estimated for next year as A were worth a price/earnings ratio of X would translate into two estimates, of earnings and a suitable ratio, merged into a third estimate of future price. Thus, fundamental forecasting becomes increasingly distant from the actual price action. And if the market itself were booming, the analyst's work might get tilted toward a more optimistic earnings forecast, along with an expectation of a higher ratio; the stock, already up, would look all the better to recommend at a time when customers would be all the more eager to buy.

Following is a weekly chart of Sony (but the daily charts during this time span show much the same details). The stock had been declining for a year, finally to reach a low at 6. At that price, estimated earnings of $1.10 for 1980 meant a relatively, perhaps even enticingly, low price/earnings ratio of approximately 5. But no one cared, as you can see from the low volume during that entire time span. It was only the chart that gave the first clue: during the extreme silver panic Sony held above its low, and two weeks later crossed its long-term moving-average line on sharply increasing volume. Obviously, at this point buyers became interested, probably due to someone's favorable fundamental analysis. But all you needed to see was the volume on the breakout across 7. Again, after a consolidation around 10, the stock broke out again on even greater volume. Another consolidation took place between 14 and 17, and, it seems, as soon as the moving-average line was successfully tested, SNE broke out for a third time and carried on up to

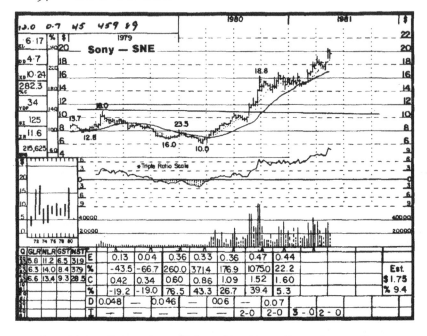

the mid-20s. It wasn't until then that the earlier estimate of $1.10 was proven wrong; actual earnings were $1.52. As a result, analysts raised their forecasts for 1981 and got all the more excited about the stock. In a report on various portfolio managers' activity, we read: "Recent buys include Sony," and "He would be a buyer of Japanese stocks such as Sony." Where were those high-paid money managers at 7 or 11 or even 17? What happened to bring them in at 22 or 23 instead? The rising stock created an ever-rising expectation. The actual market action, as depicted in the chart, was ignored; only when corporate results and fancy analytical reports coincided with the strong stock were they willing to believe. Note that even though the stock had nearly doubled, nearly tripled, there were profitable buy points for Sony. A stock does not necessarily become overpriced just because it is up. But at some point the potential buyer is mesmerized by the expectation of still greater gains . . . and he's the one who buys near the top. There were analysts shrewd enough to foresee what was changing at Sony, and to recommend the stock in anticipation. But all we needed to see were the twin clues of upside breakout and confirming volume, and to ride the stock as long as its moving-average line was unbroken and still trending upward. The only thing that can keep us objective in considering any fundamental opinion is market reality: how is the stock itself acting?

A stock does not have to go up to be strong; in a declining market, resistance to decline is a sign of budding strength. What we are seeing is that for some reason—and we don't need to know why—big money believes enough in that stock to start buying. Others will come in later, when they feel more secure about the market. As a result, such stocks usually turn out to have the most dynamic fundamental stories, leading them to produce the biggest bull-market gains thereafter. And once the market improves, there is a craving for recommendations, so that the fundamentalist's opinion begins to produce more and more price action for us to evaluate. Meanwhile, other opinions are being rejected because of taste, anxiety, or disbelief. Whatever the reason, however brilliant the analysis, it doesn't matter unless and until it has an actual effect on the stock's price. Someone with money has to start buying, and that's what we can see. Strength proves validity. Weakness breeds suspicion. What ought to go up, and doesn't, according to our aphorism, is doubly significant.

RCA is a case in point. In March 1981 there was excitement about the introduction of a new product. What a great chance to write a report on the company. With some embarrassment in the face of the eagerness of all this excited fundamentalist belief, we'd keep insisting, whenever asked, that the chart of RCA (see following page) didn't show anything special no matter how we looked at it. Note the lack of volume at point A, and the successively lower rally peaks. If all those recommendations were around, how come buying wasn't having much of an impact? Then along came a dreadful earnings report and the stock tumbled despite a strong market. The market in its collective wisdom knew what the new-product story didn't . . . that RCA still wasn't doing well.

After all, we—you, the bank-trust officer, the pension-fund manager, the floor trader, the brokerage-firm analyst, the salesman—don't know very much. There are varying degrees of ignorance; someone else, it seems, always knows more, or knows about some

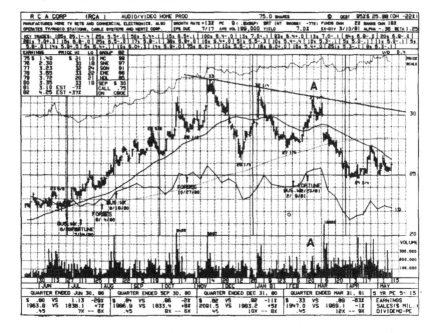

other stock, or has a different perspective. The only objective thing you have to go on is the stock's own action within the action of the marketplace.

Despite your ignorance, if you weigh all the factors, you can come out ahead. First, you need to have market timing on your side via what the various indicators are saying. Second, an ample list of buy candidates—as evidence that the anticipated move will be broad and robust; a lean list is a warning of a potentially paltry move—will serve both as an indicator in itself and as the source for your selections. And third, you need provable-action points to enable you to focus on those stocks with the most potential at the moment they begin to demonstrate proven strength. If you follow these guidelines, you'll be amazed at how often the reason you made a good bet comes out later.

6

HOW TO USE
THE
INDICATORS

Technical analysis exists in its own enclosed and narrow world. The stock market is all. One of the deans of the art, John Magee, is reputed to have sat in a room with the windows blocked off, letting the daily newspapers pile up, unread and yellowing, outside the door. All that counted to him was the action in the marketplace itself. Knowing anything at all about how the companies were doing, or the economy, or political events, was thought to cloud objectivity and affect judgment. The concern was only whether stocks should be bought, held, or sold. The basis for the decision was in how they were trading, not in how nice or how speculative they were, or whether the Gross National Product was rising.

At the other extreme are the economists and market analysts who scrutinize every bit of news, ranging from corporate quarterly and annual reports to broad economic statistics, congressional attitudes, and world politics, in search of data that they believe will help them decide what the stock market is apt to do. They think the market will, should, ought to respond to every news announcement and press release as if it is a push-pull toy. Reporters, and the business sections of our newspapers, fuel this approach, because if they did not try to tie in the events of the day (mostly press releases) with what the market was doing, they would have nothing to write about the day's action. "The market went up today because there were more buyers than sellers" makes for a very short column.

We're not about to sit in a closet with a ticker tape and our charts, but we do admire John Magee's legendary austerity. The best rallies come "out of nowhere." The dynamic portion of the rise that was launched in late February 1981 occurred when a down-10 Dow-point morning was reversed into an up-8-point day. Reporters were anxious to find a reason for this dramatic afternoon reversal, but without anything to pin it on, the move was dismissed as a mere technical aberration. Well, the reason was, perhaps, that prices had sold down to support (see chart of the DJIA in the preceding chapter, p. 84), and there was no follow-through on the downside. To the technician, the reversal itself was the key; a successful test of the low had occurred. The fact that it was not news-induced was significant; it meant that market forces had driven the turnaround. Hence the fresh strength was likely to continue—as it did; the Dow rallied 10 percent in less than two months.

Good News, Bad News

Generally speaking, news-related market or individual stock moves are emotional and short-lived. Or, rather, the market does what it wants to do and uses the news as an excuse. An illustration of this can be found in President Eisenhower's two serious illnesses. At a time when a rising market had already begun to form an intermediate top, the President's heart attack set off the decline that was becoming imminent anyhow. Conversely, the market had been plunging before his ileitis attack; it sold off emotionally for about an hour, and then began to rally off the low that technicians had already begun looking for. Unexpected news can have a short-term impact in the expected direction—good news up, bad news down—but it will probably not affect the long-range outlook.

Indeed, good news is *always* deceptive. Never buy on good news even if you think you can get away with it. Openings will be sharply higher and the professionals will be selling into them. Recall how difficult it was to make a long-side profit on the enthusiastic response to President Nixon's first economic game plan in 1971, and that not long thereafter the market began a full-fledged intermediate-term decline. What's more, it is even worse if there is little or no response to favorable news; this can be a serious warning of an imminent reversal to the downside, since it means that the market is overbought already.

If you can maintain objectivity, therefore, it is helpful to know the news. As we mentioned before, *what's important is not the news itself but how the market reacts to it.* If you heed our warning that good news is always deceptive, and often a signal that the bull side is exhausted, then the chief value of that aphorism in terms of when to buy applies to bad news. With bad news, the market consistently does what it wants to do, but what it does can be valuable trading information. There is the example of RCA cited in the previous chapter: the stock was not acting well beforehand; the bad news broke the price down below support and initiated a serious downtrend. In this kind of situation, the break that comes on the bad news can cause technical damage that will take a long time to repair. On the other hand, refusal to go down in the midst of a barrage of bad news (see USI's action despite persistently lower earnings reports) is highly favorable action. This can happen to a market that has already fallen extensively and is beginning to form a base in the face of dire economic statistics (as in December 1974), or to an individual stock that is becoming sold-out even as the directors are ommitting the dividend or announcing a massive write-off (see Northern Telecom's chart in the preceding chapter). A market or stock that holds despite news that otherwise might be expected to take it lower is announcing that it is already sold out.

In addition to keeping up with news-ticker items, it is helpful to know what the general opinion is around the Street. Over and over again, a consensus opinion will be proven wrong. (In part, this is because market action will have already reflected that opinion, leaving few others to later propel the move in the expected direction.) Headlines and quoted comments in articles are excellent, although difficult to quantify, indicators. (Recall the previously quoted gloomy *Wall Street Journal* commentaries as the market was making an important low in April 1980.) Negative front-page articles on the market often appear in the *Journal* eerily close to reversal days; similarly, big black headlines in other newspapers can be useful—to start you thinking in the other direction. If you can maintain your objectivity, knowing what the majority believes can help you form a useful contrary opinion. *Never join the majority.* Playing the devil's advocate is an intelligent stance in the stock market.

But while it is helpful to know whether the news is good or bad, and what the consensus is, the news itself is hardly ever pertinent to our narrow task of trying to forecast the action of the stock market. Obviously, a Presidential illness or a Russian adventure in Afghanistan does not directly relate to corporate business results. Even the extremely rare instance in which a news event does have economic impact, such as the 1973 OPEC oil embargo, can be dealt with in technical market terms: in this case, the Dow was already topping out and was due for a correction when the news of the embargo emerged; the only mistake that could have been made was underestimating the impact of the news by buying back too soon.

But even if most political and international news has only short-term emotional effects on prices, it would seem that the state of the economy would have a direct influence on the price trend of securities. In one way, of course, this is true. Such data gets factored into the opinions of investors, and, in turn, these opinions get translated into actual buy-and-sell decisions. But if the market anticipates, if good news persistently comes out near tops and bad news near bottoms, published economic statistics can at best be past history, at worst deceptive.

Let's take a minute example. The market has been declining and discouraging; it has been trying to hold temporarily but looks as if it could break down again. At that moment, a negative economic statistic is announced—let's say it is even worse than expected. Prices open lower in reaction to the news; then trading dries up; by the close, prices are actually higher. Which is more important then, the news or the behavior of the stocks themselves? The former is telling us of trouble, the latter is alerting us to a market that doesn't want to drop any further and would rather go up, regardless of the trouble. The game is being played by its own rules, not those of the economy, and we are players in the stock market, not economic theorists.

The government publishes an Index of Leading Economic In-

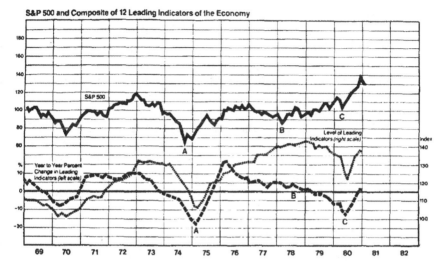

S&P 500 and Composite of 12 Leading Indicators of the Economy

dicators which has been constructed to predict economic patterns with a lead time of several months. The series had gone up, on the average, three and a half months before an economic recovery, and down nearly nine months ahead of the start of a recession (suggesting that it can be at least of some help in warning of a top). But note that it signaled the economic upturn in early 1975 (A–A), months *after* the stock market had bottomed and was already rallying. It was of no relevance to the broad rise in stocks that began in April 1978 (B–B), and its reversal in 1980 (C–C) occurred a month *after* the bull market that began that April. Actually, studies have shown that one of the components of this Index, the stock market itself, has the best record of any of the twelve components of this Index for anticipating economic trends. The stock market predicts. Little wonder, then, that the fundamentally oriented money manager—who waits to get verification from the news —so often ends up throwing up his hands and cursing the market, insisting that it is impossible to time.

Some Closely Watched Statistics

Let's briefly run through a few typical and closely watched economic statistics to see if they can tell us anything helpful at all. For example, among the statistics fundamentalists use is Real Personal Income. This reflects the purchasing power of the consumer, and thus measures both economic activity and consumer confidence. Over the years, the changes in real personal income and stock prices have moved in vague tandem—in hindsight. Note that this statistic peaked in late 1973, nearly a full year after the market topped out (A–A–A). Rather than Real Personal Income itself, it was the year-to-year change in this statistic that provided an early signal, for its peak came coincident to the market's peak. Similarly, the rate of change was only a month or so late at the major 1974 bottom, while the actual statistic said nothing at all (B–B–B). Thus, encouraged by this approximate relationship, you might have tracked Real Personal Income's year-to-year changes, only to miss totally the big stock-market rises that began in 1978 (C–C–C) and again in 1980 (D–D–D). Relationship yes, useful signals no.

How about Industrial Production? There was a sharp falling-off from the end of 1974 through the first quarter of 1975 (A–A). In other words, the decline in this indicator coincided, not with a top, but with the major bottom for stock prices. It actually went contra to the market. What seems to happen is that excess inventories retard production even after the economy has begun to recover, so that at market bottoms this series has invariably lagged, not led. Compare, too, the action in 1978–79 (B–B) for another missed buying opportunity, even though (see C–C and D–D) there seems to be some coincident value at tops.

The relationship of Housing Starts to market action has a slightly better record, even if still of little value for our purposes. Housing Starts measures stimulus within the economy, is credit-sensitive, and highly cyclical. These statistics (see p. 104) topped out during 1972, hit a low a few weeks after the market bottom (A–A) in late 1974, and then rose steadily along with a prolonged bull market. But note how the 1978 stock-price rise was totally missed (B–B), because housing construction simply was not going to boom in a high-interest climate, even though stock prices defiantly did.

In addition to the inconsistencies and failures of these statistics, there is a problem even when the data are approximately in gear. Note that we refer to the month a statistic turned. But this is

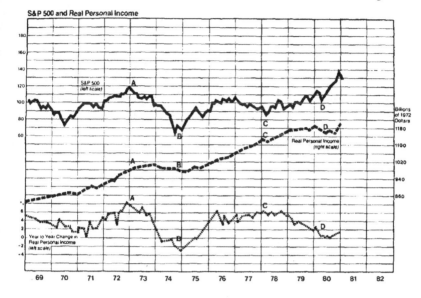

S&P 500 and Real Personal Income

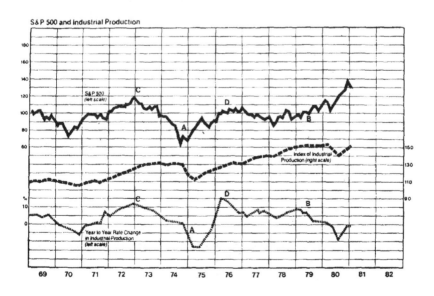

S&P 500 and Industrial Production

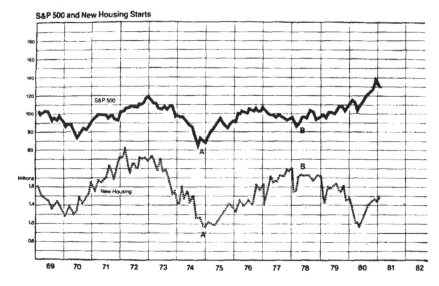

S&P 500 and New Housing Starts

hindsight observation; in addition to the delay before the month's statistics are announced, at least another month or two of statistics are needed to confirm such a turn, so that even when it's on target, this data does little good. Hindsight does not provide useful signals. Such data, though filling the newspaper pages and of relevance to the economy, have no practical use in timing the stock market. The market itself has a better record for predicting economic trends than the other way around.

Federal Reserve Board statistics, however, cannot be so readily dismissed. First, the degree of available money—whether it is tight or easy—affects buying power. In periods of easy money, there is a lot more speculative money available, particularly during the early stages of a bull market. The Fed begins to ease its prior monetary restrictive policy to help stem the recession and put the economy back on track. Since the recession tends to start at approximately the time the market is bottoming, there is far less incentive to use the easier money promptly for such business purposes as building inventory during the recession, than to play the stock market with it, at least temporarily, especially since the market is, of course, already anticipating the end of the recession ahead. Second, the action of the Federal Reserve has a direct future impact on business and corporate results, so that its data tell us not only about current policy but about the potential climate ahead as well. Third, the level of interest rates directly competes with the stock market for funds. Bonds and Treasury bills are alternative investments, so when their yield is high, money can be and is diverted from the stock market. And, in addition, lower interest rates increase the temptation to buy on margin; higher rates will eventually cause liquidation in margin accounts. Finally, as a practical matter, the track record of certain monetary statistics work often enough, although far less well than our technical market indicators, in relation to the trend of the stock averages, to make them viable indicators.

It is this last point that is most important for our purposes. The economic statistics don't work, so we cast them aside. What the Federal Reserve Board does has an effect that ripples into the stock market, so we pay attention. The relationship to some degree, we believe, is due to the fact that both the stock market and the Federal Reserve actions anticipate. A change in Fed policy, not in what is said but in what is being done, is designed to create a future change in the monetary conditions of the country. Thus, the rate of change that can be observed is also an anticipatory indicator. In this regard, changes in money supply have become the most closely followed statistic, but it seems to be more emotional than practical, more inconsistent than useful. Good news is deceptive; bad news provides us a measure of the shape the market is in; but good news can, on differing occasions, mean a rise in money supply or a drop. Even the longer-term rate of change has lagged behind the stock market (in 1974 and 1980) or missed a rise entirely (the start of a big boom in secondary stocks in 1978).

The Federal Reserve statistic that has the best batting average as an indicator relating to the longer-term trend of the stock market is Net Free or Net Borrowed Reserves. Here, changes in the cost of money and the demand for it are reflected in one statistic, and that change has often anticipated stock-market direction. For example, the level of Net Borrowed Reserves hit an extreme in mid-1974 (A–A) and started diminishing ahead of the stock-market

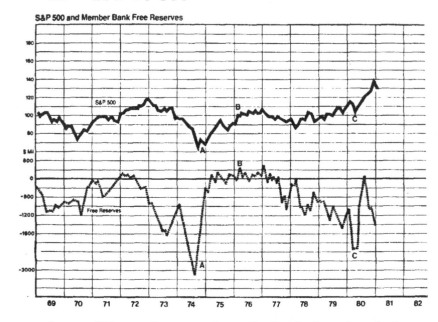

S&P 500 and Member Bank Free Reserves

bottom. This was also true at the market low in the spring of 1980 (C–C), although with less anticipation. In general, a rate of change toward less and less borrowing is favorable for the market (although sometimes the market can rise without it, as in '78), and readings which get up into the Net Free Reserve area (B–B) have usually coincided with bullish climates for stock prices.

There is an even more direct correlation with interest rates, but again a far from perfect one. Traditionally, higher short-term rates act as a damper on the market—as an alternative investment, for one reason; for another, it is a symptom of tighter money; and third, buying on margin is increasingly costly, while selling short to earn high interest becomes a professional tool. But when rates peak and then start to come back down, it has usually proven favorable for stock prices. This has been a leading indicator for long enough now to be respected. Rates peaked, for example, in September 1966, June 1970, October 1974, and March 1980; in each instance, stock prices were higher (an average of 7 percent) three months later and six months later (an average gain in the DJIA of 19 percent). Accordingly, it's a good idea to pay attention to the direction of interest rates, even though there are periods when the stock market ignores such a factor (as in the secondary stock rise beginning in 1978) and when falling rates are so widely expected they provide a sense of euphoria to a dangerous market. Just don't forget the value of contrary opinion—even in an indicator that has worked before—when something is so obvious that you read about it everywhere. Ask yourself: If everyone is buying in anticipation of, in this example, a decline in interest rates, who will be left to buy if and when that decline actually takes place? An indicator is most likely to fail when it is most closely watched.

Here again, too, we have the problem of knowing of such a peak in rates only in hindsight; little fluctuations might serve only to deceive. A way to deal with this has now become possible with the recent introduction of a lively market in various financial futures —a commodity-type way of playing Treasury bills, bonds, etc., for future delivery. Chart-oriented traders can keep an eye on the action of this market by watching the charts published by Commodity Research Bureau or by maintaining one's own charts. The futures market is, as the name indicates, played by people betting on the direction of interest rates. Although such charts develop in much faster fashion than is customary for common stocks (and is more like commodity action), the chart patterns are similar— head-and-shoulders, trend lines, etc.—and thus reveal evidence of potential dynamic changes in direction. Watching the futures market can give you a leg up on what might happen to interest rates, and when the stock market is sensitive to such swings, this can be well worth monitoring.

Last, the relationship between short-term and long-term rates has often been a useful stock-market indicator, chiefly because it reveals a traditionally favorable—or unfavorable—climate for share prices. A simple measure that has come to be known as the "Alert" indicator measures the ratio between three-month Treasury bills and long-term AAA-rated corporate bonds. (These statistics can conveniently and consistently be found in the weekly pamphlet available free from the Federal Reserve Bank of St. Louis.) When, in the past, the ratio has begun to rise across 1.20, it has been a bullish signal; a rarer crossing of the 1.40 level has represented a major stock-market buy signal.

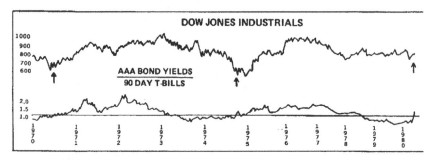

As you can see, the closer a statistic relates to the stock market, the more useful it becomes. Thus, changes in interest rates are the most useful fundamental indicator, while something as remote as the Consumer Price Index is of no help at all. Years ago, Garfield Drew, the originator of the odd-lot indicators, made a spoofing case for using the score of each year's Rose Bowl game as a market indicator. Nowadays, that indicator has received new life as the Super Bowl indicator, based on a pattern of what the market does in years when the AFL, or the NFL, wins the ultimate prize. From that, it is but one step to indicators based on historical precedence whenever something occurs with more than random frequency. That is, the first year of a newly elected President is usually a down year for the stock market. It makes political sense for a new President to try to clean house economically in the first year, so that by the time reelection looms, the economy has been brought back into an upswing. (Note how, despite a deceptive spring rally, 1981 finally conformed to this pattern of behavior.) The most consistent of such historical patterns is known as the January indicator: the action during the first five trading days of January (or for the full month itself) often foretells what the market is likely to do for the rest of the year. Actually, and rather amazingly, this calendar indicator has an excellent record (again, note its accuracy for 1981). The problem is that you never know whether the forthcoming year is going to be one of the exceptions or if it will conform to the pattern, or if, even though the yearly pattern fits, the market will find some perverse way to fool you anyhow. Such indicators are more to be written about than to be used as the basis for betting real money. They can never foretell when the next exception will occur, just as a high batting average doesn't guarantee that a baseball star will get a hit his next time at bat, even if he hasn't had a hit all day and is certainly due. While they can alert us to a possibility, a tendency, historical indicators do no real forecasting.

The more pertinent indicators can be generally divided into two types. One grouping can be called the sentiment indicators, those which measure the way people feel about the market. Examples are the odd-lot studies, insider purchases and sales, specialist and member short-selling. The other broad grouping is those indicators relating directly to market action, such as the Advance/Decline Line, the High/Low Differential, the Overbought/Oversold Oscillator.

Sentiment indicators, by revealing what is in the minds of various segments of market participants as shown by their market activities, enable us to determine extremes of opinion that develop at what prove to be key market turning points. We treat professionals—specialists and other Exchange members—with respect, and generally want to be on the same side of the market they are on. But we know that amateur odd-lot short-sellers and institutional money managers are often wrong at important turning points. Too much bearishness on the part of the majority is something we want to go contrary to; that's why the sentiment indicators are used to reveal extremes of opinion. When the consensus is convinced, history has shown that they are about to be proven wrong.

On the other hand, indicators based on internal market action don't signal extremes. Because they are directly related to what is happening in the marketplace itself, they reveal potential trend changes via divergences, confirmations, or non-confirmations. While one or the other of these two broad groupings may provide the earlier signals, it is usually necessary to get both the sentiment and the internal indicators in gear before a meaningful move can evolve.

With that as background, let's review in detail those particular indicators which have been useful over the years in forecasting important market bottoms and buy points.

The Sentiment Indicators

Let's start with the sentiment indicators. When a worthwhile bottom is made, everyone, including you, is frightened. The market

has become scary. With prices dropping and stocks acting as if they
never want to rally for more than an hour, the feeling is generated
that prices will keep plunging, that the bottom is still far away.
Often, late in a decline, an important and closely watched level of
support gets broken. In March 1980, for example, the area that had
hitherto served as support—around Dow 780—gave way, making
the market look even more bearish and ultimately leading to the
panic-selling climax.

What's more, the prevailing news will be negative, with intima-
tions that there's even more bad news ahead. Often, such news is
associated with rumors of some sort of fiscal crisis. At first, bad
news reinforces the decline in stock prices. The bottom is not yet
at hand; there are still sellers around. It is only when prices no
longer respond to negative announcements that we get a clue that
the market is sold out. Of course, it still looks as if the next piece
of bad news will make prices plummet even further, so you are
intimidated. Everyone knows "the time to buy stocks is when
nobody wants them," but it sure is hard to do in such a climate of
negative news and falling prices. After all, if you'd bought yesterday, you'd have a loss today, so why risk buying today? Nevertheless, someone has to be on the buy side of every transaction, even
if reluctantly. That's where the specialists on the Exchange floor
come in. They are required, as part of their franchise, to make a
fair and orderly market in all the stocks they handle. To do this,
they have to buy when no one else is willing to, even if they are
just as scared, just as bearish. Late in a decline, they are already
amply loaded with shares they've been compelled to buy already,
yet still the sellers predominate. And, on any little bounce, it is
hard for them to profit by selling short because they must sell
stocks first from that by now substantial long position. Because
they have so much long stock to dispose of first on any upticks, and
because this position is constantly being replenished when they
have to buy in the absence of other buyers, specialist short-selling
diminishes considerably as the decline extends itself. When it
reaches an extreme, we get a signal. Historically, whenever the
ratio of specialist short-selling to total shorting diminishes to less
than 40 percent, a bottom is being made.

These figures are available slightly late. That is, the data are
gathered by the specialist firms and turned into the Exchange

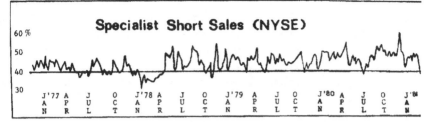

during the week following the action. Exchange personnel then total the various reports and release the data a week later—that is, on the following Friday, two weeks after the actual trading time span. This delay is relatively insignificant, because as major bottoms are formed, this index provides repeated favorable readings, appearing, for example, under 40 percent as early as August 1974, well ahead of the first low in October and the second, double bottom, low in December. Similarly, in early 1978, there were weeks of favorable readings (see accompanying chart), including a dip down to almost 30 percent, just ahead of a major rise in secondary stocks as well as a powerful upside breakout, in April, in the blue-chip average. In general, single-week signals under 40 percent come more quickly and closer in time to the actual low, but on less important bottoms. When it truly counts, the specialist short-selling ratio speaks in plenty of time, setting the stage for a low-risk buying climate at major market turning points. Also note, on the chart, worthwhile buy signals, for good trading rallies, after the October crashes in '78 and '79, and as the market was poised for a 10 percent bounce in February 1981. You'll find these figures published conveniently in two different places. They appear in *Barron's* each weekend, and in Monday's *Wall Street Journal.* The calculation is simple. The amount of total short-selling is divided into specialist shorting to get the percentage of the total. Trust this indicator. If it isn't speaking, don't try to pursuade yourself that you are otherwise seeing a bottom. Rationalizing indicators is foolish. If the ratio remains in the neutral zone of the mid- to upper 40 percent area, it isn't a buyable bottom yet. This indicator merits waiting for a signal and not taking risks until you get one. The kind of bottom we've been talking about has *always* been accompanied by such low specialist short-selling figures.

Our second, related, sentiment indicator is found in the same statistical place, but in the case of the *Journal,* a little extra addition is required. The Member Short-Sales Ratio adds together specialist shorting, off-floor member trading, and the much smaller amount of on-floor member shorting. The total of these three aspects represents all the short-selling done by Exchange members for their own or their firms' accounts. It is then divided by the amount of total short-selling—that is, including the public activity —to see what percentage has been sold short by professionals.

While specialists often are required to sell short—when they have no long position—to keep the market in that stock orderly, other members have no such restriction. Specialist short-selling, therefore, is, to a considerable degree, involuntary, and its percentage is affected by the degree to which they are forced, by a severely declining market, to be on the buy side instead. Thus, the Specialist Short-Selling Ratio depicts an extreme. But other members, whether on or off the Exchange floor, can exercise their own judgment. Apart from having to adhere to the law that all short-selling must be done on a plus or zero-plus tick—a price higher than the last different price—they can sell short as their opinion as to market direction or that of an individual stock dictates. Since they have years of experience as professionals, one can expect them to have a good idea as to such trends, and since their job is to make profitable trades, they are good people to join rather than fight. Over the years, the buy-signal level for this indicator has gradually been creeping upward. The market bottoms in 1962, 1966, and 1970 saw readings down near 50 percent, but the two important bottoms in 1974 and 1975 found member short-selling dipping to just under 60 percent. More recently, a ratio of 75 percent has proven favorable. The advent of the options market probably accounts for this shift, since a considerable amount of short positions are actually nominal, being used to hedge against long-option positions. This has been especially the case when high interest rates have made selling short—and collecting the interest on the money received from the sale—a profitable activity in itself, without taking a market risk, since the position is hedged in the option market. Nevertheless, this indicator serves as a useful extra dimension in revealing professional sentiment. The key thing to watch for is a significant shift in sentiment, regardless of level. If this shift toward less and less short-selling by all the Exchange members is matched by a low reading in the specialist's ratio, you've gotten useful confirmation of a favorable market climate for buying. It means that trading members are less and less interested in playing the short side because the market, they feel, is approaching a bottom at last.

A third related indicator, which also takes just a few seconds to calculate from the *Barron's* or *Journal* statistics, is known as the Public Short-Sales Ratio. This provides a view of public sentiment. Since dividing non-member short-selling by total shorting would just give you the balance of the percentage already calculated above, this ratio is calculated with a different divisor—total NYSE volume for the week involved. Therefore, you need to keep track of what that total volume was for the week dating back to the week of the statistics, that is, two weeks prior. (An easy way to keep track is to save each week's Market Laboratory Page from *Barron's*.) Here we are looking for the converse of professional sentiment. Little shorting is done while prices are rising, and even less when optimism rules near market tops; rather, the public is inclined to step up its activity on the short side well after a decline has gotten underway and when it is convinced that the short side is at last the side to be on. Here, too, the advent of options trading —selling calls or buying puts to bet on a bearish opinion—has reduced the signal level in this indicator. As a guide, it would be deemed favorable if the ratio were above 1.50, but what we are looking for is a rising ratio—increased bearishness—while prices are declining. This would indicate intensifying public fear. A further sharp spurt to the 2.00 level would add to the signal of an important bottom. This ratio works particularly well during the test of a low, as public investors tend to become convinced that the decline is being renewed in full force and sell short even more avidly.

An additional value of the Public Short-Sales Ratio is that it tells us about the trading activities of a different sector of the public from the more frequently watched odd-lot indicators. The stigma attached to odd-lot short-sellers, who are accused of coming out in great numbers only near the bottom, seems to apply equally to round-lot traders. But the latter figures are available only after a two-week delay, whereas the odd-lot statistics can be obtained daily. Odd-lot short-selling has lost some of its luster lately because of the considerably reduced degree of trading available for our information. The demise of the full-fledged odd-lot broker system on the Stock Exchange floor and the withdrawal of Merrill Lynch to keep its own trading to itself has caused far fewer shares per day to get listed in the published data. This is not as serious as it seems, however. There is a consistent correlation between Merrill Lynch's private statistics and those available publicly, and even more important, because we are dealing with a ratio, whether the inputs involve 2,000 shares or 20,000 shares, it is still a proportion of overall odd-lot trading that provides us with a signal. Thus, the figures are still well worth watching, even though the guidelines have shifted over the years.

The details are available in two places. The latest figures, for the previous day's trading, appear regularly on the Dow-Jones news ticker (colloquially known as the "broad tape") each morning before the opening (usually at around 9 a.m.). If the market has been plunging, it is worth asking your broker to get these figures for you promptly; a substantial increase in odd-lot short-selling even on a one-day basis can herald an imminent bottom; failure to increase says it is still too soon. Otherwise, the same figures are published the following morning in daily newspapers such as *The Wall Street Journal, The New York Times,* and other financial sections around the country. The Odd-Lot Short-Sales Ratio is obtained by dividing total odd-lot selling into odd-lot short-selling. Nowadays, readings above 1 percent on a daily basis are favorable, but we'd want them to get up over 2 percent for them to be calling for a bottom after a steep market fall. We also keep a ten-day moving average of these figures to see if there is a sustained trend toward increasing odd-lot bearishness. The more negative these amateurish traders—as marked by the fact that they deal only in small quantities—become, emboldened by a falling market and scare headlines, the closer the market is to an important bottom. The accompanying chart, calculated by a slightly different method, shows four times (A) when excessive short-selling by these little traders came at an important market bottom: November 1978 and November 1979, when the odd-lotters ventured forth near the end of the successive October massacres; in March 1980, and again in January–February 1981. This kind of excessive short-selling provides evidence that the climate has become comfortable for buying.

This particular sentiment indicator also has some timing value. After the market has been plunging, a sudden spurt for one or two days to a much higher level—say, 2 percent or more, such as suddenly popped up in March 1980—almost always times a true reversal. Traders can use it with confidence, buying skillfully into what typically is a lower opening the next day. It's worth noting, too, that relatively high readings that persist while the market is up indicate a continuing comfortable buying climate. The fear that the market is about to collapse helps keep prices rallying instead. Similarly, minuscule odd-lot shorting must be regarded as a warning not to buy, that optimism, even complacency still exists.

The regular, shall we say old-fashioned, odd-lot indicator itself —dividing total purchases into total sales—is a readily calculable statistic from the same data source. However, over the years this indicator has lost much of its potency. Formerly, odd-lotters would

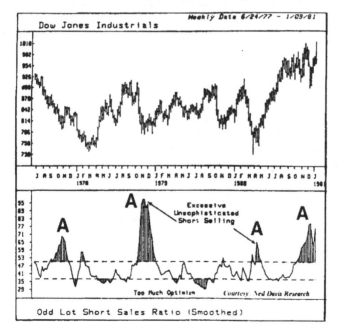

buy for a while during a decline, thinking they were accumulating bargains, but then, as the decline accelerated, there would be a noticeable shift toward more selling. However, in recent years there has instead been relatively heavy odd-lot buying in proportion to selling at bottoms, proving these small investors right, while at virtually the same time their cousins are blatantly wrong selling short.

The advent of options trading has produced another valuable sentiment indicator to take the place of the odd-lot ratio. We are dealing here with true bettors, because options are much cheaper to play than the stocks themselves, and the style is almost like going up to a window and saying, "I want to bet $200 on IBM getting to $65 by April." Further, it is possible to express an opinion on the short side without waiting for the required uptick to sell a stock short, and this is more readily done by the public because the bet entails a limited loss and an appealingly greater potential percentage profits. When market bettors become frightened and bearish, they shun buying call options and buy plenty of puts—the right to sell the stock at a designated level—instead. This is identified by a low reading in the Call/Put Ratio (dividing put buying into call buying). This chart illustrates how too much optimism, reflected in huge call buying, occurred in August–September 1978 (A), ahead of the first October massacre, and again in late 1980 (B), as warnings not to buy stocks. Low levels in November 1979 (C), April 1980 (D), and February 1981 (E), reflecting extreme bearishness on the part of option speculators, proved to be excellent buying opportunities. By telling us what this speculative sector of the Wall Street community feels about the future course of the market, this indicator has developed an outstanding track record.

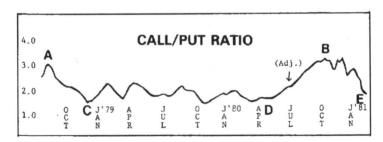

One more sentiment indicator is worth noting here. This is the by now overpopularized—because it has worked—percentage of advisory services that are bullish or bearish (see chart below). This statistic is conveniently calculated by the Investors Intelligence advisory service. The remarkable thing is that the very advisory services which purport to be helpful in telling you what the market is likely to do turn out to be predominantly trend-followers themselves. As the market rises, they tend to be increasingly bullish, while a declining market will produce more and more bearish commentaries. Indeed, this indicator is one way of quantifying what otherwise we are trying to find in headlines and news articles —that is, what the majority is thinking. It may be that different advisors are right at different turning points, or that the same few are consistently right while most others are of little use. On an overall basis, too much bearishness is a good indication that you should be going against the consensus and getting ready to buy. For example, every time in early 1979 that there were 50 percent bearish readings, 60 point Dow rallies followed. At point 3 on the chart,

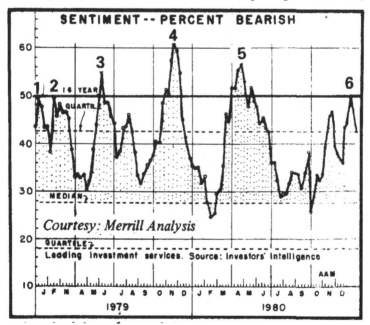

SENTIMENT -- PERCENT BEARISH

Courtesy: Merrill Analysis

Leading investment services. Source: Investors' Intelligence even greater bearishness was followed by an 80-point rise. The October debacle that ended in November 1979 produced over 60 percent advisory services on the bear side (point 4) and was followed by a 120-point rally. In April 1980 (point 5), the extreme bearishness was so wrong it missed a 250-point rise, while, in early 1981, persistent bearishness over 50 percent was followed by a 100-point rise.

Another way to calculate this indicator is to divide the percentage of bullish services by the total of both bulls and bears. As you can see on the second chart, a massive tilt toward bullishness occurs at major tops, while for our buying purposes you can also see the degree of bearishness at major bottoms. Note the favorable signals given at the major low in 1974 (A), and again starting in 1978

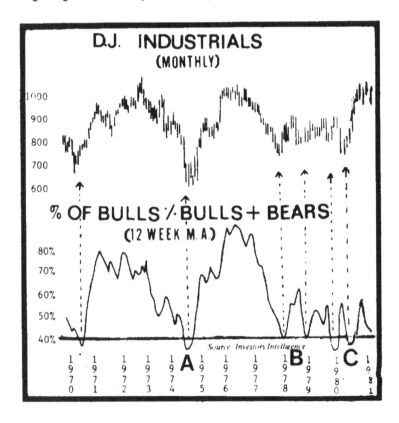

(B), when the broad market launched a huge upward move. Again, in 1980, at a major market low (C), the bearishness returned with an almost venomous fervor.

Extremes of bearish sentiment swing with both intermediate-term and major bottoms, but do not necessarily show which is which. The first quarter of 1981 produced what was at the time the most intense concentration of bearish sentiment ever seen. Odd-lot short-selling was persistently high, the Call/Put Ratio had reached new record levels every week, advisory services were steadfastly more than 50 percent bearish, the Public Short-Sales Ratio reached a peak, and there was a lot of talk that a whole new bear market had started. In contrast, member shorting lessened to near 75 percent and the Specialist Short-Selling Ratio dipped to under 40 percent. Meanwhile, stocks (see charts of Du Pont and U.S. Industries in the previous chapter) had already started to improve. This confluence certainly made for a favorable buying climate, yet the ensuing rally, although it took the market to new high ground, fizzled a few months later, when the indicators began to give sell signals instead. The difference, of course, was that, despite the array of favorable sentiment indicators, the signals were coming after an already extensive rise and not, as in April 1980, after a severe fall.

Sentiment indicators are not particularly good timing devices (with the exception of an abrupt and substantial increase in odd-lot short-selling on the heels of a steep fall). But they are invaluable in helping to keep you objective, while all about you others are betting on their emotional fears and anxieties. By making you aware of the crowd's opinion, sentiment indicators alert you to the chance to do the opposite.

The Market-Action Indicators

Now let's look at the market-action indicators. The first, and broadest, we have discussed previously. That's the relationship of the market averages to their long-term moving-average lines. Reviewing briefly: these lines identify momentum, direction, and, when crossed, provide breakout signals. Nothing truly bullish can get underway while the longer-term moving-average line is still heading downward. When the current price action gets far away from the moving-average line, a rally to redress this will develop, but will prove to be just a bear-market interruption. Time is needed to halt the downward momentum and to turn the line upward instead. Following this base-building time, the best upside break-out comes when a previous rally peak and the overhead moving-average line are crossed at about the same time, on a confirming increase in volume. This is a coincident buy signal of impeccable accuracy. You'll find that it will come *after* most, if not all, of the sentiment indicators have shown that there is too much bearishness around for the market to continue to decline as they expect. Thus, the climate will be ripe for a reversal, but you will still want further confirmation—and timing help—from the market-action indicators as well.

You may also find it useful to construct your own market average in addition to monitoring the published ones (the Dow, Standard & Poors, etc.). Such averages are weighted in one way or another, while an unweighted average can provide a broad gauge of how stocks in general are doing. You can readily make your own unweighted average from the QCHA (for Quote Change) figures published each week on *Barron's* Market Laboratory page. (In turn, they derive from the Quotron machine's calculations.) The Dow Industrials, as you know, consists of thirty blue-chip companies, with widely differing multipliers (to adjust for stock splits) used for each component of the average. Both the S&P and NYSE Composites are calculated by multiplying a stock's price by the number of shares outstanding, thereby giving heavy weight to the action of the major, heavily capitalized companies with millions of shares issued. But there are times when meaningful action is going on elsewhere, and this can be seen only in a completely unweighted comprehensive average. Quotron's data provides the collective percentage price change for all common stocks at any given moment, as it relates to the previous day's close. A reading of, say, +.50 means that the average percentage change from the day before at that moment for all common stocks is a gain of one half of 1 percent. If the DJIA, for example, were at that same moment up 10 points from 1,000 to 1,010, you'd see that the blue-chip stocks were doing twice as well as the general market.

To construct your own average, simply take the daily changes from the Quotron machine after the close of trading each day, or as published in *Barron's*. Start at an arbitrary base number such as 100, and multiply by the closing percentage change. If it's a gain, add it to the base number; if a loss, subtract. Do this for each trading day by multiplying the percentage change by the previous day's level. (You can also construct a similar average for the American Stock Exchange, via the percentage change figures identified for the Amex as QACH.) Plot your average on a large piece of graph paper, allowing room to record small daily changes with accuracy. Leave some room, too, for plotting an appropriate moving-average line as well. The easiest way to do this, if you are doing your math by hand, is to add Friday's closing figure each week, and drop the Friday's closing figure of 31 weeks earlier. This will give you a simplified 30-week moving average for your own unweighted average. (This is, of course, easier to do on a calculator and, even easier, in this modern age, programed into a home computer.)

The following chart is an example of the virtue of having this alternative average so you can judge what the real market is doing in comparison to the Dow Industrial Average. Point A on the chart represents the low made on Silver Thursday. Point B reflects a matching higher low. It is at point C that a useful divergence arrives. Clearly, the overall market, as represented by NYUA (the *Professional Tape Reader*'s name for its unweighted average), was much stronger than the blue-chip average. This is bullish, since it shows that the market was much better than the Dow made it look. It should be considered highly favorable whenever it occurs.

Thus, the unweighted average is a valuable tool in comparison to the Dow. Similarly, when it comes to making comparisons for other market-action indicators, we use the blue-chip average as the control. It may seem old-fashioned, but we've never accepted the argument that the DJIA is passé; it still represents the basic market structure, is closely watched, and is the root of emotional responses. The kind of signal we are constantly looking for in relation to this average is a divergence, such as the one just discussed. While our basic rule is that *any* divergence is a signal for a forthcoming reversal, divergences wherein the indicator (as in the unweighted

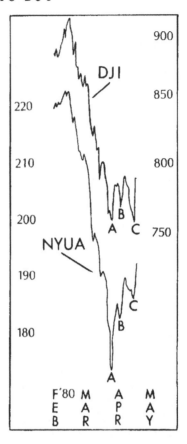

average above) is performing better than the Dow are easier to identify, and more readily acceptable.

Let's study the most basic of all market-action indicators—the Advance/Decline Line—next. This requires a simple calculation of the net difference each day between declines and advances, and then maintaining a running total. If there are more advances than declines, you will add that differential to the current total (or subtract if the day's action produced more declines than advances). For example, assume that a given day has 1,000 advances and 500 declines, for a net difference of +500. If your previous day's total was −51,000, then you have an improvement to a new total of

—50,500. We're using a negative illustration here because, for many years now, the Advance/Decline Line has been on the minus side. The minus sign has no indicator significance; it just means that you have to be careful in your calculations; a plus differential reduces the running total, or Line; a day when there are more declines than advances will mean increasing the previous total. In any event, the Advance/Decline Line you are now tracking should remain in approximate gear with the Dow Industrial Average. If the DJIA makes a new low during a decline, the A/D Line should, too. But when the Advance/Decline Line fails to confirm such a move, you've got a budding divergence. Often the A/D will catch up a day or two later, but if it refuses to, the divergence assumes significance. What usually happens is that this sort of divergence appears on the final wave down for the Dow and helps to identify the internal market bottom. Fewer stocks are now participating in the decline. That's a market success compared to the blue-chip action.

When this happens, you are being told that individual stocks have already begun resisting further decline. There have been times when this divergence continues for a more prolonged period. On the surface, this may be discouraging, for you'll spot what seems to be a bullish divergence only to find that the decline is renewed after a brief spell on the upside. But in practice—if you follow our guidelines for buying individual stocks—you'll find that you have already placed your bets on some developing winners. They'll go up on the rallies and not come back as far, even if the DJIA dips to another new low. This condition is indicative of a major bottom forming for a whole new bull market ahead, whereas a simple divergence—the Dow down to a new low while the Advance/Decline Line holds about its comparable low—is more of a key to an intermediate bottom. But this is guessing at what you don't know yet; what you do know is that you have seen a divergence, and that's a buy signal.

There are also times when the reverse might happen. That is, the Dow Industrial Average might have a successful test of a prior low while the Advance/Decline Line diverges by making a new low on its own. As odd as this may seem, it is still a bullish signal. The rule, we repeat, is that any divergence of any sort is a signal of a trend reversal. The bottom of the 1969–70 bear market, for example, saw the DJIA make its low on the climactic selling at the end of May 1970, whereas the Advance/Decline Line's low came in early July while the Dow was holding above its May low. This, too, counted emphatically as a bullish divergence.

While you have in hand the calculation of the net difference between advances and declines in order to plot the running total, you can also proceed to deal with another valuable indicator—the ten-day Advance/Decline Ratio (otherwise known as the Overbought/Oversold Oscillator). You simply keep a ten-day moving average of the same daily net differential between advances and declines. Short-term market moves rarely last longer than this ten-day time span before becoming exhausted. This oscillator can show you just how oversold—when enough is enough, so to speak —any decline has become, in mathematical terms, rather than by hunch or guesswork. Historically, a level of −4,000 is oversold territory, but there have been times, due to the abrupt and violent nature of some recent sell-offs, when this indicator has gotten down as far as −6,000 and, in October 1978, to a record oversold reading of more than −8,000. Since what we are talking about is an extreme, so we can assume that the selling has just about exhausted itself, we'd like to see a reading in the neighborhood of −6,000.

It is even more helpful to be able to anticipate when such a severe oversold reading is likely to occur. This is easy because you can observe which numbers are about to be dropped from the ten-day moving average. You can anticipate, for example, if you have a string of plus days as the market begins to fall, that not only are you dropping those pluses but you are also adding in fresh minus

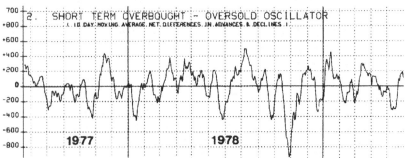

days; this can get the ratio down deep into negative territory very fast. But when you've reached the end of that string and foresee that negative numbers are about to be dropped, you can calculate that the oscillator will have reached its worst reading by then. Often, therefore, you can estimate a few days in advance just about how many more days a sell-off can last before there is at least a fluctuation back up. This observation can help keep you from joining a panicky crowd late in a decline. A truly oversold market will look its worst, but it will be too late to sell. Rather, it may be time to get ready to do some buying—if other indicators are turning favorable.

More than mere short-term buying signals, however, can be seen by observing a diminishing degree of oversold conditions on successive sell-offs. While the first may reach, for example, −5,000, a subsequent decline—while taking the averages to new lows—may not sink quite as deep, stopping perhaps at −3,500. Note the steady improvement in early 1981, after a −6,000 reading in December 1980. This is a valuable sign that downside momentum is ebbing. Just as on an individual stock chart, higher lows are worth noting.

The major companion divergence indicator is the High/Low Differential. This simple measure is a 10-day moving average of the net difference between the number of stocks making new highs and the number making new lows. Simply subtract to find the net difference between the two numbers—plus if there are more new highs, minus if there are more new lows; for example, if there are 47 new highs on a given day, and 53 new lows, your daily reading is −6. This answer is then plotted as an entry in a 10-day moving average. This gives you a rather broad figure to compare with the

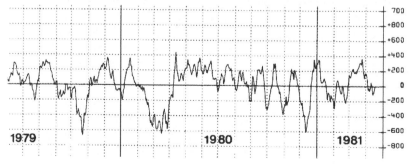

level of the Dow Industrial Average. By broad we mean it has to swing down and up noticeably and then down again, because we are looking for a divergence. When the Dow makes a new low, it should be accompanied by a new low in the High/Low Differential; if it does so, the decline has been confirmed; everything remains in gear. But eventually certain individual stocks will start holding, and even though the DJIA resumes its decline, they won't make new lows any more. Thus, on the next decline in the Dow, this differential will refuse to tumble to the same level it had achieved on the previous decline, creating a favorable divergence. As you can see, such non-confirmations don't occur within a few days but on broader market swings as a base begins to form. In late 1974, for example, the differential got no worse in September than it had been in August, despite a further DJIA fall, and was far better in December even though the Dow retreated again to a marginal new low. Divergences in the ten-day High/Low Differential which occur over such prolonged time spans identify major bottoms.

But do not ignore the raw data. Often this can be as telling an item. An abrupt one-day divergence frequently marks the exact day to start buying. If there were 270 new lows when the DJIA fell to 905, and only 195 two weeks later when the blue-chip average hit 895, this divergence would be a buy signal for an imminent rally. Indeed, even on such major bottoms as in 1974, when the differential is giving a broader signal, that one day when the Dow makes a new low but there are fewer new individual stock lows than previously, can serve as an excellent timing signal in itself. It is also possible, of course, that you can virtually guarantee such an occurrence in advance, and get your buying list ready for action; if there were 600 new lows on the first Dow low, but as the blue-chip average retreats again toward that level the daily number of new lows is around 80 or 100, or even 200, you can see that there is no way a new Dow low would be confirmed by this indicator—hence a buy signal can be accurately anticipated. Accordingly, we always keep a running record of the daily figures as well, to match against previous readings. Furthermore, we've noticed during wild swinging markets that when the DJIA has continued to decline sharply, but the number of individual new stock lows is fewer than on the previous day, simple divergence is a valid signal of an immediate short-term rally. Traders may find such fine-tuning helpful, especially if it coincides with an oversold reading in the Overbought/Oversold Oscillator.

It is also possible, if you have a minute's extra time, to add another calculation—a 30-day moving average in addition to the 10-day. The 30-day average, encompassing more time, will depict a broader market move; you'll find that the 30-day remains above the 10-day while the market is still declining, because it is dropping older numbers. Eventually, the rate of decline in the 10-day moving average will begin to temper, as individual stocks begin to resist further decline. This gradually begins to be reflected in the 30-day as well. You can see, in the accompanying chart, how the 10-day moving-average line began to move sideways first. A timing buy signal is rendered when the 10-day moving-average line breaks out across the 30-day. This chart, as of the beginning of April 1980, shows how you can begin to anticipate that just that sort of breakout is becoming possible. Two weeks later, as the DJIA was completing its successful test of the March panic low, the breakout buy signal in this indicator helped put buyers in almost exactly at the

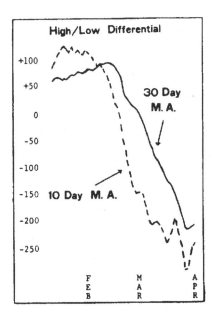

market's reversal point. By using such a signal, you will be sure to get in on meaningful moves and increase the chance of avoiding whipsaws.

Obviously, you can construct the same sort of relationship in the Advance/Decline sector, by adding a 30-day ratio to the 10-day we've already discussed. The basic guideline is the same. The 30-day moving average will be downtrending well above the 10-day for a prolonged period, and should, of course, get deeply into oversold territory itself. (For this 30-day MA, that is at least − 3,000.) The 10-day moving average will at first be even more oversold, but, being more volatile, will begin to move sideways. When the 10-day comes leaping back up across the 30-day moving-average line, a buy signal is given. This is evidence of an important buying juncture, with the signal often coming conveniently just ahead of a turn in the averages. What's more, it is infrequent enough to make it well worth heeding when it does appear. In recent years, such a signal was given only in late 1974, October 1978, October 1979, and (as the chart shows) April 1980.

Last, we need a market-action indicator that tells us about indi-

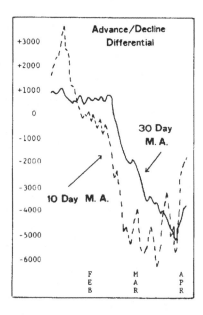

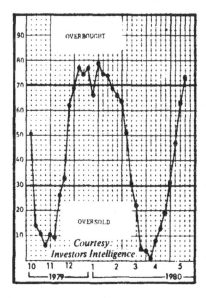

vidual stocks in greater detail. This is calculated in different ways by certain market services. For example, the Investors Intelligence service maintains an overbought-oversold indicator which measures the percentage of stocks above their 10-week moving averages. While a market decline which knocks so many stocks down below their averages that the reading is less than 30 percent can be said to be oversold, we want an extreme greater than that, and don't really care until the reading gets closer to 5 percent. This means that all the water has been wrung out of stock prices and there isn't room for anything but improvement. Similarly, the Trendline Chart Service measures the percentage of stocks above their 30-week moving averages. In the past, a drop to 30 percent has also been considered favorable, but, obviously, the more extensive the decline, the more sold-out the market, and the lower the percentage will be. The John Magee service uses a slightly different calculation, ranking all stocks strong, neutral, or weak. When their percentage of strong stocks gets down near 5 percent—meaning that just about every stock has been hurt in the decline—the market can be said to be thoroughly oversold.

While these varying statistics can be helpful indeed, if you keep your own charts, or subscribe to a charting service, you can establish your own, and perhaps even more useful, gauge. Tabulate your own lists of stocks under such categories as basing, buyable, sell, and sell short. Then you can see when the list begins to shift toward the favorable side, and begins to expand. Such a list should have important names on it, along with secondary stocks (i.e., Du Pont as well as U.S. Industries). When you begin to see—and you will —head-and-shoulders and triangle bottoms forming, and moving-average lines starting to arc sideways, you'll know what to buy as well as when.

In sum, we have—in addition to the action of individual stocks themselves—two basic sources of data to determine what the internal market action is in comparison to the action of the Dow Industrial Average. What counts, in both the Advance/Decline and High/Low indicators, is perceiving a change in the behavior of stocks that might otherwise be masked by the averages. These shifts, proven through divergences, will usually come in a climate already made more comfortable by favorable readings in the sentiment indicators. In our opinion, these indicators are sound enough, successful enough, and revealing enough to provide all the evidence you'll need to identify important market bottoms, to get you oriented to the buy side, and to convince yourself, even though everyone else is still scared, that it has become safe enough to buy. Not all indicators will signal every bottom equally well, but the majority will, and you'll be amazed at how often many of them will begin to turn favorable at about the same time.

Working with the Indicators

For those of you who want to quantify the signals even more, here's a checklist. There are seven sentiment indicators: the Call/Put Ratio, Odd-Lot Short-Selling, Member Short-Selling, the Public Short-Sales Ratio, the Specialist Short-Selling Ratio, Advisory Service Bull/Bear Ratio, and your own reading of consensus opinion in headlines and articles. Favorable readings from four or five of these should mean a positive climate for buying stocks. Similarly, there are six market-action indicators: the direction of the longer-term moving-average line, both the High/Low Differential and the

10-day/30-day crossing, both the Advance/Decline Line and the 10-day/30-day crossing, and either the oversold individual stock readings provided by an outside source or your own tabulations of basing stocks. Provided the sentiment indicators are in favorable ground, we would begin buying as soon as three or four market-action indicators have given signals. You must see the moving average begin to change direction; you must get a divergence in either (or both) the High/Low Differential or Advance/Decline Line; and you must have good stocks to buy. Thereafter, the more unanimous these indicators become, the more fully invested you should be.

You may have noticed that a number of other indicators, some well known, have been bypassed in this discussion. The Dow Theory, for instance, is basically a divergence indicator; the Short-Interest Ratio and the Mutual-Fund Cash Ratio (noted in Chapter 2 as a very reliable long-term guide) are sentiment indicators. And there are others, such as the number of secondaries, the speculation index, the London market, the most active stocks, big block trading, margin debt, insider activity, upside/downside volume, and the like. These have considerable validity, but they are, for our money, secondary or peripheral, and are better read about in other publications (*Barron's,* for example, calculates the Short-Interest Ratio every month and the *Professional Tape Reader* provides regular evaluations of many) than fussed over.

We're not being lazy. The more experience we have, the wiser it seems to concentrate on these few major indicators, and get their message straight, than to try to make a whole stew that might have several conflicting or confusing or exotic flavors tossed into the pot. It's better to use the time to keep daily charts on ten additional important stocks and truly feel the market's behavior under the tip of your pencil than to sit and calculate how many big blocks were traded on the upside that day. If the tried-and-true indicators are speaking, you'll need nothing more esoteric. The other indicators would only provide added confirmation for what is already an emphatic case. And if the big ones aren't signaling, we certainly aren't going to bet our money by relying on the others instead.

The fact is, though, you aren't going to get confused. You aren't going to get a market in which some indicators are giving bearish signals while others are determinedly bullish. Oh, you may see a period when there are no messages, or when a few indicators are beginning to turn bullish while others are still working off previously bearish readings. This can be frustrating. You may try to wrench a bearish or bullish posture from what little you have to go on, but such efforts will be ill-rewarded. Your own desire won't create a lively market. Time and time again, you'll take losses by playing the game when the climate is wishy-washy, until you learn to wait until enough evidence accumulates.

Nor will that evidence appear in the same way every time. There may be periods of favorable sentiment readings but no timing signal yet. At other times, one or two market-action indicators may begin producing divergences while the sentiment indicators haven't reached an extreme yet. *Absences* of signal-level readings are just as important, in a market that goes on and on forever, as actual signals. If something is lacking, something is wrong. If the indicators are unclear, that message may be, truthfully, that the market is unclear . . . and to stay away. Don't try to force an opinion when there is none. You not only have to learn to read the indicators; you have to learn to read between the lines.

Patience counts. You may be a short-term trader, but remember that you are going to be playing the market for many years. You may get only two or three terrific signals a year, but isn't that enough? If you learn to act on them when they come, we guarantee they'll be enough. The indicators won't all speak loudly at once, dragging you out of your chair—why should our task be easy?— but if you are truly patient you'll get sufficient evidence to be able to start buying comfortably.

We are not presenting you with a magical formula in these indicators that will time a market upturn to the precise moment. That demand is what frustrates fundamentalists, who disdain technical analysis because it doesn't work like a magic wand or a Ouija board. The profits that come from true market timing in reality come from buying individual stocks well. What our indicators do is present, in objective fashion, when the climate is ripe. These tried-and-true indicators don't fail. Or, we hasten to add, at least they haven't failed thus far. True, a closely watched indicator, one that has become fashionable because it worked so well the last time around, may become like the case of the watched pot. The same rule of the consensus being consistently wrong applies to an indicator, too. The more you read about a particular indicator, the more popular it has become, the less likely it will work as well the next time around. That's why we insist that you track several indicators and get signals from a majority of them before the case is proven. But once they speak, think of them as the cushion, the security blanket. Keep just a few, and trust the ones you keep.

In order for these indicators to work, time has to elapse. Their signals do not come on short-term moves for a few days or a couple of weeks; rather, a batch of such swings, over time, creates the climate for divergences and emotional opinions. No indicator jumps from a negative reading one week to a favorable one the next week. Once a worthwhile signal has been given, it remains in effect; you must rely on the last previous batch of indicator signals, paying particular care as to how late it might be in the rise. In a market which has as its predominant characteristic that it fluctuates, there'll be short-term corrections along the way up. You'll want to buy the first, and perhaps the second, correction when the market, or the individual stock, becomes oversold. Thereafter, you are on borrowed time.

But when the indicators have established the climate as safe, you can look for such corrections as the chance to do additional buying, or to buy stocks which are only then beginning to emerge. Following is a chart of the start of the great 1980 rise. You can see the "ideal" time (A) on the secondary test of the climactic low in April. Note that the first correction was a pullback in May (B) to the top of the base area, to, in effect, the breakout point. At this time, a lot of investors thought the rally was over; unaware of the power of the indicator signals calling for a worthwhile move, they got scared much too soon. (It often is a characteristic of the first such correction to be quick, sharp, and scary.) After the opportunity at B, the next buying juncture was on the breakout across the moving-average line, and you can see that the ensuing short-term correction (C) came back to that support and went no lower, for another

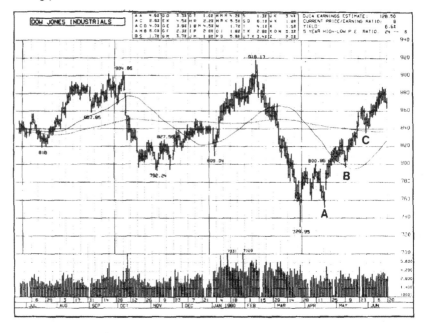

opportunity to "buy with the major trend and against the short-term trend." The market then proceeded virtually straight up another 100 points before the third correction (and many more thereafter). By that time it was already late in the uptrend and it became increasingly difficult to make money with low risk.

Such short-term swings can be bought by awareness of where you are in the uptrend. But what kind of uptrends are we talking about? Short-term moves are the true whims of the marketplace, the evidence of its fluctuating nature. Historically, the useful indicators we've described, and recommend tracking, give their signals on what is known as intermediate-term moves. These swings used to last from three to six months, but in recent years the market has been speeded up considerably and entire intermediate-term moves can now be encompassed in as little as six weeks. Their virtue is multifold.

First, they are identifiable. They encompass sufficient time and distance to be readily seen as an entity. (The longer-term moving average helps to define that passage.) Second, the swings are consistent. They contain short-term fluctuations, build bases (or tops), relate well to support and resistance areas. Third, it is on intermediate-term moves that the indicators speak. The readings we've pointed out earlier all come about after such intermediate-term declines. Thus, they are reliable as well as consistent. Fourth, every major bottom will also coincide with an intermediate-term low (although, of course, there'll be intermediate-term signals that will come at other times as well; the bottoms after each of the October debacles in 1978 and 1979 are such instances). Thus, if you buy whenever the indicators are giving their reliable intermediate-term bottom signals, you'll never miss a major bottom.

Investors, looking for long-term capital gains, frequently wait. Because they believe they are investing in the market for much longer time spans, they think they ought to wait until a major uptrend is proven. In this example, that might mean waiting as late as when the long-term moving-average line is finally and definitively crossed (C). (In practice, however, this type of investor often waits even longer—until prices have risen so high that it finally seems safe.) By then, of course, the rest of us have already had chances to buy on the climactic low, the secondary test, and the first short-term correction or pullback. It does not pay to wait for such absolute proof (and there is no need to wait, once the indicators have spoken). Our rule is that everyone—whether a long-term investor or a shorter-term trader—should buy for the trade and to hope that the stock will ultimately produce those desired long-term gains. Be a trader, and then let the profit run until there is definitive evidence of a top, rather than waiting for the definitive evidence of the uptrend and thereby buy too late. Traders can profitably become investors if they buy right; investors who buy late often become locked in involuntary investors. Another way to put this is: Buy for the foreseeable move.

Intermediate-term moves are best to swing with because they are identifiable, consistent, have indicator signals, and will coincide with major bottoms (as in December 1974, April 1978, and April 1980). But there is one last point to make about doing your buying in terms of the intermediate-term cycles. You don't have to watch the market all day every day. Leave that game to the professional traders, and to brokers who have to sit there every day anyhow.

A few hours each week to do the analytical work we are recommending will be ample to keep you in touch with the intermediate trend. So long as your long positions are carefully protected with stop orders, you won't be so caught up in the minute fluctuations that you miss the big moves.

7

A BASIC BUYING
STRATEGY (I)

If true market timing comes from buying an individual stock as close to the right time as possible, it would make sense to look at the actual moment of decision.

Each new auction market begins with the quotation: the bid and offer (or asked price). After every transaction, there is a new auction, when, if there are competing orders, the rules of precedence and priority come into play to determine which order gets executed. Often, a flip of a coin between competing brokers is the fairest way to decide, and you may someday get a report back "matched and lost," but since brokers try to cooperate with each other, these facets may never affect you. The bid and offer prices may remain the same, or they can change, depending on whether the previous transaction has cleaned up all the shares at the previous price level.

In addition to price, the quotation also includes the size: the number of shares bid for or offered. The quoted size represents one or more of three potential sources. First, there are the limited price orders left with the specialist and entered on his book, or directed to the specialist as agent via computerized order-flow systems. Second, there may be brokers standing in the crowd—that is, at the post where the stock is traded. Usually, the broker will let the specialist know what he is interested in doing at a particular price, or will directly bid or offer on behalf of the order he is representing. At times, however, a broker will stand there and not show his order or the full extent of it. His responsibility is to do the best he can for his order, in whatever way he chooses. Third, the size can also include whatever the specialist is interested in doing for his own account. If there are no orders from either of the first two sources —the book or other brokers—the specialist, in order to maintain a fair and orderly market, must bid and/or offer for his own account. Depending on the volume of trading and interest in a stock, the specialist has a consistent idea of what kind of size he wants to make and what sort of price variation between sales is reasonable, in keeping with his responsibility to keep the market fair and orderly. A typical variation will be a quarter of a point on either side of the last sale; lower-priced issues may trade at eighth variations; higher ones at half-point variations. Similarly, a relatively inactive stock might have a simple size of 100 shares bid for, 100 offered, ranging up to 1,000 and even 10,000 share markets for more active issues. If you watch any stock long enough, you'll learn what the typical quotation and size is, and this will give you a pretty good basis for presuming some of the things that might be going on in the stock at that time.

Symmetrical quotations—balanced on either side of the last sale price—and straightforward sizes, also balanced (such as 500 shares bid for and 500 shares offered), are evidence that no one is particularly interested in that stock, for the moment at least. Such quotes and sizes are often the sign of a specialist's market—that is, he is making the bid and/or offer for his own account in the absence of other orders. You may think a stock looks terrific, but the quote and size will be a clue that it isn't very exciting to anyone else. While this is useful for many stocks, it is especially true for the more active, better-known companies; you can expect to see some size in the market for an Eastman Kodak, for example, so if the reported size is 500 by 500 or even 200 by 200, you can see that interest has virtually vanished, at least for the moment.

Let's say a stock has been showing a quotation and size of 34 1/2 bid for 500 shares, 500 offered at 34 3/4. It then trades at the offered price and the new market is 34 1/2 bid, for 500 shares, and 10,000 offered at 35. You can see that it has run into a price at which there is a lot of selling waiting. Or, if the quote is a simple last-sale 35, bid 34 3/4, offered at 35 1/4, and then becomes 10,000 bid for at 34 7/8, 500 offered at 35 1/4, you can see that a more aggressive big buyer has arrived on the scene. Thus, one of the most dynamic clues to an increasingly strong stock appears when the bid, or buy side, has begun to show some intensity via a higher bid, or a larger size, or both. A stock which has begun to rise and suddenly shows not only that the previous offer has been taken but that the bid is now at the same price as that offer indicates a very eager buyer. Thus, any deviation from a symmetrical quotation, or from the customary size, is always useful information.

Price

As a trader, we prefer to wait for such clues as evidence that there is life on the floor. If you enter an order in a stock reflecting a symmetrical quotation and balanced size, you are likely to be the instigator, and can therefore expect to have your order filled in accordance with the quotation. Put in 500 shares to buy at the market when the quotation is 500 shares bid for at 34 3/4, 500 offered at 35 1/4, and you should buy those 500 shares at the offered price of 35 1/4. Put in a limited-price order to buy at the last sale price of 35 and the report should come back that it is now your bid at 35, 500 offered at 35 1/4. If the normal expectation does, indeed, occur, this also tells you something—that things on the floor are as they seem to be.

But the market is rarely so straightforward. Even in this simple example, you may now be faced with several variations. First, you might get a report back that you've bought your 500 shares, entered "at the market," at the offered price of 35 1/4, but instead of having cleaned up the previously announced size, you discover that there are still more shares offered at that price. Where did they come from? Perhaps the specialist has decided he's willing to sell more stock at that price; perhaps there's another sell order lurking. In any event, that can be discouraging, suggesting the stock lacks appeal, again, at least at that moment. Even more disheartening would be to get a report back that you bought the stock at 35 1/8 or even 35 instead. How come the stock has been buyable at a better price? A stock that is *too easy to buy is never a good sign.* This, too, may be a momentary condition; the market is constantly changing. But what you have been told is that someone else is willing to sell you the stock at an even better price than you were willing to pay. If you were testing the market with that initial order, and this is often a wise way to start buying a sizable position, you'd want to hold back and do no more buying for the time being. It's possible that a broker with a sell order is standing there, or that the specialist himself doesn't think too much of the immediate upside potential. You learn—unfortunately, only after the execution of your order—that the stock wasn't such a good purchase at that moment. Similarly, if you had entered the order at the limited price of 35 (the last sale price) and immediately got a report back that you'd bought your shares, that, too, would be a sign that the stock was too easy to buy. That's not just an idle phrase. Just as a stock that's too easy to sell tells you there's still an aggressive buying interest, a stock that is too easy to buy probably still has sellers around to impede its upside progress. What you really want, ideally, is a stock that is hard to buy, meaning that other, aggressive buyers want it, too. If you are the bidder, and no one sells to you, but the stock keeps trading higher, that's an example of a stock that's hard to buy.

Another possible variation in this moment-to-moment climate is to get a report back that you have been "stopped" at 35 1/4 on your market order to buy. This is a cousin of the more familiar "stop" order. It means the specialist is willing to guarantee you an execution at that price while trying to do better for you. He'll probably bid 35 1/8 on behalf of your order. That's nice of him, but it means that he's using your order to make a closer, more orderly market, because there's enough stock available for sale for him to be willing to fill not only your order but another. If someone else comes in to buy, that order will be executed at the offered price of 35 1/4, and automatically causes your order also to be executed at the guaranteed price of 35 1/4. If a seller comes in, you'll get the better price. Being "stopped," therefore, tells you that the specialist himself didn't think as much of the upside potential as you did. Usually he is not judging any longer-term potential but is basing his willingness to stop your order on what he deems an ample supply of available shares for sale. Of course, that supply of stock might be from his own holdings, and that tells you that perhaps you don't really want to buy that stock at that particular moment. It is sometimes worth cancelling the order immediately under such circumstances, especially if you are a trader betting on an imminent rise.

Now let's examine what might happen if you have become the bid side of the quotation with your limited-price order at 35. In the first place, it is worth pointing out that if the prior quotation and size had suggested that it was likely to be the specialist's bid (because the quotation was symmetrical and the size standard or customary), and the stock was quiescent, you might find it feasible to bid 34 3/4 rather than 35 to the same end. That is, you are bidding so as to be the next buyer if someone places an order to sell. Since it is the specialist's own bid at 34 3/4, and he is not allowed to compete with a public order, when your order comes to the floor, he'll step aside and it will become your bid at that price of 34 3/4. If a market sell order were to come to the floor next, you'd buy it at 34 3/4 as readily as if you'd bid 35. You should get —a good broker will give—a report that it is your bid at 34 3/4 or, alternatively, that there is stock bid ahead of you (in which case you can then raise your bid to obtain priority).

But if you are playing this cagey game, you must keep an eye on the quotation, because while your bid sits there, another buyer might come along and top your bid or, perhaps, take the offer at 35 1/4 and leave you far behind. The quotation might then become 35 bid, offered at 35 1/2. The specialist is maintaining the symmetrical quotation, but because another buyer has become more aggressive than you were willing to be, you have a more difficult decision to make than you did before. In its own way, the stock has become hard to buy.

Size

So far, we've been sticking to price. Now let's turn to the size aspect of the quotation. Once the size gets lopsided, it is valuable new information. If, after the stock has been bought at 35 1/4, the quote and size become 35 bid for 5,000, 500 offered at 35 1/2, you've learned not only that a more aggressive buyer arrived (to take the offered stock) but that the same party (or another) wants to buy more stock. Should that added size appear on a higher, and thus unsymmetrical, bid price—35 1/8, or even 35 1/4—the signs of an aggressive buyer are increased to almost action level. The stock wants to go up right then and there. This is especially true if such action occurs as the breakout level on the chart is approached. If a lopsided bid follows transactions at the offered price, the *very short-term* action can be said to have intensified dynamically; as a trader, we take such clues almost as we would a "hot tip." But all is not always as it seems.

Such aggressive dynamic quotes and size are exciting, but only *momentarily.* A lopsided size means something different if there is no further action, or if the stock is quiescent. Many amateur investors would think that the size of 35 bid for 5,000 shares, 500 offered at 35 1/2, is bullish. They see that there is a sizable buy order entered that both provides support on the downside—so it shouldn't go down much—and suggests that someone else thinks highly enough of the stock to be willing to buy that quantity. But, in fact, the bidder has decided that the stock is unlikely to run away from him on the upside, so he can afford to wait. The aggressive favorable aspect no longer exists. Instead, what has happened is that, while he can't buy on the offer because the size is too small, it has become easy for someone else to sell to his bid.

The rule is simple, although it isn't a guarantee. *Price tends to move in the direction of the size.* Thus, our 5,000 bid for, 500 offered, situation is said, in the terms of old-timers, to be a "down book." If it were the other way around, lopsided on the sell side, it would be an "up book." A quote of 500 bid for at 35, 5,000 offered at 35 1/2, would probably look to a potential buyer as a "no need to hurry" situation because it would seem there was plenty of stock to buy. Such a buyer tends to think that if the stock starts to trade at 35 1/2, then he'll act. But what often happens—assuming good stock selection—is that a big buyer will come along and take the entire offer. The tape will print 5,000 shares at 35 1/2 and you'll realize you've been left behind. In many cases this happens at important price levels—old resistance points, breakout prices, prior peaks—where there is a substantial amount of supply. That's one contributing factor to how and why volume increases dramatically on breakouts. There may be 30,000 shares offered and all of a sudden, while you are watching and waiting, the tape will print 20,000, another 10,000, and perhaps even more, in a string. There's got to be a lot of stock offered in order to create that kind of opportunity for a big buyer.

Just remember that a stock usually moves in the direction of the larger size. Symmetry means little, but a lopsided size is worth analyzing.

The Machines

We always like to see life in a stock we've been watching. There is, of course, the aggressive sort of life when a buyer is willing to pay up and bids just under the last sale or even at the same price as the last sale. Conversely, it is bothersome when the bid lags. Suppose we have a narrower market of 35 bid, offered at 35 1/4; the offer gets taken, but the quote remains 35 bid, offered at 35 1/2. An even more uncomfortable quote in this vein can come when a 39 5/8 bid, offered at 39 7/8, quotation is followed by a sale at 39 7/8 and the offered side becomes 40 while the bid side remains at 39 5/8. Where, we wonder, is the drive, the potential follow-through that might assault the 40 level? A bid of 39 3/4 would certainly show more interest on the floor, and if we saw a bid of 39 7/8, that might get us up out of our chair. But when the bid lags, more evidence is required before buying.

The source for all of this information is, of course, the widespread availability of desk-top interrogation machines such as Quotron, Bunker Ramo, etc. Not only are these machines invaluable when the tape is running late—as discussed already—they consistently provide us with useful current quotations and sizes, which in turn tell us what is going on down on the Exchange floor.

Let's pause here briefly to discuss these machines. In addition to the ready availability of quote and size information, those with access to the market-minder feature should consider programing specific items in addition to tracking stocks of current interest. What we have in mind (using the Quotron designations) are TICK,

TIKI, TRIN, and QCHA. You will want, we assume, handy access to the changes in the Dow Industrial Average, overall volume, and perhaps even upside and downside volume, but these other indicators provide very specific and useful details.

TICK is the net difference at any given moment between those stocks whose last transaction has been on an uptick (a price higher than the last different price) and those which have just traded on a downtick (a price lower than the last different price). For example, you might have 800 stocks having traded on upticks and 700 on downticks; the reading would be plus 100. A few minutes later, 50 stocks might bounce back from their lower price and trade on upticks, making 850 up and 650 down, for a reading of plus 200 —a sign that within that brief interval the market had improved quickly and well. Good rallies run up into the +300 to +500 range; feeble ones falter at +100 or even less. Rallies, therefore, should be measured by whether TICK readings are in gear with the extent of the rise in the averages. Sell-offs are comparable on the minus side, so that a decline in the DJIA, for example, with a modest minus reading in TICK, is a favorable sign, indicating that relatively few stocks are actually declining. There have been extremes near the 1,000 level, but more often 700 is extreme enough. Thus, you can use TICK to learn about the quality of a move, by comparing it with the action of the Dow. It is also an excellent intra-day overbought/oversold indicator. Because markets consistently fluctuate, a very high plus reading tells you it is too late to buy right then and there. The rally may look more and more exciting, but if you are coming to it late, a high plus reading suggests you'd be better off remaining calm and waiting for the inevitable, even if minor, fluctuation back down.

Similarly, a deep minus reading can alert you to an impending reversal. The most effective use of TICK, therefore, when you are interested in buying, is trying to time such a reversal. The first ingredient needed is a minus reading at a momentary extreme. Then look for improvement even if the averages are still falling. TICK, being more sensitive than the Dow, invariably starts improving early. Two changes upward can be enough to tell you the decline has been stemmed. This is especially so if there has been a prolonged—several minutes—period when TICK wavers around its extreme readings; when it then starts to improve, you can surmise that the worst of the selling is over. Even in a flat market, TICK improvement can announce that a rally is getting underway at last. Sudden improvement out of dullness, especially late in the trading day, is an excellent sign in this regard. TICK should be used as a warning, too; relatively low readings while the Dow is rising suggest that the rally is narrow and not as powerful as it might look at first glance.

TIKI is sometimes even more sensitive, but often it's too much so. This calculation is the same as TICK, but with reference to only the 30 Dow Industrial components. It swings around so wildly that it is of little use during the normal course of action. But there is some internal information contained in its readings. Minus readings while the average itself is up can tell you that the move is centered in only a few components. Swings back and forth from plus to minus after a rally can tell you that there are sellers around, and that the market isn't just shooting upward. Primarily, however, TIKI should be used for its supersensitivity. When it reaches an extreme—customarily -20—in conjunction with an extreme for TICK, it will usually start recovering even sooner than TICK. TIKI will sometimes get back up close to a zero reading or even to the plus side while TICK is just beginning to improve. Thus, it can help identify extreme lows in selling climaxes or deeply oversold conditions when you are looking to buy. Use it for sensitive, very specific timing.

TRIN (which stands for Trading Index) is a little more complex. It is the ratio of two ratios: advances over declines and upside over downside volume. Thus, if advances and declines are equal at that moment but the advancing stocks show more volume than the declining stocks do, there will be a positive TRIN reading. Equilibrium is 1.00, so when readings are below that level, you are seeing positive upside volume; above that level means a tilt toward more downside volume. Upon occasion, TRIN will lead TICK and start improving from a deeply oversold condition, thereby announcing that some volume buying is starting to come in on the floor of the Exchange. More often, TRIN should be used for judgment. Healthy rallies should show TRIN in gear with the market averages; the readings should get progressively lower. However, extremely low readings aren't as marvelous as they might seem because they represent an at least temporarily overbought situation; the potential for selling (that is, profit-taking) then exists. But TRIN readings comfortably under 1.00 confirm the substance of a rally. However, if TRIN starts fading toward 1.00 while the averages are rising, this is a sign that the rally is deteriorating under the surface. A rally in which TRIN does not improve is also suspect; if TRIN stays near 1.00 while the Dow advances, it is also worrisome. Be very careful about doing any buying under such circumstances.

While these three readings can be used to measure shifts in the moment-to-moment flow of buying and selling, QCHA (for quote change) is primarily a measure of what is happening to the market as a whole, for all stocks rather than just the thirty blue-chip stocks that make up the Dow Industrial Average. In the previous chapter we described how to construct an "average average" from QCHA's closing reading for the day as published in *Barron's*. During the day it tells at a glance what the entire market is doing as well as providing a comparison to the Dow. During the long stretches of time when the Dow was selling in the 1,000 area, such a comparison was easily calculable. Because QCHA is a percentage change of all stocks at that moment, a reading of +50, for example, means that the overall market is up one half of one percent. A comparable reading for the Dow at 1,000 at that same moment would thus be up five points. Consequently, if the Dow were up only two points, it would show that the general market—the typical stock—was then much stronger than the blue-chip average; conversely, if the Dow were up 10 or 12 points, you'd see that the general market was badly lagging the action of the blue chips. This latter experience typically occurs late in rallies and is a warning not to get too enthusiastic just because the Dow makes it look as if the market is strong. QCHA is saying that it actually isn't.

For those who have the use of such an interrogation machine, such as brokers, awareness at all times of the readings of these four aspects can keep you well informed as to what is actually going on on the floor of the Exchange. You should also use the market-minder function, if available to you, for selecting stocks to post. Here are a few suggestions based on our experience. First, it is a waste of a slot to use the market minder for something quite inactive. Better to ask the machine for that stock's readings when needed. The machine should be used for current information. It helps to post market leaders, not just IBM or General Motors, but the primary stock in a particular industry group you are interested in. If you are interested in buying paper stocks, for example, put International Paper on the market minder as well as the particular stocks you want to follow. Try to have several different groups represented so you can see, via rapidly changing prices, where the action is, or isn't. Think about what you are seeing on the machine. For example, we've gotten a very valuable feel for the market when the Dow is up quite a bit but the stocks on our market minder have shown only eighth- and quarter-point price changes. Last, if you find that you are getting bogged down, or not with it, change the stocks you are watching. It'll provide a fresh start and perspective.

Even though much of this is of use only to a broker or trader who has constant access to such a desk-top machine, everyone who speaks to his broker over the phone should know what the machine can "say." If you are in this position, it is helpful to start the conversation with questions about what TICK, TRIN, and QCHA are doing in comparison with the Dow. Then proceed to ask about individual stocks. If interested for possible action rather than mere price information, get a quotation and size, too. Then go back and see if TICK has changed. Be careful, however, not to let momentary action in the market affect your judgment. There is no reason, except sheer luck once in a lifetime, to believe that the random moment you happen to be on the phone is the ideal time to buy that particular stock. This can only happen in an intelligent manner if you are staying on the phone to try to catch climactic turning points, or a shift from a downswing to a reversal during the day. In all other instances, it is a sound business practice to take the information, hang up, and think about it.

In many ways, the usefulness of this newfangled machine has supplanted pure tape reading, or rather, it has provided a multitude of instant comparisons that make us better-informed. But old-fashioned tape readers still derive a sense of the market from the pace of the ticker tape itself. A quiet tape that begins to hum as it accelerates is a bullish sign, if prices begin to tick up ever so slightly. Similarly, overloads marked by tape deletions, announced, for example, as "Repeat Sales Omitted" and the like, should serve to curb enthusiasm. In terms of individual stocks, a strong stock is likely to be due for a pullback when it rather abruptly fades from the tape and transactions are far fewer. That can give an interested viewer a chance to buy under calmer circumstances. Similarly, if you are interested in a stock that has come under temporary selling pressure, its disappearance from the tape suggests the pressure has lifted.

The Broker

If you don't have access to a ticker tape, or to an interrogation machine, you've got to rely on your broker. It is too glib to advise you to remember that a broker is basically just a salesman, trying to get you to do business with him. A good salesman knows his product and when it is suitable for you. There are fools—we've seen them—and those who scarcely pay attention, those who seemingly watch and read but don't seem to understand, those who are so full of pressure tactics that you'll never find out what they truly know, those who simply and dutifully spout the brokerage firm's view for the day. Nor can even a good broker be expected to know everything—stocks, bonds, gold; blue-chip investments, speculative stocks, OTC technology issues; how the tape looks at that moment, and market timing, as well; indicators, charts, earnings, cash flow, etc. A truly useful broker should be good at some one aspect, present his strength, and acknowledge what he doesn't know (but he should at least know where to find it out). If he provides recommendations, they must still be verified in your own work. And if you do your own work, you won't need a full-service broker at all; in such instances, a discount broker as agent for executing orders is the way to do your business.

For our money, a broker should be no more than an agent, providing information that you want and need, and acting as a conduit for your orders. The decision is yours. In *When to Sell* we wrote of analyzing your tax return to see how and why and when you'd sold stocks, so that you could understand where your successes and mistakes originated, spotting the patterns and learning from them. On the buy side, we believe a similar analysis of your relationship with your broker will be useful. Keep a log. Set down every conversation, noting what information was given, what recommendations were made, what forecasts were offered. Note who originated the conversation, at what time of day, what the market was doing—why, indeed, the conversation was initiated to begin with. Include in this diary how you feel you were talked to, whether there was a sales pitch involved, or if it was simply reporting and keeping you informed. And make sure you describe how you yourself acted in response, because it isn't just the broker's personality that's involved here, but yours, too. And, of course, you'll want to look for the usefulness of any advice. How good was his moment-to-moment feel? Was the market already strongly up by the time he told you to buy something? Do his recommendations pan out, and if so, when (sometimes the stock can be better bought later; sometimes a "hot" broker can be good at timing), and if not, why not, and does he hide if they don't? In sum, what use has he been?

Above all, look for a pattern of behavior. You might find, for example, that you paid unnecessarily high prices, or bought a stock you didn't really want, every time you made a phone call to your broker in the middle of the day, even if, or especially if, you had just phoned out of curiosity about what was happening. You might notice that when he called you with a suggestion or opinion about the market, it frequently proved out—that is, when he thought he knew something—but when he called just to keep you informed, the conversation went on too long and led to an almost accidental, too casual, decision to do something. You might come to realize that whenever you took the time to consider a choice (that is, thought about it and called back) it helped, or that you did best by never getting emotionally involved during the trading day, that it was better to make decisions before the opening or not at all. Or you might realize you weren't in touch enough and had become too dependent, or, conversely, that he was only in touch *after* the market had already moved for a few days in a row and created some excitement. In all cases, you ought to analyze just what information you want, need, and have access to. And always remember that it is not just the broker who is being analyzed; your own behavior is equally a part of this process.

The purpose of all this is to establish a comfortable arena for you to play the game in, one that fits your style. The market universe is vast, complex, and tricky. Hacks-of-all-trades are masters of none. When you find out what you do best and how to do it best, you will have increased the odds for your success.

8

A BASIC BUYING
STRATEGY (II)

Sometimes the decision as to how to buy a stock can be more difficult than what to buy, at least at the moment when you are confronted with which type of order to use. Although there are several more esoteric order formats available, the two basic choices are "at the market"—which is, in effect, an order to just buy the stock at the best price available—or at a limited price, risking that if you don't get your price you may not buy the stock at all.

Buying "at the Market"

Most often, you are best off buying at the market. In that way, you are sure of an execution. Too much pussyfooting, or fine tuning, never helped produce a string of winners. And, the argument goes, an eighth or quarter of a point, or even half a point, isn't going to make the difference between a profitable purchase and a loser; that is the job of sound stock selection. In terms of the kind of stock selection we are going to describe in the next chapter, the technical action has already done sufficient fine tuning; when a stock looks like a buy, it isn't even a question of simplicity and a guaranteed execution but, in fact, of sound tactics just to go ahead and buy "at the market."

One such time to enter market orders, of course, is during the previously described selling climax/late-tape situation. The market is on the verge of turning and you want to get on board. In such climates, the timing as to the market bottom has already been honed to the moment; you can't afford to compound the difficulty by also limiting your bid, or you'll probably miss a fast-moving market. Even at other times, the basic guideline is that if you want to buy, just buy.

The only caveats we would offer are that you've got to be careful not to get caught up in the emotional game by sending down to the Exchange floor a buy order in an already rapidly advancing stock, and you don't want to buy at all, despite the excitement, when news is going to lead to a market opening so full of sharply higher prices that you know, upon a moment's reflection, that the specialist is going to have to be a seller. Yes, there are times when even a sharply higher opening in a particular stock turns out to be the low price for the day, but let someone else have the thrill of guessing such a low; if the stock is worth buying, it will fluctuate back down and give you a quieter, safer time to buy. It is better to stick to the rule of never reacting to an emotional climate. Remember, good news is always deceptive.

As we wrote in *When to Sell,* the simple question to ask when the market looks as if it is going to open higher is: What is the specialist going to have to do? Remember, it is his responsibility to take the place of absent orders in order to keep the market fair and orderly; public orders heavily weighted on one side of the market will compel the specialist to be on the other side. Thus, when it comes to selling, such openings, replete with overeager buyers, are an excellent chance to be on the same side as the specialist and to get a sharply higher price for your shares. If you are thinking of buying, if the specialist is going to be on the sell side, why do you want to argue with him?

At the opening, the specialist who handles that particular stock matches all the orders that are left with him by various brokers. If a stock has 500 shares to buy and 500 to sell, it would open unchanged. The opening price should, in all instances, reflect the balance of orders. If there are more buyers than sellers, the stock should open higher—that is, at a level where the specialist either has limited-price sell orders on his book and/or is willing to deal for his own account. Therefore, if you enter an order to buy 500 shares at the market in this example, you have altered the supply/demand equation. If you are planning to buy in size, you have to give some consideration to the effect you might have on the opening price. In a stock that doesn't trade in much volume, a large order can have a disproportionate effect (that's why it is a good idea to know what a typical size is in the stock you're interested in). At the same time, however, because the opening represents an accumulation of orders, it is possible to trade in greater size than at any other time. If your buy order is going to tip the scale to an imbalance of buyers, that's not serious; it lets the specialist match all the orders in hand and decide on a fair opening price. But it is only to this modest extent that it is okay to buy at a higher price on the opening. Otherwise, we vote no.

Consider that in a market obviously about to open higher there are buy orders all over the floor. It may simply be that the previous day's action was so strong, or there was bullish monetary news, or the government has announced this or that. What does the specialist do when confronted with a batch of buy orders that far outweigh what he has in hand to sell? He not only opens the stock higher, he opens the stock high enough; by high enough we mean that price at which he reasonably thinks he can make a profit, however small, from his forced selling from his own account. He may be wrong; the buy orders may keep flooding in. More often, of course, he is at least temporarily right. If he is going to establish an opening price high enough to suit his own selling, that certainly would be auspicious for any holder who wants to join him, but it should be a warning to any potential buyer.

Obviously, therefore, while buying a higher opening is dangerous, it is a sound tactic to enter a buy order "at the market" when a lower opening is expected. Here, too, the specialist is establishing a price that not only matches all orders, and is fair in relation to those orders, but will also, he believes, enable him to make a profit during the ensuing trading. That is, he's being forced to buy, when the buy orders in hand don't match the sell orders, and experience tells him that the stock is likely to rebound after the opening, so that he will be able to sell at a profit what he's just bought. Now, we don't want you to buy just because the stock is going to open down. But if the stock meets all our other criteria, a lower opening is an excellent entry point. Indeed, it is also valid to buy on the opening at the market simply because the technical action says the stock is safe to buy and ready to move; if it has had a decline on the previous day, a continuation of that short-term trend (remember, you are trying to buy *with* the major trend and *against* the short-term trend) can lead to a lower opening or, at most, a flat opening. In such cases, rather than try to guess at a potential limited-price level at which to enter your order, we'd rather let the flow of orders, and the specialist's judgment, determine the price.

Consider that the stock opens at 34 1/2, off half a point from the previous day's closing price. If you entered a limited-price order at 34 3/4, you'd get 34 1/2 along with everyone else. If you entered a limited-price order at 34 1/2, you might or might not get an execution. The rule is that market orders have precedence, so if all market orders can be matched up with sell orders, you might be left as the bid without getting an execution, watching as the stock rebounded and not realizing until you got a report back of "nothing done" that you'd missed your chance. Similarly, if the stock opened at 34 7/8 or unchanged at 35, you'd also have missed the opening, one which showed that the stock wasn't as weak as you expected. Now you are left with a difficult decision. It is to avoid such quandaries that it is better to buy at the market on the opening.

Suppose you wait to see what the opening transaction is. Now, after opening at 34 1/2, it is quoted 34 1/4 bid, offered at 34 3/4. What do you do with what you thought was the virtue of waiting? If you bid the opening price of 34 1/2, then you might just as well have bought on the opening. Try to do better by bidding 34 3/8 to see if another seller comes in, or 34 1/4, trying to fine-tune it even more. Here, too, you might get left behind on any immediate rebound, and see the stock back up to 35, unchanged, before you blink. (Remember that the specialist, in all likelihood, has bought for his own account on the opening at 34 1/2 and expects to make a trading profit.) And if you take the offering price, you've paid a quarter of a point more than you would have on the opening. Why get embroiled in any of those alternatives?

In *When to Sell* we argued that the best time to sell was on the opening. Added experience in trading stocks every day has convinced us of the rightness of that stance. We prefer the psychological advantage of making an objective decision that the time has come to act and then let the specialist determine the fair opening price. If the opening is higher, the seller gets that benefit; if it is lower, it confirms that the stock is weak, and the seller is already out without having to make an extremely difficult decision under pressure while the tape is running. There is the frequent price advantage of getting the opening price rather than later having to sell to the bid, which is invariably a down price from the previous different transaction price.

The advantage of acting on the opening isn't quite as far-reaching for buying as it is for selling. The difference is twofold. First, we don't want you to buy on openings that are going to be sharply higher, but second, and even more important, there isn't quite the urgency on the buy side. You don't *have* to buy. Indeed, there are times, such as on a breakout, when price specificity is the key. The opening is not pertinent to such purchases. (There is a single exception to this. Stocks which open on a gap—a price higher than the previous day's highest price—across the breakout point are signaling an extremely convincing breakout. This is an instance of having to buy even if you pay up; an alert trader should be able to foresee such a possibility and buy in anticipation late the previous day; otherwise, one has to be alert to buy on a quick minor pullback.)

The advantages of buying on the opening are that it gets the job done without unnecessary and potentially mistaken fine tuning. As we've said, it works well when you are trying to buy into a short-term decline, whether in the general market or for a particular stock. Once the decision is made to buy, entering the order before the opening "at the market" avoids the added pressures of trying to make a decision while the tape is running. Here's another hypothetical example. Suppose the stock opens at 35, unchanged from the previous day's closing price. It sells down an eighth and you think, "Ahha, I was right not to buy on the opening." Now the stock is quoted 34 3/4 bid, offered at 35. Because it has dipped, you decide to wait to see if it will dip even more. If it sells again at 35, that seems okay, because it looks as if it still isn't going anywhere.

Note that even if you decide to buy now, you've got to pay the same price (35) as you would have on the opening. But if it suddenly trades at 35 and then 35 1/8, you are in a quandary, to say nothing of perhaps being so angry that you could have/should have bought on the opening that you sit there paralyzed as the stock goes up even further.

If the overall market has become oversold, there is no point in trying to guess if it can become even more oversold. In such instances, the market will open lower the next trading day, or at best flat, before resuming the rally. Thus, the opening is your best chance for lower prices. Here's another example. The stock has been very strong, shooting up from 33 to 38, and you want to buy it back on a pullback. It has drifted down three days in a row to under 36 and late in the day has ticked up to 36 1/4. It is clear that the stock has come back down far enough and you decide to buy. Your first instinct is to enter a limited-price order near the previous day's low. After all, it sold as low as 35 5/8 before recovering, so why not enter an order to buy at 35 3/4 or 7/8 or even 36? But now you are trying to outguess the market. If the stock is going to open slightly lower, fine, you'll get the benefit anyhow. If it doesn't, you may never get that dip and chance to buy. Better, we believe, to just go ahead and buy on the next day's opening without worrying about that fraction of a point, thus avoiding an additional emotional hassle. You might, as we'll discuss later, want to limit the order on the upside, but not on the downside. That's when you want to buy at the market. (A limited order, at 36 1/4, for example, will also get you in on any flat or lower opening.) This is, of course, especially useful for anyone who has his own business to tend to and isn't going to be, or doesn't want to be, available to an equally anxious broker on the phone.

As for buying during the trading day, we have to presume that your decision to buy at any particular moment is reasonable and not random. That is, you have given some thought, if not to the possibility that the stock is due to move higher imminently (or that the general market is about to rally), at least to the notion that the stock is holding well and is unlikely to decline in the near future. You've decided that you want to own the stock and that there is no virtue in waiting. If so, we believe that as long as you are buying no more than the current size offered, you should use a market order to buy rather than a limited order just to try and save, if possible, a minuscule fraction of a point. There are exceptions to this, however; it is not as simple a guideline as always buying a lower opening at the market. Naturally, if the stock has already become active (this is something you have to rely on your broker to tell you—or you have to learn to ask—so that you don't get hurt, as did our boardroom-sitter friend Harry, by trying to buy a stock that has already moved excitingly), a limited-price order can protect you from paying too much. If the stock has been quiet, then you can take the offered size with a market order. But suppose you'd like to buy 1,000 shares and there are only 500 shares offered. If you hesitate, someone may take those 500 shares ahead of you, lifting the quotation to 34 1/2 bid, offered at 34 7/8. Then, just as you are ready to act, it sells at 7/8 and becomes 34 3/4 bid, offered at 35. Caught up in the budding excitement, you rush down your market buy order and then watch the tape as the stock prints 3,000, 8,000, and 10,000 at 35 ahead of you. It doesn't take more than half a minute for your order to get to the floor and out to the trading post, but because of those few seconds you wind up paying 35 1/4 and 35 3/8, and the stock, after that burst, settles back to trade at 35 again. In such volatile situations, a limited order would be the better course of action. More money is lost over the long run in such emotional situations than profits are missed, since it's a rare stock that will zoom ahead right from that moment on.

Buying at a Limited Price

Let's go back to the problem of a small size compared to the amount of shares you'd like to buy: 34 1/2 bid, 500 offered at 35. You don't want to enter a market order for 1,000 shares to buy because you might run an otherwise quiescent stock up only temporarily, and disproportionately. A limited-price order for 1,000 shares at the offered price of 35 can occasionally entice the specialist to sell an additional 500 shares. By using, under such circumstances, an "immediate or cancel" order, the immediacy, and even the sense of urgency, of the order sometimes can gain the additional shares. Such an order is a variation on the limited-price order, wherein the floor broker will buy whatever stock is available for sale at the limited price, while the balance of the order is canceled. At worst, you'll buy the 500 shares offered. In any case, your order has now been canceled, and this has a very important virtue. An ordinary limited-price order would leave you as the bid; if the stock were then to advance for a while, and then retreat, your bid would be touched off on the way down—that is, when the stock is falling and not doing what you wanted it to do, which was to advance. Hence, if you are a trader bidding at a limited price, and the stock gets away from you, you should cancel your buy order rather than leave the bid sitting there. The stock has advanced; if it comes back down, whether to buy it or not becomes a fresh decision, not a leftover one.

The virtue of an "immediate or cancel" order is that this cancellation is done automatically. Thus, it can be used as a short-term aggressive tactic. We want to add, though, that on both the Amex and the NYSE floors we have rarely seen an instance when an "immediate or cancel" order made the user look like a genius. It is a convenience at best. (However, a cousin, the "all or none" order, is a foolish device. It can deprive the user of getting even a portion of the desired shares, and has no standing in the marketplace.)

Limited-price orders limited to the offer side are useful, therefore, primarily to help you avoid paying too high a price for a stock in a fast-moving situation, or to deal with a limited size without running the price up too much oneself. A more frequent, and more desirable, use of a limited-price order is on the downside, to get a better price by waiting out a market that is generally, or in a particular stock, coming down. There are times when even the trader who spends all day in front of the ticker tape can miss such a dip in an individual stock by being distracted by another stock, or out in the men's room, or at lunch. Thus, a limited-price bid can be a useful tool for the investor who is tending to his own business while the market is open.

As noted earlier, such a bid can be placed to try to catch the pullback from an upside breakout. It can be extremely useful during short-term corrections, gauging where support is and placing the bid slightly above that level. (In such circumstances, you may want to use a "good till canceled" order, so as to retain priority on the specialist's book.) Entering such a limited-price order takes the pressure off having to make an extra decision during the trading day. Without such an order, even after the stock has come down to your selected price, you may think that it will keep on falling, so you procrastinate, watch the stock dip another quarter of a point (which makes you feel you were right to wait), and then see it coming bouncing back vigorously without you. Remember: you aren't trying to catch the bottom eighth. If you've made an objective decision in advance as to approximately where the stock should hold, enter the order rather than play with the idea in your head.

This applies specifically to buying on a minor dip. The more typical application of a limited-price order, in trying to become the bid as of any particular moment, is less useful. As noted already, in a market quoted 34 3/4 bid, offered at 35 1/4, last sale 35, there isn't much sense in bidding 35. Yes, you might then be able to buy the stock, but why? Is the quarter of a point worth the risk of missing the purchase? Or, to put it another way, if you don't think the stock is ripe to rise, why are you buying it at all at that moment? There is, of course, the recognition that it is the specialist's bid at 34 3/4 and that, therefore, your bid could supplant his. In that case, if you bid 34 3/4 instead of 35—a more sensible choice—it might be worth the mental haggling. And, we suppose, there are quiet times during the trading day when you do expect the stock to move, but for a brief time span you think you can do better as the bid. In general, though, a limited-price order has its best application when you are trying to buy during a short-term dip—that is, with the major trend and against the minor trend.

But what if you want to buy in larger quantity than is offered? In this case, you wouldn't want just to take the offer and run the price up before you've bought all you had in mind. And you might think the market too lively to chance being a big bid under the market. The answer to this, and any other question related to size, is to take advantage of the floor broker. The appropriate means to do so is the "not-held" order.

The Professional's Order

As you may know, an "at the market" order means that the floor broker is required to go to the post where the stock is traded and get the best execution he can immediately. The broker, in being ordered to buy at the best price available in the market at that time, is *held* to the transactions as they occur (and must make financial amends if he misses the market; the prints on the tape are the measure). A "not-held" order removes that requirement. Instead of striding over to the post and having to act virtually automatically on behalf of a market order, he can decide to wait, to bid, to buy a little or all, if he thinks the situation warrants. In certain instances, the floor broker may find out that he can fill the entire order at the offered price (despite the smaller size on the interrogation machine) and would do so. Or he may use his rapport with the specialist to ascertain if he can do better by waiting, or becoming the bid. He may be able to find out just how much more you might have to pay to complete your order, and report back such information to you. He might learn that there are other buyers around and that he'd better be aggressive on your behalf. Alternatively, he might be told that there's a big seller around and that discretion is more advisable. In sum, a "not-held" order is an excellent tool for developing a link with the Exchange floor. Professionals use it all the time so they can get the advantage of having the broker on the floor work with them.

Naturally, to use a "not-held" order, it is important for the floor broker to grasp your intentions, by means of the same sort of code bridge players apply in their bidding. A simple order to buy 2,000 shares "not held" tells him to use his own judgment. If you add a limited price, say, to buy 2,000 shares at 35 1/4 "not held," that tells him that you don't want to run the price up but you are willing to pay the offered price if you can fill your order; you've given him some leeway to make a decision or two on your behalf, with the implicit instruction to try to do better for you if he can. Indeed, an order to buy at the market rather than at a limited price usually will have the same effect. A good floor broker isn't going to plunge ahead wildly the way he might have to were he to be held, but if he needed to—because other buyers are competing; because it's a strong market—he would have the leeway to proceed according to his best judgment at the moment. Often, if the situation warrants, he'll check back with you before he acts, especially if there are any problems. Thus, you might add to the initial order, or reply, "Take your time," or "Want to buy before the close" or whatever can tersely express your desire. A "not-held" order isn't surefire, but at least it presents a chance to use the mechanisms of the Exchange to your advantage. There are two things to remember. A "not-held" order is to be used only in terms of size. And if the broker does a good job, be sure to compliment him, as you would the chef, but if you are disappointed, accept your execution quietly. It may make no difference, but then again it just might, and it costs you nothing extra for the potential help.

Stop Orders

Other types of orders, such as "at the close," or those involved with time or contingencies, are mere gimmicks that will work against you more than they can be useful. Stick to the basics, with one additional exception: the buy-stop order.

This is the opposite of the sell-stop order, used to protect an already held long position from any further decline. A buy-stop order is most often used to cover short positions if they go against the bear—that is, to protect against further losses—but it can also be effectively used to buy on upside breakouts. A buy-stop order is entered at a specific price *above* the current price and becomes a market order to buy as soon as a transaction takes place at that specified price. (On the American Stock Exchange, buy-stop orders must be entered with a limit beyond which you will not pay.) The appropriate time to use a buy-stop order is when you are unable to pay close attention (or can't count on your broker to do so), but you have spotted an exciting breakout price. You want the stock to trade there, to prove it can do so instead of dying just before that level, and you believe that if the stock can cross that price it will be starting an important move. By entering the buy-stop order, you guarantee that you'll be a buyer as soon as that price is reached. You can't do so as well if you enter the order in size, because the weight of your order might produce a transaction much higher than the breakout price (especially if the stock is thinly traded). But it can work for a few hundred shares or so, and has the advantage of instantaneous purchase at the moment of breakout. It is a tactic primarily useful for aggressive traders.

Lastly, a reminder about using sell-stop orders. This is covered in detail in *When to Sell,* but it is imperative that you keep such protection in mind when buying. Briefly, a sell-stop order is used to limit your loss (or to lock in a profit). There are some mechanistic approaches to placing such orders, such as trying to limit your loss to 10 percent, but we advocate a more market-oriented formula. A stop-loss order should be placed just *below* the last previous correction low, because if the stock were then to go still lower, it would have established a sequence of lower lows and that, simplistically put, is a sign of a stock in a downtrend. No one is perfect, especially in the stock market, so the use of stop-loss orders prevents you from finding it emotionally difficult to sell because of the loss involved, precisely when you should be selling to protect your capital. They can also be useful buying tools. Locate the price level where a proper stop-loss order would be placed as protection. If the price of the stock is then more than 10 percent or so above that level, the odds are great that the stock is too high to buy at that moment and that it is likely to have a dip soon, instead, affording you a safer entry point.

What Day of the Week to Buy

Having discussed what type of order is best to use when, let's take up next the question of when to buy in terms of the general market and certain repetitious patterns of behavior.

Monday is the most difficult day of the week. This is especially true of Monday mornings. Yes, there have been days when the market has gone straight up from the opening bell on Mondays, but we don't remember them. Almost always, a Monday gain has been due to a weekend news event that produced only a temporary lift. Much more often, the market will trade higher for perhaps half an hour on an accumulation of orders and then drift; at best, it will stay up most of the day before dying, or, alternatively, stagger around from the start. Usually Monday is a carry-over down day in a troubled market or, in a strong market, a difficult day for any further advance. Every once in a while, the market will hit bottom late Monday afternoon, start holding, and become buyable in anticipation of a rebound. As a general rule—and that is all this can be —Monday-morning openings can be an excellent time to sell, but we never like to buy then. The day is best used for watching and planning, as if the market is—as many people are when the work week resumes—just regenerating for the action during the rest of the week.

But Tuesday can be a fun day. Far more often than not, a correction will end on a Tuesday morning, be it a selling climax, as in May 1962, or following a short-term dip. If Monday has been a down day, and the market has become oversold, look for a turnaround on Tuesday morning. This happens often enough for Tuesday morning to be considered a good time to buy, and it is also true that in such cases the opening prices are likely to be, for many stocks, the lows of the day. Conversely, if you are looking for a correction and Monday has wobbled about without prices giving way, the decline is apt to begin on Tuesday. The key point to remember about Tuesday mornings is that a trend is most apt to end then, and reverse, so it can be an excellent time to buy after a decline.

Wednesdays are typically trend-following days. Good markets will carry through; weak ones will continue to falter.

The next useful time to watch out for is Thursday afternoon. Early-week declines that are in the nature of profit-taking dips rather than more serious corrections—that is, within a true bull trend—often rebound in the last hour of trading on Thursdays. It's not a consistent enough pattern to anticipate, but rallies that start at this time are almost always good ones. If you are itchy to buy, for sound reasons, be alert to taking action on Thursday afternoons.

Fridays, too, tend to be trend-following days. The era when traders kicked out all their positions so as to go home without anything at risk over the weekend seems to have passed. Selling is done only when the market itself seems vulnerable. A strong close on Fridays, therefore, is a sign of underlying health, even though there may be little short-term follow-through on Monday. But because there is typically so much of a struggle on Mondays, Friday afternoons are not a time when it is imperative to buy.

By the time you get to Friday afternoon, you have probably become overloaded with moment-to-moment action that seems more significant than it really is. It is usually better to wait for the weekend for a chance to do some quiet, more objective thinking once again. Just remember, if you get bullish about the market or a stock because of your analytical work, Monday morning is still going to be as difficult a time as ever.

If you keep track of the indicators we've suggested, you'll be amazed at how often signals coincide with these market patterns. This is particularly true for turnarounds on Tuesday mornings and Thursday afternoons when the market has become oversold. Indeed, you'll often get divergences on a Monday's action that tell you to start buying Tuesday morning. That was the case, for example, in April 1980, when Tuesday morning's opening launched the start of the major rise after Monday's decline proved that the test of the low was successful.

What Time of Day to Buy

While these day-by-day patterns are generally useful, the market has its own intra-day cycle that it adheres to with even more consistency. The opening phase lasts from thirty to forty-five minutes. An extremely late tape may make it look as if this opening phase is lasting longer, but the initial half hour or so will contain almost all the price changes. Following the rush of early activity comes a customary reversal. That is, if the market has opened lower, once the selling is out of the way, prices will try to rebound. If it is a true low, it'll be the beginning of a good rally; in a bear trend, this sort of temporary attempt to hold and recover will be just that—temporary. If the market has opened higher, there'll be a spate of profit-taking and a downside dip. In-and-out traders often use such a turn to take profits in a market that has been strong; as soon as TICK begins to falter, they sell. Similarly, if they want to buy, they wait, before stepping in, until an upturn in TICK shows that the selling has run its course. Because latecomers who want to buy into strength see this little dip as their chance, an up market often develops in two stages. The initial retracement is mild —more of a leveling-off rather than a pronounced dip—and the market then comes on again in the same direction as in the first half hour. This second wave can last until nearly noon and usually will involve fewer stocks or just one conspicuous group, while other stocks are milling around.

Mid-day is always a difficult time. Often, there is a lunchtime return to the direction of the short-term trend, particularly on the upside. But we do not trust mid-day rallies; they are isolated, often deceptive, and frequently fizzle thereafter. A close onlooker, such as a broker, can get caught up in such action, but it rarely has any staying power. Similarly, don't trust rallies that start too soon in the afternoon. They usually peter out. As a general rule, it pays not to enter any orders whatsoever in the middle of the day; the chances of being deceived by moment-to-moment trivial ticks on the tape are too great. Because this is the longest stretch of the trading day, it will be the time when many people receive phone calls from their brokers. Do not be affected by the random time you happen to be phoned.

What we watch for, thereafter, is the action during what we've dubbed the "magic twenty minutes." This phenomenon was pointed out to us by an excellent member trader and it calls attention to the market action between 2:20 p.m. and 2:40 p.m. NYSE time. It was noted that the market often stages a minor reversal during that time span. If prices have been rallying beforehand, and then ease back during that twenty-minute period, the likelihood is then great that the last hour of trading will be strong, so it is a good time to buy. Similarly, if prices have been fading, a little rally during those "magic twenty minutes" is a warning—and perhaps a chance to sell—since the market will then customarily slide again with greater vigor toward the close of trading.

Don't hold us to that precise time on the clock. Sometimes the shift in tenor takes place a little earlier, but it tends to encompass that time span and to last just about twenty minutes. All other things considered, this is often a good time to buy stocks. It works particularly well in relationship to a potential last-hour Thursday-afternoon rally, but it can also help give you a better entry point for any individual stock whenever you are looking to buy before the day's end of trading. It is far better, if mid-day action is tempting, to be patient and wait for such a timing message during this "magic" time span. It will help confirm morning action, and dispel uncertainties created by mid-day fluctuations. Thus, even if you do nothing, the market's behavior at this time can give you some idea of health or trouble. And, last, this pattern is consistent enough to have a consistent exception. If such a minor trend reversal does not take place, the odds are very great that any trend in motion that began too soon—that is, before 2 p.m.—will die well before the close.

That brings us to the question of buying near the close. Never buy weakness near the close, because the odds are that you can do at least as well on the next day's opening. However, when the market is just starting a new move, it pays to buy strength near the close, even if prices are already up a point or more on the day. This is particularly true when the Dow Industrial Average is clearly going to close above a key breakout point, or an individual stock you've been tracking is close to its breakout level. What you are doing is anticipating a gap opening up the next day. But you are generally better off to do any such buying as the magic twenty minutes nears an end. You ought to know by then what you want to do. If you don't, you may be setting yourself up for an emotional rather than an objective purchase. If, however, you have decided to buy but have held back because the rally seems modest, only to see it increasingly gather power, it will pay to buy into the strength late in the day.

In all instances, therefore, the rule is: Never buy just for the sake of buying. Don't be an impulse buyer; have your shopping list prepared in advance. If you are pressured into looking frantically for something to buy, you are apt to get overemotional and make a mistake. And if there is nothing that seems sensible to buy, take that as a warning to skip the action. It is too tempting in such moments to leap for a laggard just because it hasn't moved yet. Better to buy more shares of something you already own that has started up strongly.

In fact, regardless of days of the week or times of day, it is always better to buy proven strength. Many years ago, it was possible to buy laggards in an industry group because speculators played the game that way, starting with the leaders, switching into the secondary stocks, and then finally picking up the stocks that hadn't moved yet. (When you finally saw a stock like Hupp Corporation on the tape, you knew the rally was over, because every other stock had already been given its fling.) But it doesn't happen that way any more, largely because institutions now dominate trading and such big money won't play the tertiary stocks. This makes buying strength even more important nowadays. It is a Darwinian world, where the strong get stronger.

A case can be made that one should sell a bit early in order to get out safely and surely, but one can buy a bit late. That is, it makes sense to pay up for strength because the market action is proving what you want to know: which stock is most likely to be a winner. In the next chapter we'll show you how to act on such proof without buying *too* late. But once proven, don't delay. Buy on the basis of the current available information—that is, the price action—rather than bidding underneath the market and hoping for another decline first. A good stock doesn't give you a second chance to buy at a bargain price. There is always an offer in this continuous auction market, so the rule is: Take it.

9

WHAT TO BUY:
INDIVIDUAL STOCKS

We've discussed when to buy, and how to buy. But the most important aspect of all is what to buy. A litany on this subject has already been running through this book: buy strength; don't guess at bottoms; if there isn't much to buy, don't buy; wait for the stock to prove itself; etc. Overall market action tells us when to buy, but the individual stock can also signal the proper timing. Since we are always looking for a betting edge, we want the stock itself, as compared to all other stocks, to tell us that now is the time to buy it.

The first point to make, therefore, is that it is during major market bottoms—the selling climax, the test of the low—that we will find the most buyable stocks. They'll be basing, after a fall, just as the market averages are. But while the average functions like a single stock in that it goes up, down, breaks out, pulls back at one specific time, individual stocks do not all coordinate with the averages. To a great extent, they tend to fall together, but when it comes to bullish action, each stock proceeds at its own pace. Often, industry groups will have some unison—enough to rely on—but beyond that, each individual issue must be viewed in its own time frame. There might even be a good-looking stock or two emerging at a time when the indicators are negative; but while a stock may look buyable on its own, there's no sense in buying when the market climate is not right. There is always the choice not to buy, remember. In general, the emergence of a number of favorable stock patterns is one of the best, if not the best, indicator of a market bottom. The more you see, the more you can start buying with confidence.

Buy a Stock Whose Trend Line Signals Success

What are we looking for in a stock? That's easy to answer, even if there are infinite variations. We are looking for success in holding, to begin with. A stock that has just made a new low is clearly not successful. A stock that manages to hold above its prior low on the next sell-off has accomplished something positive. Similarly, a stock that manages to rise above its previous rally peak has also achieved a success. A stock that has higher lows and higher peaks clearly is trending upward. Simply stated, that is the art of charting.

Now let's put that a bit more visually. A stock that has held above its previous low makes it possible for a trend line to be drawn connecting those two points—the initial low and the low of the next dip—and this line points upward. If there is a third wave of selling that holds above these prior two lows and at or close to that line, we have confirmation of the validity of that line. Similarly, as part of the market's flow of fluctuations, we have rallies that fail. A trend line can also be drawn across those rally peaks which are thus far containing the upside progress. This trend line can be essentially horizontal, connecting two or more rally peaks; at other times it can be downsloping, as the second rally fails to get as high as the first.

Thus far, we have lines coming up from the bottom and lines above the recent action. In one way or another, the basic chart patterns conform to these trend lines, so that, in actuality, all we are going to describe is a play on trend lines, despite the seemingly esoteric names. You don't need to know anything more than that trend lines measure successes (or failures). Occasionally, there are more extended trend lines that define the major direction. After a stock has made a top and starts to decline, there will be intervening rallies from time to time; a line can be drawn connecting the peaks of such rallies; two peaks make a line, while a third peak serves to validate the line. Call this the longer-term downtrend line; when it is broken—finally crossed by a rally— it is a definitive signal that the back of the downtrend has been broken. However, such action typically occurs early in a base formation; even though breaking across the line is trumpeting a change in trend, it is not a major buy signal in itself. For such signals we must return to the shorter-term trend lines that develop as the base forms.

First, a word about what a base actually is. Like motherhood, it has its mythic meaning, as a marvelous though never really scrutinized ideal. But, like motherhood, a stock-market base has concrete qualities. First, it must come after a serious decline. You can't have a base perched up on top of a rally. (That kind of formation is called a consolidation, but might turn into a top instead.) What a base is, then, is that point after a decline when buyers begin to step forward with enough money to stem the decline. We have to assume, somewhat simplistically, that such buyers, having money after the decline, are shrewd enough to have done some selling near the top—hence their buying power—or are big enough to have plenty of money to back up their judgment that a particular stock is now worth accumulating. On the other side are people not in such a healthy position; they've missed selling on the way down. In addition, the decline has scared them. Unlike the buyers, who believe the fall has created a lower-risk situation, they are fearful of a still further decline. Any little rally seems to them the chance to get out at last. So they sell into rallies, stemming them, while the buyers bid near the lows, holding the stock up. This is sometimes described as shares going from weak (scared, anxious, pessimistic) holders into the hands of strong (confident, cash-rich) buyers. Thus, a base is really that point where ownership of the shares is changing from the weak to the strong hands.

If that is the nature of a base, we should now look at what a base signifies. First, the bigger the base, the more shares have gone into strong hands (which aren't going to take a three-point profit and run), and this accumulation gives the stock greater upside potential. Second, the livelier the swings between the basing lows and the lid put on them by anxious sellers, the more dynamic the base, and therefore the more dynamic the upside potential. This is especially true when the base is formed after a substantial decline, meaning the stock is really sold out, and also when the base forms at a prior support area, meaning the decision to buy makes sense on a technical basis even for those who are buying for fundamental reasons. That is, the fundamentals are confirmed by the technicals. Last, what a base does is to point to which stocks—among the hundreds we could choose from—are the best buying candidates. It provides protection in the refusal to go down further, and upside potential in the way shares are being accumulated.

Buy a Stock That Forms a Head-and-Shoulders Bottom

When it comes to spotting bases, you may hear all sorts of fancy names: flying saucers, double dips, and the like. And, we suppose, the head-and-shoulders bottom is, to the novice, another such oddity. To us, it is the best bottom of all. It is easy to spot, contains within its formation a triangle (which is another important bottom formation), and can in its dynamics help reveal the degree of upside potential. Head-and-shoulders bottom formations are, of course, upside down from the human appearance of a head and shoulders (right-side up would be a top formation); the components are a left shoulder (representing at that time a new low in the decline), a first rally followed by another decline to an even lower low (the head), a second rally which halts somewhere in the vicinity of the first rally's peak, and a third decline which refuses to make a new low (forming the right shoulder). The rally peaks are connected by a trend line, which in this formation is called, for obvious reasons, the neckline. Volume often, but not always, will show the most selling on the left shoulder, diminish for the head, and dry up as the right shoulder is being formed, indicating that selling pressure has become exhausted. As a final component, there is customarily a pullback to the neckline area *after* the stock has broken out on the upside.

We could sketch an ideal head-and-shoulders bottom pattern but they vary in one way or another in almost every stock. Sometimes the volume will not match; often there will be extra shoulders tucked into the pattern, or a double head. But the accompanying chart of Eastman Kodak can serve as an example of a near-perfect pattern to learn from.

This daily bar chart shows a decline in progress from the 60 level, but in fact EK had been declining for years from the 150 level, and more recently from a 1978–79 top at 66. In January 1980, this blue-chip stock actually broke down yet again to 44 (LS), before staging a quick rebound back up over 51 as the Dow Industrial Average itself managed to bounce to its rally high at 918 in early February. By then, however, EK was already heading back down and made a new low at the beginning of March (H). At this point, if you cover over the subsequent action, you'll see that all we have is a stock still deep in its downtrend. There is no sign whatsoever that the stock is buyable yet, with the single exception of the fact that (as you'll see on the next, longer-term weekly chart) this was precisely the price level at which the 1978 decline had halted—that

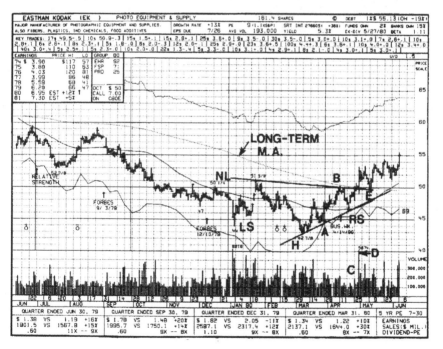

is, it was important support (wise buyers had come out in size). Volume was a little less than it had been on the prior low, but not enough to build a case on yet.

One odd little clue appeared at point A when, despite the selling-climax plunge in the market during the so-called silver crisis, EK held above its prior low. The market was rebounding and EK's move faded just over 50 on this trip up, when, as you can see (B), it ran into its longer-term moving-average line (this is a Daily Graphs chart, using an unweighted 200-day calculation), which by then was starting to lose downside momentum. The market's test of its prior low got underway, during which Kodak dipped to 46 1/2 (RS) and no further.

Having alerted us by refusing to make a new low even though the DJIA did, at this time the chart becomes exciting. Note that volume (C) has dried up considerably, signifying a lack of selling pressure; just about anyone who'd wanted to sell had done so. The latest decline established a right shoulder roughly matching the left. Including the dip at point A, the chart also shows that a rising trend line had been established. A neckline (NL) could be drawn in connecting the two rally peaks, crossing the chart at approximately the same point as the long-term moving-average line. A breakout across the neckline would also be a breakout across the moving-average line—a twin victory. An interested buyer couldn't have asked for anything more encouraging. The stock could have been, indeed should have been, bought around 50 on the breakout. Note (D) the huge increase in volume on the day the stock actually did break out. But that's not all. You can also see that two weeks later EK pulled back to the neckline support level (E), where the stock could just as easily have been bought around 50 by anyone who'd discerned this huge head-and-shoulders bottom and had the patience to wait for such a pullback. This kind of purchase is readily made by entering a limited-price order and is the best use of such an order.

It is also worth noting that within this head-and-shoulders formation exists a triangle formation as well, as you can see from the two trend lines drawn in. But before we proceed to discuss such triangles in greater detail, let's see how the longer-term (weekly) chart of Eastman Kodak looked at the same time.

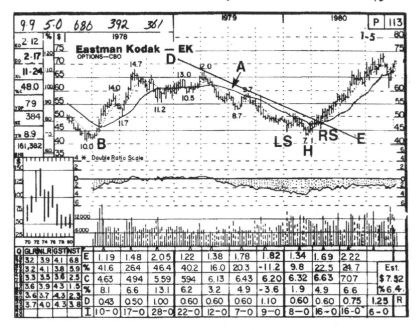

There are two things that stand out at first glance. Notice how the longer-term moving-average line (the heavy line A) rolled over and headed downward, containing all rally attempts on the way. This is a weighted 30-week line, as provided by Mansfield, and hence "leads" the 200-day unweighted line seen on the daily chart. As discussed in a previous chapter, this provides earlier clues, while the "late" daily chart's moving-average line often marks the actual breakout point, as in this instance. Also, note that the decline's 1980 low (H) matched the bottom reached in 1978 (B) before a good rally set in. Seeing where previous important support appeared is not a buy signal for the likes of us—although a big institution, wanting to buy 100,000 shares for whatever reason, might consider such a support level as a reasonable place to start accumulating shares. (And, naturally, if they did so, it would start to show, in such base building, as they bought.) The support level does alert us to a possible bottom that might form in the same area.

Next, we've picked up our handy ruler and drawn in a major-downtrend line connecting the top, the first rally peaks in the upper

50s, and the third rally peak just over 50 (D–E). This line, as well as the moving-average line, needs to be crossed on the upside in order to signal a break in the downtrend thus far in motion. Always respect the trend already in motion until it is reversed.

Last, you can see the same head-and-shoulders bottom that we saw on the daily chart. This is important. The fact that the formation was extensive enough to show up on the weekly chart is evidence of its size and potential power. You'll see many smaller bottom formations that are clear on the daily chart but which are masked or buried on the weekly. Don't ignore them, for many a worthwhile move has sprouted from just such acorns, but given a choice, always opt for the bigger base, one big enough to be seen on the weekly chart.

Buy a Stock Whose Chart Has Formed a Triangle

The other important chart formation is the triangle. While head-and-shoulder bottoms are of major significance—that is, they form at the end of declines and rarely at any other time—triangles not only appear at such bottoms but also can form as consolidation patterns along the way up. As shown, there was a triangle within the head-and-shoulders bottom formation for Kodak. This forms almost automatically, since we have a neckline above and a rising trend line connecting the head and right shoulder. A triangle, therefore, differs from a head-and-shoulders formation primarily in that it lacks the left shoulder. The initial plunge to the low and subsequent successful tests of that low set up its potential. Thus, in a market situation where so many stocks made extreme lows during the silver panic, we'll see plenty of triangle formations as bases; at other bear-market ends, such as in 1970, the market action makes for more head-and-shoulder patterns.

No matter. A base has as its ultimate key the success of rising lows. The specific type of triangle, harking back to math-class days, is determined by the overhead line. If it is essentially flat, connecting rally peaks, the pattern is known as an ascending triangle. If the second peak is lower than the first, it will look much more symmetrical. It doesn't matter. For our purposes, we need two ingredients: the success proven by the ability of the stock to hold above its previous low, and the establishment of an upside breakout point, the crossing of which will signal a new uptrend.

Here's an example of an ascending triangle formed in late March–early April 1980, beginning with the silver-panic low. All that needs to be done with that handy ruler is to draw in the lines connecting the two lows (A and B) and the rally peaks (C and D). A week later, as you can see, the stock sagged but did not even come back as far as the rising trend line (E), an encouraging clue that the stock would break out on the upside of the triangle (rather than break down). Merrill was even more tempting, because, on this little dip, volume (F) dried up considerably. But there was no reason not to wait for the breakout for confirmation, since it wasn't very far away. And, finally, note that there was even a subsequent pullback (G) to provide yet another safe buying opportunity. The stock then proceeded up to 40.

It is worth interjecting a comment here about measuring these triangle formations. As a rough guide for traders, the breadth of

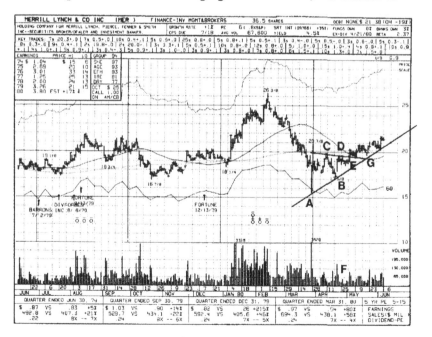

the formation can be calculated to determine how far up the stock should go on its *initial* drive. If you turn back to EK, you'll note that the distance from the peak of the first rally to the low of the head amounts to 8 points; add this to the breakout price of 50 and you get a target of 58—interestingly, almost exactly where resistance first appears. The stock hesitated there for a few weeks before resuming the advance. Similarly, for Merrill Lynch we can count about 4 points from A to C, added to the breakout point at just under 20 for a target near 24. The chart shows resistance in the 23–24 area and MER ran up to 24 rapidly before consolidating for about two weeks. Use this kind of measure as an approximation, but if it is confirmed by the presence of resistance overhead, you may consider it as a practical short-term target, never forgetting that the stock might have much further to go on a longer-term basis.

We'll discuss more bottom triangles of various sorts in the next chapter, but one more example here can be useful. This weekly chart of Atlantic Richfield shows a stock already in an uptrend, but

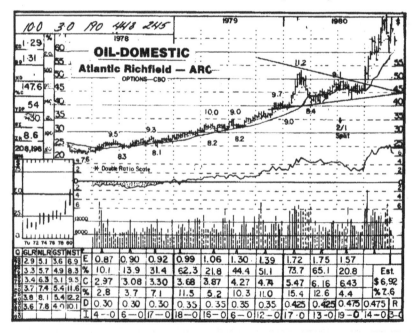

it peaked along with the market in February 1980 and got battered during the steep decline of the next two months. If you cover up the subsequent breakout on the upside, you can see that there was a distinct possibility that the stock might break down instead. We've drawn in the triangle and want to emphasize that until the breakout actually takes place you can never guess its direction. (Holders, of course, would have placed a protective stop-loss order just under the lower line of the triangle.) Since this is a substantial triangle, measuring almost 14 points, any move would have been worth following, so it was important to focus in on this particular stock. Was there any way to gain a betting edge?

That way is the use of the daily chart. The weekly chart provides much needed perspective; the daily is best used for timing purposes. Note that on this chart the overall triangle seen on the weekly chart is not in evidence; the chart doesn't go back far enough. (Only if you kept your own daily chart, and spliced back charts together, could you lick this problem.) Even more important for our purposes, though, is the fact that this daily chart shows its

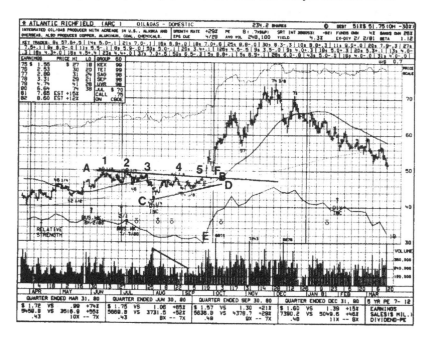

own smaller triangle. The upper line A–B is marked by five rally-resistance attempts, giving it considerable validity. The lower line C–D similarly has been validated as it held each succeeding dip successfully. Here, too, there is still an uncomfortable feeling that the stock might break down instead (and if it did so, it would break the long-term moving-average line as well). Volume within this triangle was diminishing favorably. But even so, we'd have been hesitant to anticipate an upside breakout.

But it didn't matter, except minimally. The fraction of a point anticipation would have gained wasn't really worth the risk in comparison with the ultimate profit. The breakout came on a gap above the triangle's upper line, and the combination of crossing a line that had resisted previous rallies so often plus the gap breakout made this a winning bet. For our money, the stock could have been bought as soon as the gap was created, crossing the prior high (at point 1) of 49 1/2, jumping in at the round number of 50 as volume expanded (E), or even on the subsequent pullback (F) a few days later. You can see what a good trade it would have been, even though you waited for definitive proof, and also that the measured target of about 64 was not far off the first leg up.

We've gone into this detail to show that you don't need an entire arsenal of chart-reading terms or techniques. Just as with the indicators (if the major ones aren't saying anything, it doesn't pay to heed the minor ones), it pays to wait for and to buy these few specific chart patterns. Both head-and-shoulders and triangle formations are basically trend-line structures, with proof of budding strength found in higher lows (or, in other terms, successful tests of the low) and an identifiable upside breakout point to mark the level where strength finally wins. The formations alert you as to what to buy; the breakout point helps time your purchase.

Buying a Stock with a More Complex Pattern

But not all charts are so straightforward. Often, one interesting facet will serve to alert the technician, and all else will follow. Boise Cascade has no discernable pattern on its daily chart; all there is is that powerful downtrend line, representing successively lower tops. It was clear that a breakout across that line would represent,

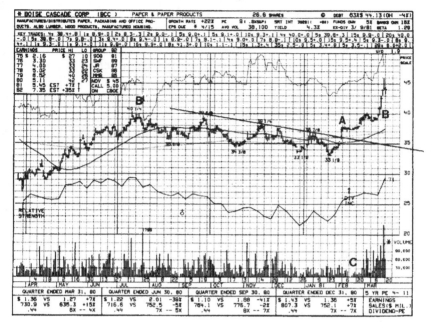

at the least, a good trading opportunity—signifying that selling pressure was stemmed—especially because, at that time, other forest-products stocks also were increasingly favorable. When the breakout came, on a gap across 36, that was a buy signal of sorts. But BCC was disappointing at first; the stock hung around the 37–38 level (A) on very low volume before it shot up again. The breaking of a major downtrend line usually requires more work thereafter, but is a good first signal. This kind of action is what makes the market so fascinating in its diversity. We wish there were a rule to cover it all, but there is none; indeed, here our pet provision of rising bottoms doesn't yet appear. The definitive move, on rising volume, actually began crossing the 40 1/4 prior high (B–B¹). Often, even though other pieces are not yet in place, the first clue is worth heeding, especially when the market climate is already replete with favorable indicators (as it was in February 1981). After the downtrend line was crossed on the upside, the daily chart began to show the desired series of rising bottoms (A and B), which in turn called the stock still buyable on a fresh breakout across the old high at 40 1/4. If you had needed another clue it could be found in the extremely low volume (C), indicating the lack of selling pressure.

But now we want to call your attention to something else. Look what the long-term chart shows—the downtrend line actually extends even further back in time and was touched so many times that it was truly confirmed as valid. What's more, albeit in a misshapen rather than symmetrical way, there is a big head-and-shoulders bottom in evidence on the weekly chart, with that trend line also serving as the pattern's neckline. It isn't exactly a bottom, because the stock is not down, being at the upper end of its trading range for the past decade. Rather, it is a consolidation—a broad sideways action lasting over a year. The upside breakout really signals a renewal of the overall uptrend. (Note, too, that the head-and-shoulders measures—from the 42 high to the 28 low—14 points, for a target, counting from the first breakout near 36, of 50; the rally high ultimately was 48 1/4.) This is confirmed on the Mansfield weekly chart via that service's highly useful relative-

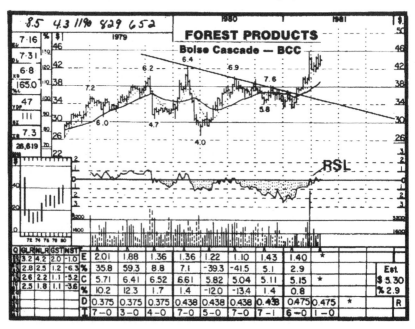

strength line (RSL), which measures the degree the stock is over- or underperforming the overall market. As the stock broke out, it crossed from negative territory (the shaded area) to positive. In our experience, after a stock has been under the "zero" line by Mansfield's reckoning, a move across that line into positive territory is often an indication that even though the stock may be already up, there is still a whole bull move ahead.

Boise Cascade is an example of the market's atypical ways. The textbook type of pattern such as we saw on the Eastman Kodak chart is actually rarer than the oddities, which, nevertheless, contain ingredients that make for a buy candidate. As a general rule, the more straightforward head-and-shoulders and triangle-type bottoms tend to appear at the overall market's bottom—in this instance, the spring of 1980—whereas more complex patterns appear later in the uptrend; Boise Cascade, indeed, missed the entire 250 point 1980 Dow rise, so you can see how late it was. Individual stocks proceed at their own pace, rather than moving as a pack. So long as market conditions are favorable—as in February 1981, when the sentiment indicators said the climate was safe—such emerging buy candidates are the ones to play.

Another example of how seemingly minor clues can be sufficient is found in the daily chart of LTV Corp. Here we see only one rally attempt (A) which failed, halting at the moving-average line, rather than the two peaks that would provide a useful trend line. But note that, in conjunction, every little dip kept holding at a higher and higher level, while there was extremely low volume (B) throughout the latter part of 1979. And when the breakout came—across the moving-average line and above the previous little peak (C)—volume increased tremendously, as if the entire Exchange floor was shouting: "Something's up." The stock was up; a purchase on the breakout produced a better than 50 percent gain in two months.

But LTV got caught in the steep market correction that culminated in the silver-crisis low at the end of March 1980. No top had formed, however (if you want to see what a top would look like, turn the chart upside down in front of a mirror), so it could be deemed just a correction, one which came all the way back, on that panic day, to support at the 8 level. What a great buy into that panic! How would you have known to single LTV out? The huge

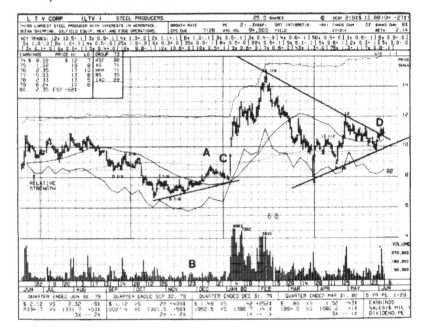

volume on the prior run-up suggested that LTV was worth a play.
All that stock wasn't bought for nothing, especially since, without
a top, it hadn't been distributed. In due time a rather oddly shaped
but nevertheless valid triangle formation appeared, again with a
sequence of rising bottoms. The breakout across the downtrend
line of the triangle (D) was eventually followed by a major rise to
25—a better than 100 percent gain on this trip. Even if you had
waited to buy until the previous peak at 12 was crossed, you'd have
doubled your money.

What we are trying to illustrate is not a lot of different esoteric
chart formations but a simple method for defining strength. Not for
us the game of guessing the possible bottom in a weak stock. We
want to know that a stock *can* go up (as it develops a perceivable
pattern) and then that it actually has the strength to start up
strongly (the breakout). *The key to picking winners is locating the
point at which such strength will be proven.* You'll miss some stocks
that never develop such a clear point, but that won't matter, because every stock you do pick will start you off on the upside with
proven strength. What's more, you'll have stocks unfolding as buys

along the way (EK at the market low; LTV and ARC a couple of months later; BCC as the market was at a correction low; and so on). By concentrating your buying on such breakouts, you will also be well on your way toward avoiding those late-in-the-uptrend seemingly alluring buys of stocks that have already had big moves and are just on their last gasp.

Remember that you always have a choice, and if something makes you uncomfortable, you don't have to buy. You can just watch and shake your head regretfully at what might have been. It's no big deal, for in a bull climate there are always plenty of stocks to buy. Patience is the key, so you can insist on an upside breakout point and proven success in holding better and better on every downside test. That ought to give you a good bet every time, particularly when that sort of downside action—successively *higher* lows—occurs against a backdrop of lower lows in the Dow Industrial Average. Divergences work for stocks as well as for indicators.

Buy a Stock That Has Support

Now let's take a moment to discuss the oft-misunderstood chart features of support and resistance. There's altogether too much confusion surrounding these terms. They represent both price areas and actions. That is, in order for a price level to function as support or resistance, buyers or sellers have to react to it as such. Are buyers willing to step in and bid for stock? That's support. And if so, are they rich enough and persistent enough to absorb any and all selling? That's good support.

In the abstract, we don't know exactly where such buyers might be willing to appear, at what price they might start buying, or how strong a stand they might be willing to take there. But in actuality we do have something to go on—not the current action, but past price history. That is, where the stock was able to find good buying during previous declines. Unless you have a head for stock prices (some Stock Exchange specialists seem to be able to remember virtually every trade in their stocks), you need to rely on the chart picture to identify where those past buying (support) or selling (resistance) areas appeared.

Support, therefore, is actually several aspects. First, it is that price area where, following a previous serious decline, buyers have appeared and the stock has held. Second, it is that price level where the stock has broken out on the upside. When we write approvingly of stocks that begin to show a pattern of higher lows, of successful tests, all we are saying is that willing buyers have raised their bids to get the stock; support is rising to a higher level. The trend line that we've drawn in on the charts represents the slope at which this occurs and becomes, in itself, the measure of where support is. That's why we don't like to see such an up-trend line broken; it suggests a problem with support, with, in effect, the willingness of buyers that we are counting on to make our bet a winning one.

When the stock breaks out on the upside, the buyers have won. The base represents a struggle between buyers and sellers who have gotten, for a time, into relative equilibrium. The buyers are willing to buy on dips, the sellers want to get out on any little rally. Thus, the upside breakout means that the buyers have finally overpowered the sellers. If they are truly right, then they ought to be able to hold that turf on any subsequent counterassault by fresh sellers. That's why the breakout level becomes the next meaningful support level; the upper-trend line (the neckline or top line of a triangle) measures that support.

If the stock then does what we expect, rising robustly, support becomes increasingly more fragile. Buyers are using up their money, and we don't know how much willingness to keep buying is left. The normal fluctuations of the market bring out a correction —a retracement of the advance. The price at which that correction holds usually is at an established support level. This could be the top of the previous trading range, the rising trend line, or the rising moving-average line. If the stock holds at or above these levels, then, obviously, fresh support has come in willingly—a favorable sign. Wherever this reaction low occurs then becomes another support level. We don't want to see any subsequent dip drop below that level, because then the chart would show successively lower lows, a clear sign of weakness, when what we need to see is strength.

If a stock holds at or above support, it can start rising again quickly. However, if it fails, and dips lower, that sign of trouble requires more effort. It may, given the market's complexities, violate one form of support—let's say, the upside breakout point—but still manage to hold subsequently just above the longer-term moving-average line. But some damage has been done. In this situation, the stock cannot immediately launch a new rally. It must do, as we say, some "work" in that area; it needs to consolidate, to make sure all this freshly revealed selling pressure has been absorbed. If successful, the new consolidation area will become a higher level of support.

An illustration should make this clear in visual terms. Here's a daily chart of Comsat, starting just after its selling-climax low in March 1980. You can see a small basing area—indeed, a small head-and-shoulders—at the outset (A), which was followed by an upside breakout. Note, incidentally, that although the breakout, in our terms, came crossing 35 when the neckline was penetrated (NL), there was a typical hesitation just under the prior rally high, followed by a second breakout across the long-term moving-average line. Support, at this point, would be considered 36 (at the top of that hesitation) to 36 3/4 (which was the moving-average line

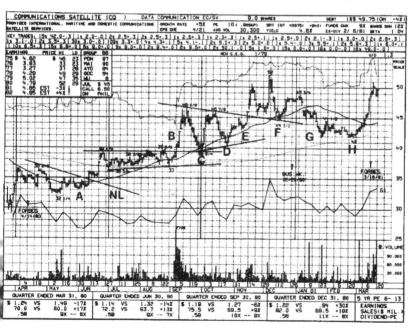

as it began to arc underneath). For the next several weeks, that support held every little dip, while every rally was contained under 40. This formation can be contained by two virtually parallel trend lines—that is, a rectangle, which is, after all, similar to a triangle. The stock was set up for another upside breakout, which came this time on a huge increase in volume, marking it as real, across the 40 level (B).

This rectangular formation then became the important support level. Others would cite support as 37–40, since that encompasses the entire prior trading range. To us, however, the meaningful support is 39 1/2–40. *For support to be proven favorable, the top of the support area must hold.* Otherwise, our rule of "going too far" comes into effect. If the stock is truly bullish for a longer-term move, it must succeed during all tests. A correction is such a test. Accordingly, either it holds the top of the support area—because it is a good stock—or it dives down "too far" into support, telling us that the selling pressure was too strong or the buying too weak, telling us, in any event, that the stock isn't as rosy as it had previously seemed. A stock that goes too far into its support zone is providing its first warning sign of potential trouble.

In this instance, CQ held perfectly, right at the top of support (C), just as it had held perfectly during the rectangular formation above its longer-term moving-average line. Indeed, on the next wave of selling, it also held perfectly (D), reaching a low that was slightly better than the previous low at C. The slightly higher lows and slightly lower highs during this period of wild swings created another triangle formation. The mild dip on extremely low volume at E provided a tip-off that the breakout from the triangle would be up, as indeed it was, for another rally. (This action at E is a good example of why and when a trader can risk anticipating an upside breakout.)

Now note that the dive down (F) after the high was made exceeded the two previous low points. Yes, the stock did hold at support—the breakout point—but the lower low was certainly a warning. That warning of potential trouble became actuality when the stock failed on the next rally. An important technical point can be made here, not just about Comsat in this particular instance, but about stocks and the market in general. When a decline carries "too far"—that is, when it breaks support, and a series of lower lows is set up—too much damage has been done for an immediate return to the upside. At points C and D, this did not occur; rather, the dips held successfully, and traders could have bought. But the decline starting with point F, the subsequent failing rally, and the action around point G are negative instead. Thus, the rallies from points C and D could go straight back up, but the relative weakness at point G required that work needed to be done to mend the damage before any rally could develop. The basic guideline in such instances is that, when damage has been done to the bullish structure, the first rally off the low will *not* be a good one.

Don't rush back into such situations, even if you think the stock looks "cheap" because it has come down so far from the peak. Time is needed to restore some equilibrium first, and then to prove that the stock not only can hold there but can advance again. Comsat trended sideways for four weeks before some renewed bullish proof came back into the picture: first, it managed to hold just above the initial reaction low, and second, it held above the support level of the longer-term moving-average line (H). Often, a stock will extend sideways in this manner until the moving average catches up, is tested, and holds. The selling pressure that has caused this sort of dip is exhausted, and the stock is ready to rally again.

Support, then, can be identified as the band of sideways action where the stock has traded for a period of time, but always consider the true support level as the top of that range, rather than, as amateur wisdom has it, the bottom price. The stock may look cheaper—a so-called better buy—if it has come down that far, but view it as a warning instead. Consider all trend lines and moving-average lines as support, too, especially if such a line has been touched and held more than twice. The third touching can be considered a validation of the line; the more such touchings, the more you must respect the line if and when it is broken.

There is, however, one time when the extreme low price is the support. This develops on major declines and relates to historic support levels. Monthly, or long-term, chart books will show many instances where a stock returned to the low level of a prior bear market, and might even do so again and again over the decades (an argument against buying a stock and locking it up). Of course, it isn't sure that the stock will hold there once again, but stocks, despite all their fluctuations, tend to repeat history.

While such repetitions can occur many years apart, this chart of General Motors illustrates what we mean within a shorter time frame. The low reached in April 1980 (A) was almost precisely matched in December (B), despite what started off as a scary renewed downside move. Clearly, this kind of support—the extremity—held successfully, and was followed by a strong recovery. Although the stock, we suppose, could have been bought on that action, it isn't a buy yet in our terms. The rally stopped at 48, where resistance came not only from the moving-average line (C) but also from the congestion area (C¹) that had formed on the way down. What happens is, those who bought wrongly during that brief sideways trading action at C¹—thinking the stock would hold, but missing the danger signal that it was a lower low—now have a chance to get out even on the rally, and do so, providing ample supply to stem the rise. The subsequent decline, in turn, held at the

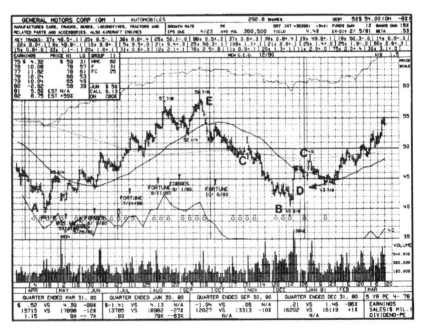

support (D) that marks the similar congestion area just before that final wave of selling. It is worth noting, too, that the stock subsequently made a similar, almost matching, "double top" like the double bottom, when it ended this particular rally in April 1981 at approximately the same 58 peak (E) that had ended the prior move. Indeed, reference to a longer-term chart shows heavy resistance areas formed in 1979 in the 58–60 area for GM. After a stock rallies extensively, it becomes too tired to have the strength to break through such resistance areas. There is persistent method in the market's madness.

If you study the General Motors chart during the 1980 rise, you'll see a series of steps upward and orderly corrections, each of which held approximately at the top of the prior rally. Extremities of price as support apply only to the bottoms of major moves. Thereafter, only amateurs call support the low of the correction; it is the top of the area that counts. By point E there was no such support, and that told us not to buy so late in the move.

Let the Charts Tell You What to Buy

We've used two different types of charts in these illustrations, the daily and the weekly. Both are bar charts—that is, each entry represents the high, low, close, and volume for either the daily or the weekly action. Our examples come from published chart services, but keeping a few charts of one's own, as we've said, is instructive and helps give you experience in "reading" the published charts and a much needed feel for what is going on. Details emerge that are often glossed over in a glance. The daily-chart paper published by John Magee, Inc., is semi-logarithmically plotted, so that the scale reveals percentage moves rather than mere point changes. It is often helpful, then, to look at the published chart for a different perspective. The more you see, the more you know.

As for the published services, Mansfield is very useful. You don't need to look at it every week, because each week only adds another line, one which you can easiy pencil in for any stock you want to be current with. Its virtues are multiple: every listed stock is published (there is a rather less adequate OTC service available); the stocks are arranged by industry groups, so the investor can perceive which groups are the ones to focus on (group confirmation is a valuable tool); the broad picture is extremely helpful, since the charts provide about three years of action; the relative strength measurement is simple to see and often effective to use; and the moving-average line, being weighted, gives advance clues even though it sometimes gets blurred in the middle of the action.

In comparison, our illustrations of daily chart action come from the Daily Graphs service. This, too, contains every listed stock. Its charts are comparable to those printed by Trendline, the chief distinction being that the longer-term moving-average line is calculated differently. Those who are only interested in the most active, most important stocks might prefer Trendline. That service provides several highly useful indicators in addition to the individual stock charts, such as the percentage of stocks over or under their moving-average lines, mentioned in Chapter 6. The indicators provided in Daily Graphs we find far less useful.

A few words on how to read these differing charts might be helpful to those readers who do their analytical work via these

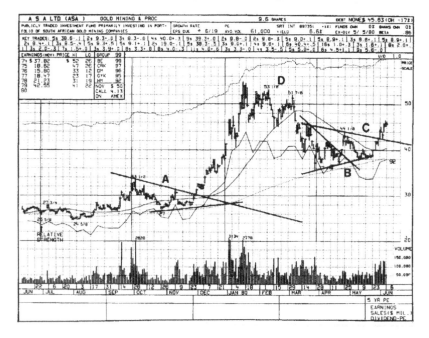

published-chart services. Let's compare two more charts to see how best to use them.

Above is a Daily Graphs chart of ASA. We've drawn in two triangle formations: the October–November period of 1979 and the March–April period of 1980. Note, to begin with, the sequences of rising lows in each instance. The first triangle (A) launched a major rise; the second (B) staged a fast breakout but then faltered, so that another triangle (C) formed, aided by those rising lows. The chief virtue of using daily charts is clear: you can identify the potential breakout point specifically, *timing price as well as day.* The chief danger, in turn, is that you can place too much emphasis on short-term moves.

You can also see that the longer-term (dotted) moving-average line served as support under the triangles, and that stop-loss orders placed just under that line, and under the lower trend line of the triangles, would have been sound protection if wrong—at 26 7/8, had you bought at triangle A; at 34 7/8 (B) raised to 36 3/8 as C formed.

Now look at the vastly different perspective of the longer-term

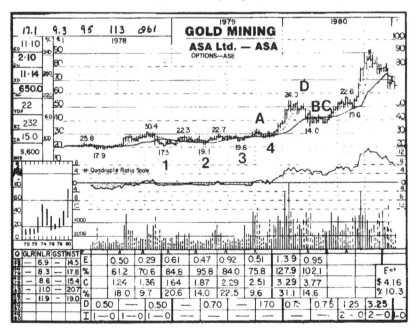

chart. The triangle at A and the two formed at B and C are hard to discern in comparison to the daily chart. That's why timing a move is much better handled from the daily. But the added perspective of the longer-term chart is also important. Note that all the action from the start of the chart through A looks like a remarkable base formation. It doesn't look as big in its fluctuations as some of the previous charts we've shown, but that's because of the chart's scale. This is a lesson everyone who looks at published charts must learn: the scale of the chart—which may be arbitrary on the part of the publisher—can have a serious effect on the way the chart looks (and this is why there is an advantage to logarithmic-type chart paper). Actually, the base encompasses a wide trading range of from 20 to 30. The four successively higher lows are thus much more impressive than they at first appear, and so, too, is the poking up above that base as triangle A begins to form. This huge base makes ASA look, at that juncture, like a terrific long-term buy. By referring to the daily chart, you could then establish the precise time and price to get in exactly when the stock began its major move.

Second, the top that formed at D can be seen in better perspective. On the daily, it looks serious—three successively lower rally highs leading to a downside break. Had you sold, thinking to buy back, you wouldn't have gained much except some sleep for a while. The longer-term chart shows that it was just a correction within a major uptrend. When the move resumed, ASA took off to its real top, where, at the end of the chart, the longer-term moving average not only was broken decisively but also finally turned downward.

The ideal, therefore, is to analyze stocks via a combination of both daily and weekly charts. This is not nearly as significant on the sell side of the market, where weekly charts can provide the perspective needed to know when it is finally time to get out. Daily charts can often look as if substantial tops have formed when, in reality, the top is far less significant to the major trend. But, on the buy side, we are trying to time a betting choice. The long-term chart provides the perspective of the size of a base and the upside potential, while the daily shows when and where to actually buy.

A word may be useful here about trying to coordinate charts

with fundamental information and especially with "hot tips." A wise old trader once told us: "If God himself told me to buy a stock, I wouldn't do it until I saw it on the tape." The chart, of course, is just a graphic representation of the tape. When someone —be he broker or neighbor—wants you to buy a particular stock, don't do it until you refer to the chart, regardless of how exciting the reason for the recommendation may seem.

Far more often than not, a look at the chart will show you that others already know about the stock—that is, the stock will have advanced considerably before your attention is called to it, leaving it vulnerable to at least a short-term correction. There's no better way to buy into an instant loss than plunging without checking. Even when the weekly chart shows that the stock is still buyable —early in a move—the daily may reveal that it has run up rapidly over the past few days and that a fluctuation back down is worth waiting for. You must always assume that, rather than being among the first to hear the story, you are among the last, that other people have already acted. The chart can warn of the risk.

The trick is to try to look at the chart as if you don't know what stock it is. Ask yourself, if you can: "If this were a chart of Hemline Fabrics, what would I think?" Try to see it in a purely technical sense. Otherwise, the story will subtly (or not so subtly) affect your bias. We recommended Data General to a group of institutional money managers one day and from the back came a voice: "I wouldn't buy that stock; everyone's looking for $10 a share, but I happen to know earnings are going to be down instead." The stock proceeded to advance 5, 10, 20 points, but every time we looked at the chart, we'd hear that voice and worry that it was going to start down the next day. Any such input will affect your judgment; what you want to believe, you are more apt to believe; be aware of this tendency and try to put it aside. Let the stock's own action speak.

You might look at the chart and say: "That's a bad picture: I wouldn't buy that stock." Don't try to rationalize any further. If the chart doesn't look good—shows lower lows, for example—ask yourself: If the story is so good, where are the buyers? Or you might see a pretty decent chart picture, but one with considerable resistance overhead—that is, the stock has little room to move. The tendency is to dismiss this resistance, especially if the story is of a potential takeover, but it never pays to ignore the chart's reality. Here heavy volume may help, but that's something you'd want to see first. Substantial increases in trading activity can provide the best advance hint that "something" is brewing.

Stories about a company's fundamentals—good earnings, new products, etc.—can be helpful on the buy side. On the sell side, you'll *never* hear the negative news in time. It is sometimes six to nine months before the reason why a stock topped out becomes evident in the news. The market, remember, anticipates. On the buy side, too, never react to good news that has already been announced. A good fundamental story is one which speaks of the future and can be treated as a security-blanket reason to buy the stock if you need such additional motivation. If it coordinates with a good chart, one which shows the potential for a robust move upward—big base, serious resistance far away, etc.—you can then determine when and where to buy.

When it comes to a "hot-tip" type of story—typically, these days, of a takeover—there are instances when the stock will be languishing and the takeover bid surprising. In one recent week there were similar stories on Kennecott and AMAX; the former was surprising, while the latter obviously had a leak at least a day or two beforehand. If you hear such a story, make the market verify it not just by a leap in price for no apparent (as yet) reason but through sharply increased volume. Place your bet if it is still relatively early *and* if you can use a stop-loss order relatively close to the purchase price, for protection against a fizzle. Rumors can have validity, but that doesn't mean the deal can't fall through later, or be long delayed, and there are times when the story is started by someone who wants to get out of the stock. A certain cynicism, rather than enthusiasm, is always helpful. The chart is your protection.

Best of all is when the chart itself is buyable even if you didn't know of any fundamental reason. Here are two examples.

New England Nuclear rose persistently on rumors of a takeover. There was no major resistance until the low 30s, NNC having made a high in '79 (before this chart's time span) at 34. On the way up, there were interludes of rising volume on days of rising prices, and each minor dip held above support. This was a good chart, buyable

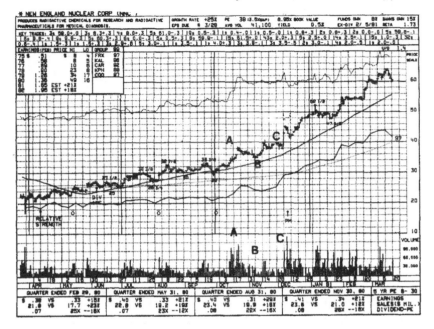

at any time if the story itself sounded good enough, because the stock never looked overextended. But note the extended sideways action at the resistance area in the low 30s. The first breakout buy thereafter came at A when the stock moved above this two-month sideways consolidation, with heavy volume appearing as it crossed the prior all-time high at 34. You could also have bought safely and soundly on the subsequent pullback (B) on extremely low volume. In both instances you would have anticipated the actual merger news, long rumored, when it was finally announced at point C. Indeed, as NNC was drifting down at point B, the market itself was sliding a fast 100 points. That relative strength coupled with the low volume combined for an excellent buying opportunity for anyone who had heard the rumors. Volume works two ways, remember. It should increase on the upside, diminish during corrections. When it does the opposite, beware.

Dillingham was a somewhat different situation. The volume on the chart (see following page) shows that there was little or no advance indication. But the price action on the chart was highly

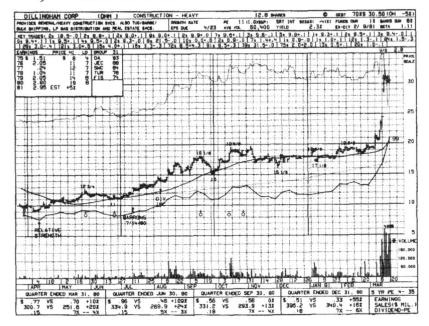

favorable. The stock had refused to go down in the face of a severe January 1981 sell-off, showed a series of rising lows, and had a breakout at 20—such round-number breakout points seem to have a mysterious but extra-special cachet—which was not only above previous rally peaks but to a new all-time high. In February, this stock belonged on a list of buy candidates simply on its own merits, and should have been/could have been bought on the breakout across 20. And even after that breakout, there were a couple of days of quieter pullback action. In sum, there was plenty of time and reason to buy the stock—without knowing anything else—before the news came out.

Nothing is ever perfect. Try to remember, when dealing with a recommendation from someone else (for whatever reason), that even if he or she is the most professional of Wall Streeters, no one is going to be perfect. Stories excite not only the teller but the believer. Believers buy. But you can be more objective. The chart tells if they've bought it up to too high a price over the short-term, or if it has reached a resistance area, just as much as it can tell you if the stock has overall merit. Stories of how marvelous things are going to be "two years out" are the most dangerous; the market is hard enough to deal with, based on what we know, without adding such guesstimates to the equation. Conversely, the best fundamental stories, in our experience, are those which anticipate that a stock in current difficulties is going to work its way out in another quarter or two. One last bit of bad news coinciding with a higher low is a positive way to coordinate fundamentals with charting. As for those so-called hot tips, many of them are more often based on guessing that something must be up because the stock is, rather than stemming from genuine inside information. Year in and year out, the investor who buys carefully, respecting chart formations, trend lines, and breakouts, will do better—in his otherwise ignorance—than the person who is constantly searching for an advantage through information. In the end, the tape—and, thus, the chart—tells all.

10

WHAT TO BUY:
CASE HISTORIES

The act of selling is psychologically much harder than the act of buying. The excitement of participating, the thrill of the bet, the pursuasiveness of the recommendation (be it hot tip or reasoned analysis) can lure even first-timers into the stock market. One can get emotionally caught up in the game and plunge in. But once having bought, it is hard to let go.

Yet the choice on the sell side is simple. Once a stock has been bought, there are only two options: either hold or sell. Nothing else applies. The fundamental reasons that might have applied when buying are no longer a factor; indeed, they have become a danger, because the good and therefore lulling news will invariably come out near the top. (Similarly, fundamental reasons for selling will always come out long after the stock has started declining.) When the stock finally makes a top, the task then is to free one's self from the emotional compulsion to hang on—greed that it might go higher; reluctance to take a loss if wrong. Once you are past such emotional entanglement, the decision to sell can be made objectively and straightforwardly.

One way to make the selling decision as completely objective as possible is through the use of trailing stops. That is, the stop-loss order, initially placed to protect your capital if the market goes against you, can successively be raised as the stock rises. A properly placed stop order—just under the most recent prior low; the trend line; or the moving-average line—will get you out automatically at the first sign that something is wrong. However, if the sensible stop level is too far away, or if the value of the profits to be protected exceeds the value of possible additional profits, careful consideration ought to be given to selling the stock outright.

On the other hand, the choice on the buy side is complex. Factors that must be considered are: whether to buy or not; which stock to buy out of all the stocks available; and when to buy it. And these considerations lead to further questions: If you don't buy now, when? Should you buy speculative, or conservative, issues? Do you buy on the breakout, on the pullback, or risk a bit more by anticipating? These choices can become bewildering. Each individual stock begins to assume its own flavor and intricacies in terms of whether to buy it and when to act (patterns which are often consistent through every cycle for that stock). You've seen this diversity in the examples we've presented already. In this chapter, several additional examples are being presented to illustrate various important technical points and to give you added insights into this intricate game.

Some Misleading Charts

Parker Drilling is an example of a mistake. It was brought to our attention because an advisory service with an excellent stock-selection record came up with a buy recommendation at point A. You can see their reasoning—a head-and-shoulders bottom seemed to have formed, and that particular day's action seemed to be suggesting a breakout across the neckline. Up to the moment when the stock traded at 32 3/4, it certainly seemed that way.

But there were several subtle problems, beginning, of course, with the fact that at that time—April 1981—the entire oil sector of the market was in its own downtrend. So there was a lack of group confirmation and, it must be added, a bit too much bottom fishing for our taste. But the chart itself has problems. Note that the stock did not actually close above that supposed breakout price; it closed,

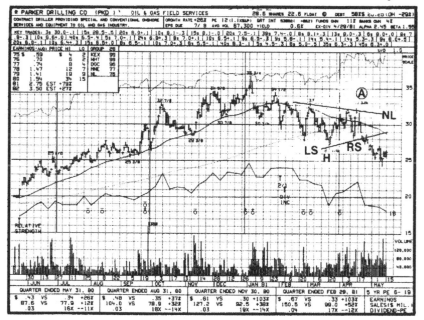

instead, back down under the neckline. Add that volume did not expand on that upward move, and it begins to look more and more like a failure.

In such instances, a bull might still like the potential of the chart pattern but ought to reduce risk by waiting for further evidence of strength. Naturally, the 32 3/4 high at point A would need to be surpassed, and with the next previous peak at 33 only a quarter of a point further plus being a round number, we'd wait for crossing 33 to signal strength. Often, downsloping necklines, even if valid in terms of announcing a true move to come, are not the actual volume-breakout level; the high of the prior peaks may be the definitive breakout point.

Given those problems of a failed rise, lack of volume, and group difficulties, a protective stop-loss order was certainly required. In this case, the proper point to enter such an order would be just below the right shoulder low at 28—that is, an order entered at 27 7/8 stop. The subsequent gap in that area as prices fell away confirms the validity of that stop price.

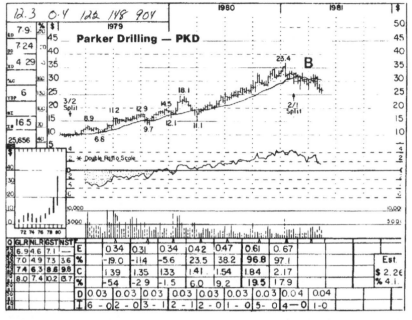

12.3 O.4 122 148 904

| 1980 | | 1981 | | $ |

Parker Drilling — PKD 1979

	%	$
ED 7.9		45 50
DD 7.24		40 45
XD 4 29		35 40
%C 6		30
YDP		25
BI 16.5		20 15
IB		10
25,656		5

B 23.4

18.1 14.5 12.9 11.2 8.9 9.7 12.1 11.1 6.6 3/2 Split 2/1 Split

\$ * Double Ratio Scale

10,000 5000 10,00 500

Q	GLR	NLR	GST	NST	E	034	031	034	042	047	061	067			Est.
	6.9	4.6	7.1	—	%	-19.0	-11.4	-5.6	23.5	38.2	96.8	97.1			$ 2.26
	7.0	4.9	7.3	3.6	C	1 39	1.35	1 33	1.41	1.54	1.84	2.17			% 4.i.
	7.4	6.3	8.6	9.8	%	-54	-2 9	-1.5	6.0	9.2	19.5	17.9			
	8.0	7.4	10.2	13.7	D	0.03	0.03	0 03	0.03	0.03	0.03	0.03	0.04	0.04	
					I	6 -0	2 -0	3 -1	2 -1	2 -0	1 -0	5 -0	4—0	1-0	

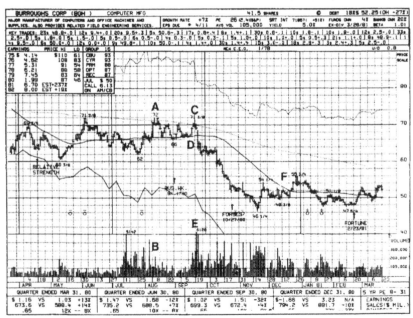

BURROUGHS CORP (BGH)   COMPUTER MFG   41.5 SHARES   © DEBT 18%S 52.25 (0H -27%)

CARNINGS	PRICE HI	LO	GROUP 16.
75 $ 4.14	$110	61	CBU 93
76 4.62	108	83	CYR 93
77 5.31	91	54	PRM 88
78 6.21	88	58	OPT 87
79 7.45	83	84	REC 87
80 1.98	87	46	JUL $ 50
81 6.70 EST+237%			CALL 6.13
82 8.00 EST +19%			ON AM/CB

A C D E B F

RELATIVE STRENGTH

FORTUNE 2/23/81

	APR	MAY	JUN	JUL	AUG	SEP	OCT	NOV	DEC	JAN 81	FEB	MAR

QUARTER ENDED MAR 31, 80	QUARTER ENDED JUN 30, 80	QUARTER ENDED SEP 30, 80	QUARTER ENDED DEC 31, 80	5 YR PE 8- 31
$ 1.16 VS 1.03 +13%	$ 1.47 VS 1.68 -12%	$ 1.02 VS 1.51 -32%	$-1.66 VS 3.23 N/A	EARNINGS
673.6 VS 588.4 +14%	735.2 VS 688.5 +7%	699.2 VS 672.4 +4%	794.2 VS 881.7 -10%	SALES ($ MIL.)
.65 12% -- 8%	.65 10% -- 8X	.65	.65	

But there is one more important point to make about Parker Drilling at this time. Despite the potential appeal of the daily chart, it did not check out in comparison with the longer-term weekly chart. Point B on this Mansfield chart shows the improvement seen on the daily but, more seriously, shows that the overall chart looks more like a top than a bottom. The moving average has certainly begun to roll over after a prolonged uptrend. It isn't dreadful, but it is uncomfortable enough to make a potential buyer hesitate. The only question is, therefore: Why take the risk?

Burroughs is another example of unnecessary risk-taking. Indeed, it is two examples. At point A we are in the middle of a strong market uptrend, full of bullish enthusiasm. At first glance, the stock looks interesting. It has held on a test of the prior low and started upward again. At 72 it has exceeded the previous high by an eighth. But the warning signs here are the lack of volume on that action (B) and the fact that the daily chart's moving-average line is still sloping downward. At point C, when it seemed that BGH might be ready to move at last, exceeding two little highs and closing in on a potential breakout across 72, volume had expanded somewhat. But if you look at the volume carefully, you'll see, at E, that those high-volume days came the days *after* the rally failed. So there was no breakout.

Anyone who had been tempted to buy at point A would have had a warning that the proper stop-loss point—under 62—was too far away for comfort. Anyone who had tried to anticipate a breakout thereafter would have been able to use a stop-loss point of just under 66 (D). This at least would have saved a small mistake from becoming a huge one.

So Burroughs tumbled to a new low. But it then went sideways for months, constantly tempting those who like to fish for bottoms. A little base formed at F, nowhere near big enough to be meaningful, but tempting to traders. A glance at the longer-term chart, however, showed how emphatically the moving-average line was still heading downward, severely limiting any upside potential. (See following page.) By March, this entire area had to be reevaluated. The original low had been tested twice, creating a slightly higher low, and then another dip held at an even higher level. But volume failed to expand on the rallies, and the moving-average lines were

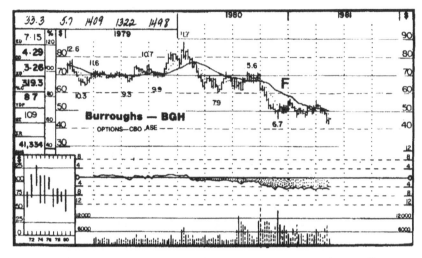

still heading down. It was hard to draw any meaningful trend line; there really was no discernable pattern. The relative-strength line remained moribund. And those little rallies seemed to be having trouble at what was, after all, just a minor resistance area around 53 1/2–54 1/2 that had formed at year end. What was tempting about this stock was that it was down so far, had a glamorous name, and had apparently gone sideways long enough. But so what? That's just guessing. The stock, in reality, was not a good risk on the evidence, especially when in that same time span there were a lot of much better candidates. Buying Burroughs was more of a guess than a good bet.

Note how in both of these examples the same elements were lacking. Volume did not confirm any potential bullishness; the moving averages were still trending downward; there was no break-out across any meaningful trend line or prior rally peak. Having only half the picture can prove costly, as can counting on the decline to reverse itself—far more costly than the loss of the point or two that waiting for proof positive will mean.

The Possibility of Anticipation

Sometimes it is the longer-term chart that can catch your eye first. Here's a potential base in Polaroid that looks terrific. It covers

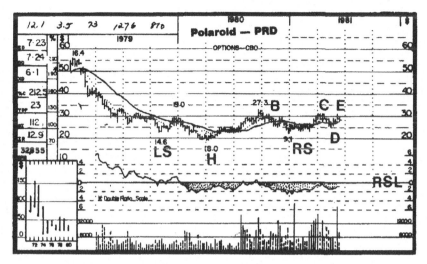

almost two years—surely huge enough—and shows enormous potential. A good case can be made for a head-and-shoulders bottom pattern within that base. Volume is on the increase on the upside weeks. The stock (see inset) is down from an all-time high over 150, in the early '70s, as well as from 50 to 20 during PRD's leg of decline depicted on this chart. What's more, Mansfield's relative-strength line has been negative (the shaded area) throughout this entire time span, but shows some gradual improvement. There is the implication that one good breakout rally would carry this line into favorable territory at long last and mark the initiation of a potentially big upside move. At point C, all is in gear, but . . .

Let's switch perspective to the daily chart. On the following page we see (B on both charts) the first swoop upward to over 32 which failed. The stock then declines through November, December, and January 1981. PRD holds the recent low in February and breaks that intermediate-term downtrend line in early March on rising volume. A short-term trader could have bought at this time with relatively little risk, paying, let's say, 26 1/2, with a protective stop at 23 1/8. But for many Wall Streeters the stock didn't become exciting until it was active on the tape at 29 and 30. Judging solely from the long-term chart, that would still have seemed cheap. But

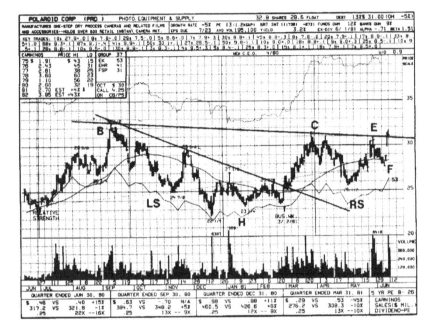

the daily chart revealed, rather, that the run-up from the breakout across that downtrend line to point C had been virtually straight up. That is, by the time it reached 30, PRD was already over-bought, at least for the short-term, and lacked the power to stage a fresh dynamic breakout. Reviewing the daily chart would have placed a curb on your enthusiasm; instead of playing, you'd have realized the stock had gone too far too fast. But you would then have become alert to buy on any subsequent dip.

Polaroid then came back down to 26—the top of a good support area. Proving that it could hold at this point made the stock a much more sensible buy; this would have been a suitable time to use a limited-price order to catch the dip. Anyone who can muster the patience to identify a potentially favorable chart pattern and then wait for an ideal entry point will show a superior record of profits over the years. On this dip (D on the long-term chart, RS on the daily), we see that volume has dwindled favorably as a right shoulder forms on the daily chart. The stock has already suggested that it wants to go up, and it is at this point—and no sooner—that you could actually anticipate a potential upside breakout. There is a neckline above (B–C) which identifies where that breakout should occur. At this time, an extravagant new-product rumor began to circulate, but again, by referring to the daily chart, you would have realized it was too emotional to jump on the rumor and buy at 29 or 30; better to wait, with that breakout line not far above. Indeed, PRD failed exactly there. At point E the new-product announcement proved disappointing; the failure extended the neckline; and the stock dipped again. But, here again, volume diminished drastically. Bulls were given another chance to anticipate an upside breakout, with another favorable clue coming at point F, when, after closing on its low for the day, on the very next day Polaroid, instead of continuing down, actually opened higher and closed at its high instead. The subsequent gap, and leap above the neckline, was apparently valid. Despite the way the technical picture was exploding bullishly, you should, of course, have placed your protective stop-loss order—in this case, just under F at, say, 26 7/8— because it costs you nothing to enter and can save a lot of capital.

We'd like to stop our tale of Polaroid here because the main point we've wanted to illustrate is the possibility of anticipation and there were two such examples here. In the abstract, it is better to wait for the actual breakout, but in reality each and every one of us would like to bet well before the breakout takes place. Being aggressive will make you wrong a few more times, but if you adhere to stop-loss points to keep from getting stubborn, that risk, too, can be minimized. The fact is that stocks do fail, and Polaroid has been one disappointment after another . . . even before the failure which subsequently evolved from this seemingly powerful bullish chart. Never, to our recollection, has a failure developed so abruptly as it did right after this apparent upside move; you'd have gotten stopped out with a minimal loss. That's the way the stock market keeps us humble.

The following chart of Western Union shows the ideal anticipation situation. Note that this takes place during the extremely difficult 1981 market climate. After hitting a low in February, WU actually formed a very potent base which evolved into a conspicuous head-and-shoulders bottom, with a clear-cut breakout point across the neckline (A–B). What's more, the downtrend line, which was confirmed at a third point (A), had been broken. And by the time the right shoulder was forming, Western Union had clearly established a pattern of rising lows. Last, volume during this decline was noticeably low; selling pressure was drying up. But while all those aspects were quite favorable, perhaps the most positive aspect for this stock was that the action was developing while the Dow Industrial Average was collapsing some 200 points. In other words, by refusing to go down, the stock was conspicuously diverging from the overall market. The message was that Western Union wanted to go up. Add all that up and the stock, as the right shoulder formed, was an excellent candidate for anticipating the upside breakout. In this case, the breakout came on excellent confirming volume, plus a move across the Mansfield Chart Service's relative-strength line's zero level as an added indication of power. There were so many ingredients in place here that it would have made sense to anticipate, but note that even if you had bought on the upside breakout, you'd have had a winner.

McDonalds is another example of how useful it is to combine a

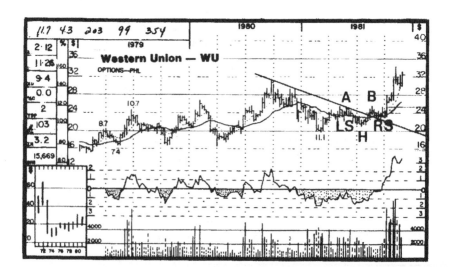

study of both the daily and the weekly charts to get a sounder perspective on a stock's potential action. Look at this daily chart first. We have a potential head-and-shoulders top, followed in October 1980, when the market itself was becoming precarious, by an apparent downside breakout to a lower low. But then something intriguing happened. MCD refused to continue on down. Instead, the stock held and made a series of slightly higher lows. The more this continued through November and December, including an unexpected spurt of volume (A) on a little upswing, the odder the situation became. McDonalds should have been bearish but was refusing to be, even as the market headed into a sell signal at the beginning of January 1981. A small base had appeared which, at the time, didn't look potent enough to exceed the resistance from the prior top area, but was certainly a sign that anyone who had previously sold the stock short ought not to be short any longer. This, of course, is closing out a position, not initiating one; the choice is to buy back, or hold, a short position already established. A potential buyer would have waited, but a short-seller should have covered his position as soon as that sequence of rising lows

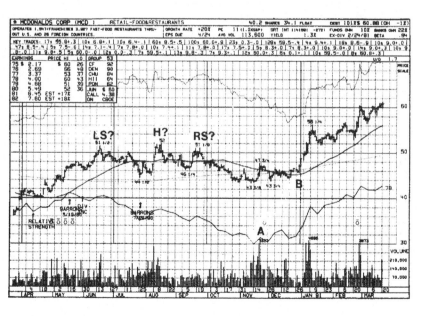

developed, certainly by point B. This is the rule of "Don't argue with the tape."

A simultaneous look at the longer-term chart would have suggested that no one should have been short in the first place. Here we see what looks much more like an overall big base, with the right shoulder forming on that deceptive short-term downside break. No wonder MCD didn't want to go down any further. That small top had shaken out the last batch of nervous holders. Encouragement for the bull case during this period came from the fact that the longer-term moving-average line was flat to rising rather than downtrending or rounding over. The upside breakout finally came across that pattern's neckline at 52, but note that this could have been anticipated a bit when volume increased as the stock attacked the 50 level. What's more, there was ample time thereafter on a series of pullbacks to the breakout level at 52 to buy the stock comfortably and sensibly. Notice, too, how the relative-strength line, having shot up across its zero line on the breakout, confirmed the buyability of MCD. The coincident move of this line from

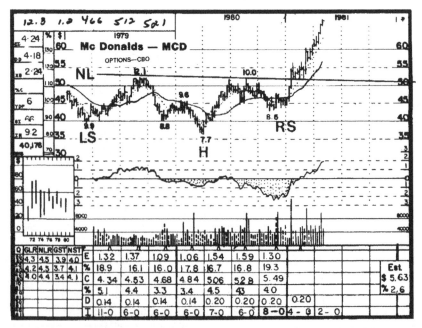

negative to positive territory while the stock itself is breaking out provides substantial favorable odds that a big upside move is in the making.

History Repeats Itself

Datapoint reveals an odd fact about stocks. History does repeat itself. That's why support and resistance levels must be given full weight in any consideration. In February and March 1980, the market itself was in the throes of a huge and abrupt decline. The climactic low, as we've discussed, came at the end of March. But even though the Dow Industrial Average was successfully testing its low, DPT went lower on its next leg down. The ultimate result was that Datapoint formed a head-and-shoulders bottom that spring. Even though the blue-chip average was already starting up, this shows how stocks move at their own pace; in a true bull move there will be plenty of buying opportunities within the first several weeks. Note, too, that the low of this particular decline, at 44 1/4,

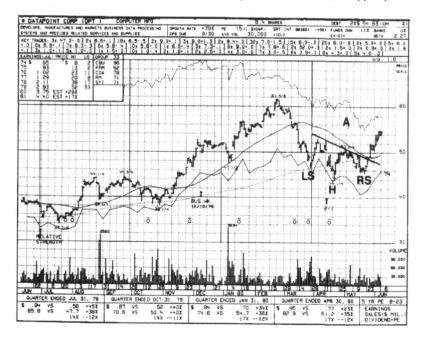

held at the top of the prior sideways area of August–October 1979. Support appeared almost exactly where it should have. This doesn't make the stock an automatic buy there; the pattern must develop further, but it does provide an added measure of confirmation to the buy side. Crossing the neckline thereafter proved to be the upside breakout signal and the stock then embarked on a huge rise.

Now let's look at the subsequent daily chart. The stock split two for one yet again, almost mirroring the prior split, as it occurred in the midst of a correction. But the more remarkable mirror image was that another head-and-shoulders bottom formed at almost the identical point where the same sort of bottom had formed less than a year earlier. It is as if the stock itself remembered where it ought to hold. In this instance, the bottom pattern wasn't as big, or dynamic; it was much later in the long-term uptrend, but the upside breakout did lead to a highly profitable trade nevertheless.

A glance at the longer-term chart shows these two formations within the entire context of Datapoint's big bull rise. The first formation was obviously better because it came while the relative-strength line was still low—a sign that the stock was nowhere near overbought yet—and came on a dynamic dash across the moving-average line as well. Note that here, too, there was ample time thereafter to buy on a pullback to the top of the breakout, and that the move didn't accelerate until after the prior peak had been exceeded. Those who worry about the desirability of anticipating a breakout should learn from this that the breakout itself (especially when it comes from a downslanting neckline) anticipates sufficiently. The second head-and-shoulders (B) bottom was far more risky, because by then relative strength was so steep that it was in itself a signal of a stock already late in its move. But the breakout—coinciding with a bullish market climate in the indicators—was real enough. No top is yet in evidence on this chart, and it can be reasoned that until the moving-average line catches up to the price level and starts to falter, the stock is okay. But anyone who bought this particular formation should be well aware of how late it is—revealed in the longer-term and not the daily chart—ready to sell as soon as failures start to appear. The next fluctuation

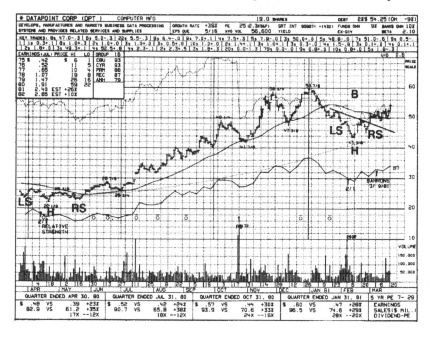

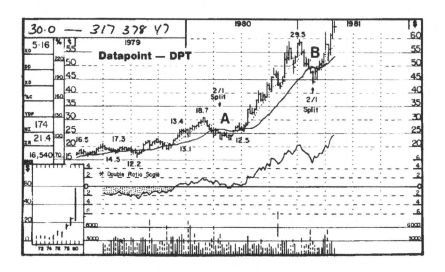

down will surely come . . . and almost as surely it will find support in that same 40–50 price range.

Here's another example of how historic patterns and price levels repeat themselves. Computervision has been one of the biggest winners of the last few years of the decade. Up from the price equivalent of 2 in 1977, and around 12 when the stock was listed on the New York Stock Exchange, it may have seemed late by October 1979, when this first triangle formed (A). But it was a legitimate formation for that particular market moment; no use saying, "I could've bought it when . . ." when a new buying opportunity presents itself. That's particularly true when the relative-strength line is still comfortably low. The triangle itself is a simple one, lacking some volume on the upside breakout but with that factor offset by the still steadily rising moving-average line.

The second triangle (B) on this same chart formed after the 1980 crash. Notice how this pattern evolved differently from Datapoint's, even though both can be considered fancy high-technology stocks. DPT had a lower low, forming a head, while CVN held

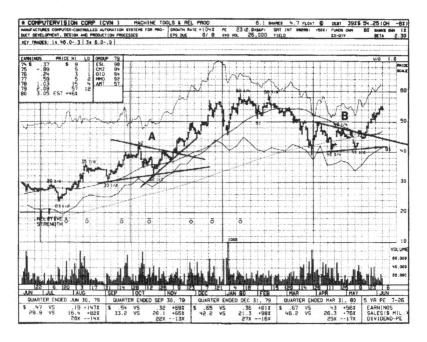

during that same market dip, exactly at the top of the prior triangle's (A) support area. The breakout across the downtrend line of the triangle proved to be a good entry price, providing anticipation enough for our money, but it actually wasn't until the stock exceeded its previous high (see long-term chart) that much more volume traded. Crossing 60, therefore, was the conventional breakout, but the triangle formation provided a buy point nearly 15 points lower, and a lot closer to a protective stop-loss level (at, say, 38 7/8).

Now let's look at subsequent action on another daily chart. This picks up approximately where the first chart left off. Because the stock subsequently split two for one, this chart is adjusted so that the move across 30 in July is the breakout to a new high. What is interesting about this chart is that there is no further safe-buying opportunity, in our terms, with one possible exception. At C you could, with a bit of effort, find a small triangle forming. (Note that CVN's pattern of triangle formations is consistent, as was DPT's tendency toward head-and-shoulders patterns.) If you put your

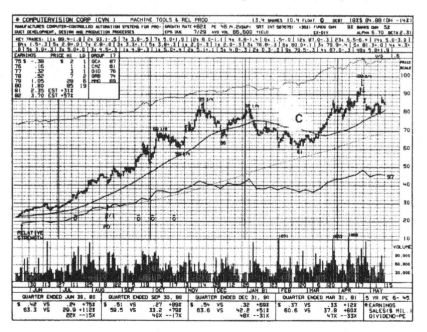

thumb over the upside action after March, you'll see why it didn't seem safe to buy. The stock could have been forming a top which would have been completed breaking 60. The small resistance area centered at 70 that formed in January just might have impeded any rally. It didn't. Instead, a dip to 61 held slightly above the prior low, and the stock was able to continue rallying instead. To us, however, it wasn't a low-risk buy at a time when there were other, even though less high-flying, buys around. In the end, if you'd paid 70 on the breakout from that little triangle, you'd have had to be an extremely nimble trader, or else would have had to sell when the stock broke 79 in June. That kind of gain isn't worth the risk this late in an uptrend. The chart can tell you that it is too soon to sell short, but it is also saying that it is too late to buy.

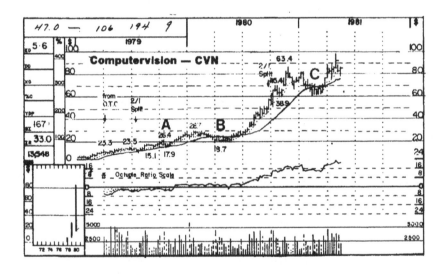

An Unglamorous Buy

Lest you think that highly profitable buys come only in glamour stocks, here's a chart of J. C. Penney. The yearly price range revealed in the inset on the weekly chart shows that this supposedly slow-moving, big-capitalization, conservative stock had been in a downtrend from its high of 100 since 1972. There were attempts to hold along that path down, so what we see developing here may seem like just another such attempt. But that is trying to outguess the future. All we know is what is factual at the moment, and JCP has a very bullish chart. Note the base that formed in the last quarter of 1980 and on into 1981. It is substantial enough that the head-and-shoulders bottom configuration shows up on the weekly chart as well as on the daily. Note, too, that this formation developed at the same price level as the March 1980 crash low, proof that the 20 level was important support that had been tested successfully on this bottom development.

The daily chart shows this head-and-shoulders bottom in clearer form. The moving average has begun to trend sideways just above the trading range and is crossed at 24 on a gap opening. Such gaps are important buy signals in themselves, but on the same trading day, on a sharp increase in volume, the stock also crossed its

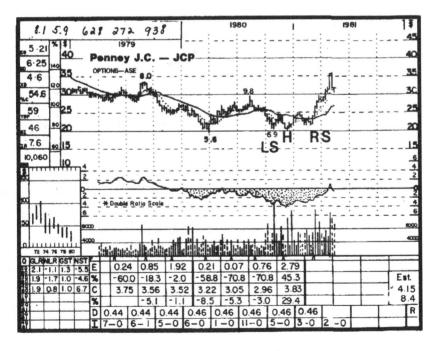

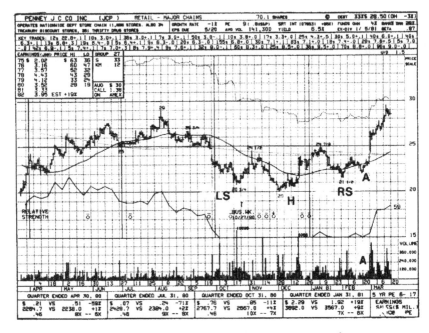

previous high at 24 7/8, thereby eliminating any lingering doubts as to the vigor of the upside breakout.

Here, too, we have the question of whether it was possible to anticipate such a breakout. Again that possibility exists not well in advance but in the few days just before the major move begins. (No need, in other words, to tie up your capital in a guess.) Note the minor dip at point A and the drying up of volume that accompanied that easing. Once the daily action indicated that a higher low had been made, it was possible to anticipate the breakout with a sufficient degree of safety for the bet. As you can see, both traders and conservative investors could have done well in Penney. The name of the company doesn't matter and can lead to prejudices. Cover the name over and ask yourself if you'd buy that chart.

The Twin Keys to Buying

Let's look at one more winning chart to see how it combines so many of these favorable aspects. This is a weekly chart of Pepsico that shows not just an ordinary head-and-shoulders bottom but a substantial one. The head was made at 20 during the silver panic, but despite the decent percentage gain from that low to point D, that wasn't the time to buy the stock. Note that while the DJIA was rising through 1980, PEP was going sideways as it formed this base. The neckline (C–D) became clear as something to watch intently for. But by the time Pepsico was starting to break out, the market itself was in the throes of trouble. Nevertheless, PEP was undaunted. It broke out on substantial volume for that week (B) and kept going up despite a decline in the averages.

Now let's see how the daily chart can be useful once the weekly picture has become significant. The time span of the daily chart on the following page commences with the head-and-shoulders bot-

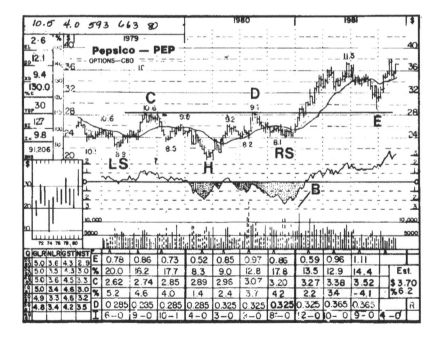

tom already well underway. We've denoted the right shoulder to
point out the seemingly minor clue that was important: the stock
held twice at 24, which, in turn, was just better than a prior dip
at 23 3/4. Volume was lower on declining days during this period
than it was when the stock lifted its head. For our money, you
could have anticipated buying PEP as soon as it crossed 26 1/4
(above the last two minor peaks). That was soon enough. But you
could have bought on the breakout as well, and in an even calmer
moment at point A, when a minor pullback to the breakout level
came on considerably less volume. Last, go back to the weekly
chart and see that on the late September 1981 low, after the Dow
had fallen 200 points, Pepsico was available for purchase under 30
—that is, it was holding its major support level above the breakout
point. This success story was clearly revealed in the charts.

All we are looking for is an advantage. At the race track, some
will study past performances, others track conditions, still others
the workout clockings, and so on. The search is for those clues that

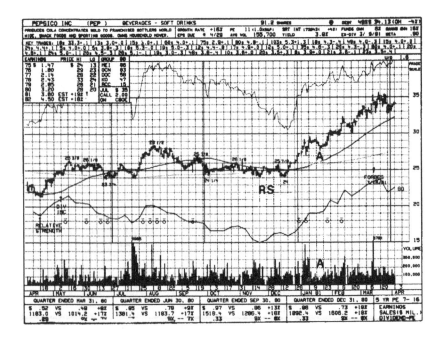

will identify one horse as more likely to win than any others in the race. But in the stock market we can do better. To begin with, the choices we have to pick from are much greater, and we are not looking for the single winner among several; all have the same odds for success. But it is the same search for that betting edge. Finding a stock with a definable base gives us the sense of low risk; the upside breakout confirms the stock's strength and ability to go up; the daily action often gives us the seemingly minor clue to be able to anticipate the forthcoming move. There are times when the individual stock will move independently of the averages—after the Dow has made its bottom, or even much later in the rise. But there are also times when we will also have a market climate freshly signaled as favorable by the indicators. Tie as many factors together as possible and we are going to be able to place far better bets than anyone ever could at the track.

11

BETTING IN THE OPTIONS MARKET

We've rarely had any success in the options market. Others may profit, but we've tried and tried and apparently it is not our game. That may be a strange confession to make in a "how-to" book, but it is an unfortunate fact of our trading life. In the preceding chapters we've written about what we know works because it has worked in our own experience both as forecaster and as trader. But in this chapter we can only discuss what we've observed and what we think makes sense, in the hope that you'll be able to do more with the comments than we have.

Oh, once in a while we've placed a bet. Buying options is a pure bet. It has the time limit a horse race has; the limited risk of a small sum, wagered on that one race, and when it is over, you know whether you've won or not. There is, while the race is being run, the chance to be in the lead, to fade, to come back strongly toward the finish . . . and to fall just short of winning, too, as happens in the options game so often. The wager is for a specific reason; that the stock is going to win that particular race within that particular time frame.

Options have been around for centuries. The current expansion of use is due to the structure devised to create set prices and time spans. Call options represent the right to buy the stock at the specified (or strike) price within the designated time span (until the option expires). It can be "in the money" if the stock is trading at a higher price than the strike price, or "out of the money" if the stock is trading at a lower price. The premium you pay for the option will vary, depending on the volatility of the underlying stock. As of this writing, almost every call option traded on the four option exchanges has a comparable put option, in which the bet is that the stock will go down—that is, the option is the right to sell the stock at the designated strike price within the length of the option.

Let's suppose stock XYZ looks as if it is going to break out on the upside, so we bet on that opinion. With the stock then selling at 41, we decide to pick the out-of-the-money option at the 45 strike price, then selling at $2, for the right to buy shares at 45, or $200 per 100 shares of stock. Let's say the expiration month for that option is December, and it is still only mid-October, so the option has approximately two more months to run. But that isn't our purpose; at expiration, the stock would have to trade at 47 (the strike price of 45 plus our investment of $2) for us to be even. What we are betting on is that the stock will move strongly soon enough to cause the option to sell at a higher price than $2. Indeed it does, rallying from 41 to 44 in a couple of days; the option price increases to $3. That's a terrific percentage profit, far better than the gain in the stock itself. But that 50 percent gain actually amounts to only $100 (putting aside commission costs for this purpose).

Of course, you could perhaps approach this differently, by buying $4,000 worth of options and making a good dollar profit as well. But you've negated the other speculative virtue of option trading —the low and limited risk if you are wrong. If you are wrong in this case, you've blown the whole big wad; if you buy the stock and are wrong, you've still got a substantial portion of your investment left.

In sum, if you had lots of loose cash, obviously you'd have made more actual dollars by buying the stock for this quick rise instead of the option. So the percentage gain itself is somewhat misleading. Two such gains would get you $200, but if the next trade is a loser, there goes the entire profit. You've hit on two out of three—surely a decent track record—and ended up nowhere.

And yet you have to take that percentage gain; that's what this aspect of the option game is all about. If you forget that what you are after is such a percentage profit—in this case, 50 percent in less than a week—you can get into all sorts of trouble. Since the option that was bought still has about two months to run, instantly the thought is: Why not wait, why not stick it out for a truly big gain? That's when you get teased; the time value begins to work against you. The premium begins to erode because there is less and less time before the option expires. You are defying the notion that the market fluctuates. A breakout occurs, but then there's a pullback, etc. The stock actually goes higher, but by the time it does, there is less and less time to expiration date, so that the option price lags more and more. It may still be selling at only $2, even though the stock is at 44, because by now there is only one month left to the expiration of the option—and remember, the stock still has to get to 47 on expiration date for you to break even on this bet. Indeed, many's the time the option is actually lower, even though the stock itself is higher. And then, finally, the option is about to expire worthless, because the stock never got to the strike price. Or it did get over the strike price, let's say to 46 1/2, meaning that if you "call" the option—have the stock bought for your account at 45, as you are entitled to—you've gotten $150 back (again, before the bite of commissions). In sum, your profit can vanish even if the stock is a fine pick, because you never took the first fast gain when it was handed to you.

What's happened is that the apparently simple options bet—a few hundred bucks just to participate in the excitement—has actually become a multiplicity of choices. You no longer have that simple need to pick the right stock at the right time. You have further to decide whether to buy an in-the-money or an out-of-the-money option, as well as pick one of the three available time frames till expiration. And, of course, this concerns only one aspect of options betting—that of buying a call. The choices in the options market are compounded by other parts of the game: buying the stock and selling the call (known as covered writing); selling a put instead of buying the call (thus betting that the stock will go up and the put option you've sold will expire worthless, enabling you to pocket all the money from the sale); doing a straddle or a spread or a butterfly, as some of the more complex option strategies are called. Instead of a simple bet with the appeal of a known dollar risk if you are wrong, the difficulties have been compounded and the chance of losing money has increased . . . even if you pick the right stock at the right time.

Does anyone make money at this game? Yes. Yes. We've watched them on the floor of the American Stock Exchange, and there are undoubtedly counterparts on the other options exchanges. The specialists make money in the time-honored way. That is, by being on the opposite side of the fluctuations, the opposite side of the emotions, they can profit. (By equation, then, the public usually loses money.) It is important, too, to remember that none of us on the outside is going to be able to sneak one over on the specialist. He knows everything we might know—breakout point for the stock, big block activity and interest, etc.—and can act much faster. That doesn't mean you can't join him; it simply means you should never assume he's missing something.

Others make money, too, and sometimes they can do so without knowing anything about the stock market, not even caring where prices are apt to go. These are the hedgers with all of their intricate calculations. They make money doing spreads, straddles, and the like because they use mathematics to protect themselves up, down, and sideways. They stand at the trading post, never leave their zone, and help create a more liquid market by constantly buying and selling. Anyone good at such mathematics who has sufficient capital and is willing to be alert to what is happening so as to act quickly can play the same game. Essentially, they are plays on the premium differences between different strike prices and/or time values. Such hedgers don't make much each time, but it is pretty well assured, and adds up. But we've seen even experienced players make mathematical mistakes, forget to put a sufficient spread on, or think that—just this once—they can get away with leaving themselves exposed.

We're not going to get into the mathematical aspects of spreads, straddles, and their various cousins. But two further points are worth making. First, as a tactic, legging into spreads can be effective. The customary method for establishing a spread position is to do so simultaneously. For example, one buys the January 45 call and sells the January 50 call when the premium difference at which the transactions can be made is 3 1/2 points. The tactic of legging in means establishing one position first and then, later, making the second transaction. Having bought some call options (preferably in the money) in a stock which then moves higher, you can set up a spread by then proceeding to sell out-of-the-money calls now that they have also gone up in price. That protects your profit and can actually compound it, for you can subsequently sell your calls as soon as the stock begins to falter and, with luck, watch the out-of-the-money calls you've sold expire worthless.

Our second point relates to straddles. Here you are trying to benefit from a stock which, at its most desirable, goes neither up nor down. Or, alternatively, the stock swings in both directions, perhaps even sharply, but essentially ends up where it started. Let's suppose the stock is selling at 50. You sell a January 60 call at 1 and sell a January 40 put at 3/4. If, by the time January options expire, the stock is neither higher than 60 nor lower than 40, both options will expire worthless and you, as the seller, will pocket both premiums. This is perhaps an extreme example, but professionals tell us that straddles are an often productive approach to the options market.

All in all, the consistent money-makers in options are those who base their decisions on mathematical calculations. Everything is hedged and protected. The profits may be minuscule, but they mount up day by day. Other books can tell you how to apply these formulas and their many variations and refinements. To us, it's no fun.

In-the-Money vs. Out-of-the-Money Options

The options market can also be a betting parlor. As we have noted, the multiplicity of choices required—which strike price; which time frame, etc.—can increase the chance of error, so that sometimes one throws up one's hands and says the hell with it, and goes back to the stock itself instead. But for those who are interested in placing such bets, let's discuss the choices further.

As you might expect, everything in such choices is a trade-off. An advantage in one area—a low premium, let's say—may be offset by a near total lack of liquidity. A highly desirable stock may already have a huge premium. A further-out expiration date may seem to give more leeway, but the added cost may be questionable.

Let's begin by examining the choice between in-the-money options—those with the stock selling above the strike price—and out-of-the-money options, with strike prices above, and sometimes well above, the stock's current trading price. Magic does sometimes happen. A week before expiration, Pfizer was selling at 44, and the chart showed a breakout at 45. With so little time left, the options with a strike price of 45 were selling at 1/8. It so happened that the stock actually broke out three days before expiration and raced above 46. Anyone who'd bought those options at an eighth was able to get a buck for them within the week.

Note that the stock actually had to get above the strike price for anyone to profit; had it only gotten to 45 1/8, it wouldn't have worked. Oh, sure, only an eighth (multiplied by the number of options purchased) would have been lost, but lost it would have been. The problem with out-of-the-money options is that the stock can move well, but still not be above the strike price at expiration time. Thus, buying such options because they are cheap can be nothing more than a sucker bet, equivalent to plunking down good money on the long shot in a race. It is a long shot because, on the evidence, no one figures that horse to win. But the horse, at least, is starting at the same time as all the other horses in the race; when it comes to out-of-the-money options, you are starting from behind.

Thus, buying out-of-the-money options is very risky. There has to be a fast profit—and you've got to take that profit without regard to remaining time value, purely because of the percentage gain. Often that's the only solid profit, with the risk increasing greatly, otherwise, of not only missing the gain but handing back your investment entirely. As time passes, the option will lose value; the premium will steadily diminish as the chance of the stock getting above the strike price diminishes. The stock can actually sell at a price higher than when you bought your option, but because of the loss of time left before expiration, the premium is less and your option will sell at less than you paid. Because out-of-the-money options are much cheaper in dollars, they have speculative appeal as a pure bet. But to win, you must be right by getting a fast move relatively soon after purchase, and take your percentage profit promptly.

Yes, there is also the rare chance, as in the Pfizer example, when the overall market, or an individual stock, may be ripe to rise quite close to an expiration period, so that you can place a bet on one of those one/eighth or even one/sixteenth call options with a few days left to run, and see it soar. The stock must be close to the strike price, of course, and you must be prepared to lose your entire investment with a shrug if the explosion doesn't happen, but it can be done.

While buying out-of-the-money options are pure bets, the virtue of in-the-money options is that they will participate proportionately if the stock advances. Because they have an intrinsic value, since they are in-the-money already, their cost is much higher. That makes the potential percentage gain less, and the downside risk, if wrong on the stock itself, greater. But one of the most deceptive of all salesman's pitches is: "That's all you can lose." Playing out-of-the-money options, the bettor too often simply does lose it all—that is, the option stays out of the money. In-the-money options have a greater dollar risk because the investment is greater, and it is possible for the stock, in a slide, to drop below the strike price and make the option worthless. Thus, you must be aware of the premium you are paying, for it is the premium that is the cost of buying the option instead of the stock. Premiums, too, are a mathematical calculation. Naturally, the more time remaining before the option expires, the higher the premium; you are paying for trading days. So, too, if the stock is volatile or is currently actively swinging. A high premium—no matter how much you like the stock's chances—is a warning not to bet on the option. But if the premium is minimal, and it looks as if the stock has a good chance to move soon, you are, in effect, buying the stock relatively well. For example, if calls in ASA with a strike price of 50 are selling at 3 1/2, while over on the NYSE the stock is offered at 53 3/8, you are only paying an eighth more to buy that option than the stock. Of course, you must like the stock for itself; if you do, that kind of bet might be worth it. But if the premium is two points, the stock has to make that up, while time dwindles, and that can be your loss, built in.

Note the differences: If you buy the ASA 50-call option—stock at 53 3/8, option at 3 1/2—and the stock rises to 54 1/2, let's say, the option should pretty much go up in line with the stock; at expiration it would sell for about 4 1/2, and you've made money. If you buy the ASA 55, out-of-the-money, you've lost it all. If the stock goes down a point instead, to 52 3/8, you've also lost all your money with the ASA 55, but if you've bought the ASA 50, it still has some value; you'll get 2 3/8 back. But if the premium is greater —two instead of an eighth—you may end up losing more money than on the pure bet of buying the ASA 55, even if they turn out to be worthless. All in all, placing bets on options, whether in- or out-of-the-money, calls for a strategy of taking the first worthwhile percentage gain.

Expiration Periods

The problems of the premium are also a factor when considering which expiration period is worth opting for. The premium, naturally, is greater with the lengthier expiration periods, because you are buying more time. Why would you do that? If you are buying because you think the stock is imminently due for a rise, the extra months don't matter. If it isn't due, why in the world are you buying it? Let the hedgers, with their various mathematical gimmicks, play with the other expiration periods. Your bet must be based on a current potential.

As you can see, the most deceptive aspect of options is the time span. The fact that there is still time left before the option expires, time you've actually paid for in the premium, creates a powerful subconscious desire to play the option for, so to speak, all it is worth. But the expiration date is actually an artificial date that has nothing to do with market action (except for the action the date itself sometimes inspires). You are placing the bet for a move, not for time. Treat time as your enemy, rather than thinking that it is still on your side as long as the option hasn't expired.

In addition to considering whether the premium is excessively high or not, another factor, too often forgotten in the excitement of the moment, must be considered—the dividend date for the stock itself. Because the stock price is adjusted for the dividend, while the option is not, buying a call just before the stock goes ex-dividend can be unnecessarily costly, especially if the stock pays a good-size dividend. In some cases, you could lose a buck off your bet in that one stroke. (Obviously, this same factor can be a virtue if you are buying a put option in expectation of a decline, or if you are selling an out-of-the-money call option.) Always know when the ex-dividend date is before you trade.

Another factor that should be considered is trading activity. The need for liquidity must be part of your decision. Often, the most active options are those highly speculative out-of-the-moneys, whereas the in-the-moneys tend to be relatively, even quite, inactive. Thus, they are harder to buy in any size, have greater spreads between the bid and offer, and are more difficult to liquidate if you want out. Avoid buying options that have virtually no public interest. And if you want to trade in an issue that is relatively thin, this can be another reason to take that first percentage profit, selling to that sudden spurt in activity that you were betting on.

How to Bet

There is one exception to taking fast percentage profits—when you are buying call options at major bottoms. Obviously, if you have the skill—and apply all the criteria we've discussed in previous chapters for timing a market bottom as well as a worthwhile base in a stock—you'll be buying calls at a time when the premium is relatively low, because few traders believe in the upside potential at such junctures, and when the market and the stock are about to launch a prolonged move upward. There is more leeway under such circumstances to let your profits run. But even so, it doesn't pay to get so enthralled by how much time you have left before your options expire as to be blind to the profit already gained, or to forget that each trading day that passes takes its toll in the premium even if the stock is still okay. The market is just perverse enough to stage a fluctuation back down while you are still holding. Always remember that you've placed a bet; when you win, cash in.

Similarly, it is possible to use call options to anticipate an upside breakout in an individual stock without committing too much capital. A glance back at some of the examples discussed in the previous chapters will show such opportunities. Buying a few calls when the stock looks as if it is making its right shoulder, for example, will give you a head start and permit you to await the actual breakout more calmly before you buy the stock itself. Such situations can prove to be good bets.

It may seem, in the above discussion, that we'd prefer to place any such option bets via an in-the-money option, buying the nearest expiration month. Indeed we do, for two reasons. Out-of-the-money options represent not only an almost pure bet but an almost pure loss as well; experience shows that the vast majority of such options expire worthless. If you are wrong, and the stock doesn't do what you expect, get out promptly. Many speculators sit and suffer as if helpless. The fact that their option still has time to run causes them to want to hang on and hope, thinking that, after all, they had made the bet with the notion that they could lose it all. But if it becomes apparent that the upside action is not forthcoming, don't wait for time to destroy option value any further. It is better to retrieve whatever money you can, and bet again some other day.

Second, the in-the-money option, while not so enticing in terms of its percentage-profit potential, provides the means, with limited capital, of controlling more shares of a stock you like, since the option and the stock should rise on an almost dollar-for-dollar basis (if you avoid paying an excessively high premium). The odds are better that you will at least make some money on such bets.

As sound as this may sound, however, it is not the most successful strategy, at least in the eyes of experienced professionals. The sad fact, they note, is that the vast majority of option buyers eventually lose their stake. The game looks enticing, but it is more glitter than substance. Granted, then, that a great many losing trades are going to be made, here's a way to survive and eventually come out ahead. Let's suppose one's available capital is $100,000. Ninety percent of this is invested in U.S. Treasury bills, and the remaining $10,000 is available for betting. Those following this strategy lose during three-quarters of the year, according to professional traders, and replenish their betting funds from the interest received on those T-bills, while during one time span they hit it big by betting on low-cost out-of-the-money options that show big percentage gains.

In our opinion, this strategy can be refined considerably. It should not be a game of "Well, we've got some money, so let's bet." Rather, face the fact that option playing is really not a good bet except under extreme circumstances—the one or two times a year when a severe decline, a selling climax, a budding major upturn, etc., set up the likelihood of a sharp and perhaps extensive rally. We don't want to lose, even if our betting funds are being replenished from interest earned elsewhere. And if we've only got a few thousand dollars to bet with, the strategy can be the same. Bet options far less frequently than you would trade stocks. Wait patiently for the major opportunity and then plunge. In sum, coordinate what we've written about market timing and stock selection with the virtue of options—low cost and a potential fast percentage profit. If you don't bet that way, you will get trapped by all the option flaws.

Writing Options

In addition to recommending the above strategy, professionals on the floor of the options exchanges would tell the public options player one other rule: Don't go short. In other words, never sell a naked option that would subject you to unlimited risk. But others play what is a more conservative game—selling options against the stock they already own. (This is known as writing the option.) For example, you buy 1,000 shares of General Motors at 40 and sell 10 options with a strike price of 45 for $5. If the stock stays under 45, you still own it and keep the money you received for writing the option. If the stock goes above 45 and the option is "called," you have to deliver the stock at 45, which, with the premium received, gives you an effective selling price of 50. They tell us this raises rates of return; they show us figures, as in this simple example, to prove it works. But the theoretical is always related to some ideal performance on expiration day. Yes, it can work, at those times when both the stock and the option are available at the mathematically desired prices. It limits your potential gain on the stock, of course, but it can be done. It seems to us that the chief virtue of this tactic is not simultaneous execution but, again, a form of legging in. That is, writing covered options can be an effective method of protecting a big gain (and can, in addition, often be used to help turn a short-term gain into long-term with relatively little risk). If a stock you own has had a worthwhile run-up, and has become potentially vulnerable to at least a short-term correction, selling a call against that holding can add to the ultimate profit. By selling an out-of-the-money call, you will offset any dip in the stock you own with the increased likelihood that the call will expire unexercised. In any case, the stock holding must be protected with a stop-loss order; it does no good to seek extra income this way only to have a loss in the stock that more than offsets the gain from the option. One alternative strategy is to buy the stock, sell an out-of-the-money option against it, and use the premium received to buy a put option as insurance against a decline in the stock price instead. In swinging markets, writing covered calls can be used as a hedge with a potentially high rate of return.

Puts

A word here about puts. We've concentrated on call options because that is the bet most frequently made by those who think a stock is about to go higher. But you can also sell a put to much the same effect, although the percentage gain is limited to the premium received as compared to the theoretically unlimited upside potential of buying a call. Selling puts is an aggressive bet that you are going to be right. In certain bottom climates such as March 1980, the premium for puts will be relatively high because everyone has become so bearish the demand for puts is relatively great. Someone with a contrary opinion can take advantage of this situation by selling puts that will become worthless if the market indeed turns and starts up instead. For our money, though, being right about such market timing would make it more desirable to buy calls. Further, we are not in favor of selling anything "naked"— without protection—be it puts or calls. There is something appealing about selling an option that could become worthless, but it does involve much more risk, if wrong, than placing essentially the same timing bet by buying.

However, now that so many stocks have put options available, it is important to note their one indisputable virtue. If the stock market is heading down, and you can't get a short sale off in the stock—because there are no upticks—you can always buy a put by taking the offer in the options market. Just be careful not to get caught up in the emotions of the moment; you might pay too big a premium, one which might quickly disappear. (Puts have scant premiums during periods of high interest rates because the interest earned from selling a stock short has much more appeal to professionals.) But if you are quick in perceiving the downturn, and frustrated because there are no upticks, buying puts is a way to get on the short side. Further, because it is usually the burden of short sellers—see the discussion in *When to Sell*—to have to be a bit early, and have the stock go against them for a while, buying puts can establish short-side positions with a relatively low commitment of capital in the late stages of a top formation.

Yes, you may have seen someone pull off a big gain—or done it yourself—by sticking out an option through market fluctuations, but we'll wager that over the years that kind of gain will be more than offset by the losses created while constantly seeking such big hits. A consistent pattern of trading behavior will invariably work better, unless you are like one man we know who enjoys the betting just as he would enjoy going to the track for entertainment and not profit. He willingly loses a few thousand dollars a year in options because he gets a lot of fun out of the excitement of the bet that he doesn't get from his much more serious, and more substantial, longer-term investing. By using those few thousand dollars to speculate, he is able to enjoy exciting markets, and by concentrating his speculation in this manner, he is able to refrain from speculating in those longer-term selections. It helps him keep his head and perspective.

We've just overheard two Amex options specialists talking about some of their hedging strategies: "Buy the calender deep and cheap," says one. "Buy anything, keep spreading," says the other.

"Let's put on double butterflies in every volatile stock," says the first. All those complexities, designed drastically to reduce risk, are there. It is the simple option bet that is sheer gambling. Buying the option is betting on the stock to perform. Buying 100 calls can be profitable if the stock moves; buying 10, or 2, can be fun. The emotional aspects of such a bet help make the Call/Put Ratio such an important sentiment indicator. This ratio is calculated by dividing total call volume by total put volume. A low ratio, in the 1.5 to 1.7 range, indicates heavy public bearishness, and hence is favorable. If you want to bet on options, it is important to be aware of what the prevailing sentiment is—so that you can go against the majority. This indicator is such an excellent measure of emotional belief in one side of the market or the other—by speculators, primarily public—that it provides a basis for contrary opinion. Adamantly and scrupulously avoid buying calls if the ratio shows heavy bullishness. (But you can then bet on puts.) Similarly, if there is heavy public bearishness, bets on calls should work out.

Just as you should not think you alone have found a good bet despite your joining the crowd, don't think you have ever discovered an undervalued option. The options market is highly efficient. The options-exchange floors are full of traders constantly adjusting relationships. Nothing remains over- or undervalued for more than one trade. You can't beat the floor in knowledge, calculations, money power, or timing. Indeed, it is tough even to beat them on breakouts, because the specialist in that option is already well aware of the same breakout point you've spotted. He is not standing there with blinders on. He'll be long into the breakout and will then sell to all the excited buyers as the stock shoots up.

That's the best way to bet on options.

12

PUTTING IT ALL
TOGETHER

"The market," says one professional trader, "is a humbling experience."

You're not going to make money every time. No one does. If you'd listened to the litany of losses, of mistakes, that we've heard from institutional portfolio managers, floor traders, and specialists, you'd realize that you're not alone in having to confront the difficulties of the stock market. The accumulation of capital over the years, as we've said, is based as much on the old saying, "It's not how much you make, but how much you don't lose," as it is on picking winners.

Some Last-Minute Advice

A successful market strategy year after year requires applying all the necessary capital-preserving cautions on the sell side, such as protecting positions with stop orders; selling when a top has formed; taking losses promptly if the market action proves you wrong; letting your profits run instead of getting overanxious and selling too soon. But it is also necessary to buy intelligently. That's why, no matter how tempting, we're wary of buying stocks that are already up, of trying to estimate an extension of a move already well in progress. The later the purchase, the greater the risk. Of course, an exciting emotional market can be tempting; a bubbling market is the easiest time to buy. Yes, prices could still go higher, but that is when you have to have the discipline to sit back and let someone else have the last few points. You won't find bottom formations then, and if you've learned anything from these chapters, it should be that when there are no longer any bottoms to be seen, it is too late to buy. Be disciplined.

Rest assured that the market will sooner or later fluctuate back down again, and when it does, those bases will form again. The hardest time to buy is when the market looks its worst. But that's what the indicators are for. Wait. Be patient. The indicators we've discussed are designed to be—and have consistently proved to be—leading indicators (at worst, precisely coincident). That's all the advantage you'll need, so don't try to anticipate what is already leading. There will still be plenty of time to buy once the indicators have given a signal. Trust them, no matter how wretched the news, how scary the market seems to be. Don't try to rationalize them. When they speak, whatever they say, accept the message. If they say nothing, do nothing. But when the majority of the indicators have turned favorable, it is time to act.

The indicators should be used to provide market timing. Don't put any more burden on them than that. Don't ask them to call little bits of moves, or three-day swings. The market has been and will be around a long time; let the indicators tell you the one, two, or perhaps three times a year when the odds have shifted substantially to your favor. Oh, it won't be easy, because they'll be speaking against the conventional opinion, against the headlines. But it might be said, with considerable validity, that when the indicators are most difficult to believe, they are most apt to be dramatically right. The indicators provide the buying climate, and then it is the turn of stock selection to take over. What to buy? There is a huge market of over 4,000 stocks to pick from. In recent years, every time there has been an important market bottom, the technology stocks have bounced back quickly and powerfully. But that doesn't matter. The best buy at a particular bottom might be a staid old utility, a cement stock, or a high-flying computer company. You don't need to know the name so much as to recognize that a base has been forming. The action of the stocks themselves will tell you whether or not to buy them. Have no prejudices.

The chart of a stock tells you two things: that there has been accumulation of the shares, presumably by knowledgeable buying interests, enough to have an impact on the market, and, by calling your attention to such base action, it can help you determine where and when to buy that stock as it emerges into a new uptrend. The opportunity to time the onset of a major uptrend can be seen in three factors: the base as it develops, looking for evidence of vigor in the swings as the base forms, and width of base for extended power; the breakout, using volume to confirm the strength; and the subsequent pullback, as a chance to get on board a proven strong stock near support. If you limit your buying to just such situations and no others, you'll miss some odd winners, those stocks that go up without a definable technical thesis, but among your purchases will be plenty of big gains, too, and far fewer mistakes.

This approach to selecting buyable stocks protects you from three potential deceptions: knowing too much, knowing too little, and knowing nothing. It requires you to deal with only what is objectively known, instead: how the stock is acting in the marketplace. Buying a stock for fundamental reasons still leaves it at the risk of the market. Buying a stock for technical reasons has underlying fundamental support behind it, or else why have those potent buyers been so active?

And if you can't find any such buyable stocks, don't buy. Put your itchy wallet away. There has never been a whole new bull move without such bases and subsequent upside breakouts. Tacking on yet another upleg is not the same thing. Rather, it can be the trap near the top. Curb temptation; your responsibility to your capital is to be patient. So long as the market fluctuates, and we know it does, then you'll get your chance to buy again, at a safer, sounder time. The person, or institution, who believes in being 100 percent invested at all times ignores market history and is admitting to an inability to deal with market reality.

The best reason to wait is that you want to act so as to reduce risk. The further away you get from what is knowable, the greater the risk. After a market has run up for a considerable period of time, it is no longer knowable how much further it will go. The majority are bullish near a top, but they are so because of excitement; there's no evidence for such confidence, compared to the evidence at bottoms of favorable indicators, basing stocks, upside breakouts. Constantly ask yourself what you know as compared to what you hope for, or what everyone else is confident of. A base, a breakout point, a stop-loss level, an indicator reading are the kinds of things you can know and rely on for objectivity; the distance to the pot of gold at the end of the rainbow is for others to guess at. Aware that the market constantly fluctuates, having as your primary intent reducing risk, you should base your betting style on what is knowable.

The virtue of the buy side of the market is that you have a free choice to act or not. Patience means you can wait for both the suitable time and the stock with genuine potential, using the market's fluctuations to your advantage instead of battling upstream against them. Keep your perspective: make the stock's own action tell you what to do. And insist on success. In *When to Sell* we spoke of failures as the key to knowing when it was time to sell. When you are buying, success proves itself. Such aspects as higher lows, upside breakouts on volume, pullbacks to support levels, all speak of success. We'll say it once again: relative strength works. Why buy a weak stock in hopes that it will improve, when you can buy what is already proven strong?

Some Hot Tips

Many reasoned discussions about what to do in the stock market end with a hot tip or two. Here are some hot tips of our own.

Today's technicals are tomorrow's fundamentals.

Don't try to defy selling pressure in a weak stock.

Ignore advice from others. Let newspapers age. Play the devil's advocate to headlines.

Always ask what the market could do to prove you wrong. Use stop-loss orders as necessary protection, placing them at the price that would indicate the stock is failing.

It is useful information if you are wrong.

After a stock starts to go up, follow it with a trailing stop, again placed at the price that would indicate the stock is failing.

Write calls on substantial profits, but keep close stops, too.

It's too easy to get lulled after buying. The stop-loss order is to protect you from being knifed in the back, but you still need to keep an eye on the same subtle clues that led to the buying decision in the first place. It may turn out that you should buy more.

Why not buy more of a stock that has already proven itself strong—on a pullback to support, for example—rather than search for another stock that hasn't proven itself yet? There is nothing wrong with owning more of a winner. It is only those who dollar average down that are betting on losers; dollar averaging up is a path to success.

Let others fish for bottoms.

Don't look for low-priced issues as if they have some special virtue. They don't.

A market in which speculative and low-priced issues are all over the tape may look appealing, but it is actually a dangerous place to bet. A good market has substance, true leadership, not froth.

Beware of a market in which only the Dow-type blue-chip issues are advancing, while the rest of the market lags; this sort of action has frequently come at an important top.

Bottom testing is bullish because it helps to form a base.

Do not buy a stock when it is all over the tape. Wait until it quiets down.

Don't wait for "one more dip" to buy a stock. If it is good—that is, it meets our conditions—the stock is unlikely to accommodate you. But you'll get all the weak stocks with that kind of net.

Head-and-shoulders patterns are the essence of bottom testing. When the right shoulder forms, it shows that the bulls are winning the test.

Triangles, however, are uncertainty patterns. If the stock trades in the upper end of the triangle, it is more likely to break out on the upside; if it trades in the lower range, it is more likely to spill downward. A move within a triangle that only goes part of the way toward the opposing trend line is usually signaling that it wants to turn around and break the trend line that it has most recently bounced off of. Make triangles prove themselves; you'll still be in early in a real move.

Lack of a base means you are guessing at a bottom. What's the hurry?

Buying laggards no longer works. It is as dangerous as buying low-priced speculative stocks simply because they are low-priced.

Don't buy a hitherto strong stock if its new high is made on less volume. Volume peaks halfway into the move. The lower volume is a warning that you are late.

Be patient.

The market is like every other business: try to buy something that you can sell later at a higher price. There is no other reason for risking your money.

Avoiding buying at the wrong time is more important than trying to be right. Use the indicators to tell you whether the climate is ripe. Don't think you have found the one stock that should go up regardless; it may, but if it doesn't, chances are you'll be stubborn about it and hang on, and the loss will be that much greater.

On the other hand, if in a favorable climate you don't buy a stock when you should, the aggravation at what you've missed could cause you to switch to a laggard or to reach too high too late.

The problem of buying is not acting emotionally but nevertheless acting in time.

A stock doesn't have to go up to be turning bullish. Merely not going down in a declining market is a sign of potential strength ahead.

It's easy to buy in a favorable market, but it still takes judgment. It is a free choice compared to selling, when all you have to decide is whether to sell or not, but you must take advantage of that choice to pick stocks with the least risk and most potential.

There is a right time to sell, but you can buy at many different times.

Bet before the race is run, not when it nears the finish line.

Don't buy more stocks than you can watch.

Do what the technical action says and do it decisively, as soon as and precisely when the charts say to do it. Not thinking things out clearly enough leads to mistakes. Don't shoot from the hip.

Follow big volume on breakouts and low volume on dips.

But remember that volume is low during bull-market dips. During a bear market, low volume is dangerous, suggesting that the big-volume part of the decline still lies ahead. A stock (or the market) that starts to break down on low volume should never be excused. Low volume is bullish only when the stock (or the market) is holding at the top of support.

Don't wait for an eighth.

You can always buy a stock back.

Traders should establish a buy-back price for stocks they've sold, and act on it.

Don't be afraid to buy a stock back at a higher price than you sold it.

Never buy a higher opening if you can help it. Buy on lower openings without trying to fine-tune the price.

You must take a chance. That's what a bet is.

The greater the chance, the greater the reward, or so it seems. In actuality, if you buy stocks when no one else wants them, it may seem as if you are sticking your neck out very far, but it may be the safest time. Besides, as long as you maintain a stop-loss order, you may get your neck bitten but never chopped off.

Develop a betting style that works for you—buying after a base forms but in anticipation of the breakout, or on the breakout, or on the pullback—and then be consistent.

Make sure the stock has room to move before buying it.

Buy when the shorts aren't around, such as on partial holidays.

Never react to good news.

Concentrate on individual stock selection. All stocks do not fluctuate in the same direction at the same time. So long as the climate is suitable for buying, profits will depend on which stocks you buy.

Try to be long the strongest stocks and short the weakest simultaneously.

When a stock goes against you, it is always possible to find a reason to justify the decline, to sit complacently with the thought that it will go up again. But when a stock goes up, it becomes a threat, a challenge. Keep what is doing well, and sell what isn't, not the other way around.

Let the market tell you. Don't try to tell the market.

Why should the market cooperate with your needs?

Made in the USA
Monee, IL
11 January 2021

57332094R00144